Cover design: Peter Labrow
https://content. productions

Illustrations: Caroline Chapple
http: //www.chapplecartoons.co.uk

Editing and proofing: Claire Andrews
http://proofreadingclaire.co.uk

CW00864734

IS IT NEWS?

IS IT NEWS?
WRITING PRESS RELEASES THAT REALLY WORK
by Peter Labrow and Robert Clarke

Peter Labrow

Robert Clarke

CONTENTS

WRITING

DISTRIBUTING

MEASURING

VOICES THAT MATTER

RESOURCES *(a collection of useful templates)*

FOREWORD:
PRACTICE MAKES PERFECT

Publicity is absolutely essential.
A good PR story is infinitely more effective than a front page ad.
– Richard Branson

Either write something worth reading or do something worth writing about.
– Benjamin Franklin

Let's be honest.

Plenty of people see press releases as easy, bash-it-out marketing.

Too many press releases are summoned into existence with the damning phrase, "Let's *just* get a press release out." They're frequently born from a knee-jerk reaction: something happened in the morning, and the world must know by the afternoon. Churned out into a world overloaded with information, occasionally one sticks.

It's not surprising that so many press releases fail:

- Most often, the story simply isn't interesting.
- Or, the writer outlined the basic facts but hadn't identified the *real* story or its impact on others. Such press releases are potentially solid, but the significance of the story is buried. If a writer didn't find the *real* story, nor will the readers.
- Finally, the story may be written soundly enough on a technical level, yet detached, dry language killed its impact. Dry? A press release isn't a coroner's report. It shouldn't be dry. News stories should be exciting.

GETTING IT RIGHT

Humdrum, vague or formulaic press releases sink without trace, but great ones can deliver excellent results.

There's no magic to writing a great press release: just some solid logic, a dash of creativity and a fair bit of practice. It takes *logic* to correctly identify what is and isn't newsworthy. *Creative* use of language brings the story to life. And *practice*? Well, as anything else, getting it right - to the point where it's second nature - takes time. You have to stick with it.

The more you put in, the more you get out. This is our gentle way of flagging that this book isn't a quick-fix guide.

Time spent learning *will* pay off. When you put into practice what we set out in this book, your press releases *will* stand out from the crowd.

We take you through our working process, end to end, sharing not just what we *believe* works, but what we *know* works.

While news media has changed, and publicity has changed, what makes a great news story remains the same. We focus on the foundation principles that *don't change*: knowing how to identify a good story and write it really well.

It doesn't matter if you work in an advertising or public relations agency, the marketing department of a multinational company or run your own business. All that matters is that you believe the *quality* of what you create *counts*. That doing things well matters.

This book is for people who want to write *great* press releases. People who want to make publicity *really* work.

The world wants news. So give it to them. But do it well.

Peter Labrow
Robert Clarke

HOW THIS BOOK IS STRUCTURED

If you're one of those people who flick through books to see how the land lies before settling down to read, you'll perhaps have already noticed that we've broken this one down into sections.

If so, you're probably keen to dive straight into section three, the *writing* section. That's understandable. After all, this is a book about writing. So what's all that other stuff?

Well, before you start writing, there's a fair bit else that you need to know. The act of *writing* press releases is just one part of a far larger process.

For example, setting specific objectives for a press release will fundamentally change how it's written – as can knowing what stakeholders' expectations are, understanding the intended audience, creating search-engine optimisation goals, and so on.

The structure of this book broadly follows that bigger process, to address a critical reason why many press releases fail: they were written without adequate preparation. However well-crafted the prose, if press releases aren't correctly planned, targeted, structured, distributed and measured, they won't hit the mark. Being a great writer isn't just about *writing*. Words conjured from thin air are merely invention. Successful press releases are based on facts and directed towards a predetermined need. They are informed by an agreed, structured process.

That said, we know many people prefer to dip in and out of books such as this. So, to help 'hunt-and-peck' readers, each chapter can be read on its own. If you just want to know how to write a great headline, dive right in.

But we would encourage you to explore and embrace the whole book; to read about publicity-writing within that wider context. It can genuinely transform what your press releases can achieve.

INTRODUCTION

WHY PUBLICITY?

Publicity is a powerful part of the marketing mix.
Indeed, it has the potential to be the most powerful part of it.

You will learn that:
- publicity can be an unmatched marketing tool.
- the world is hungry for news.
- the newsworthiness of your story is vital.
- press releases are a key tool for making announcements.

When you get publicity right, its benefits can outpace those of many other forms of marketing. Being published by news outlets and other influencers gives news stories far greater credibility.

Publicity is a very different beast to most other forms of marketing. With, say, advertising, you control the message entirely. However, with publicity, a story is usually subject to assent by news outlets, influencers, journalists, editors, commentators and so on. A press release is a starting point, not an end product. These *outlets* are gatekeepers. They decide if a story goes out to the world. In many cases, *they* decide exactly *how* a story will be told.

And the story?

Publicity can help you to:
- launch a new product or service.
- invigorate older products and services.
- transform your organisation's visibility.
- enhance your perceived worth.
- improve your company's reputation and credibility.
- respond well when something goes wrong.
- keep your company in the mind of your customers.
- affirm your expertise or leadership status.
- open up new markets.

Publicity can do this – and more.

You can undertake publicity with budgets large and small.

Publicity has long since proven its value in the marketing mix and yet, for many, it remains a baffling challenge. When companies find it hard to get stories picked up by news outlets and equivalent influencers, they can reach the erroneous conclusion that 'publicity doesn't work any more'.

Nothing could be further from the truth: good publicity works just fine.

The main ingredient for success is the quality of the story. If it's news, it can snowball. If it isn't, it will vanish without a trace.

Just as the story must be *newsworthy*, so the press release has to be well-written. It needs to tell the story well. And not just *tell* the story, but also *sell* the story. This isn't a cakewalk: to tell a compelling story in a scant few hundred words is one of the most creatively challenging writing jobs there is.

Every press release has to compete with many more distributed that day. Many more press releases are created each day than there are outlets to deal with them. Having said that, outlets and other influencers *want* news. It's what drives their business. But they won't take just anything. You have to grab their attention. Your press release has to be a good story, well told.

Getting it right counts. Great writing is vital if you want to make news stories fly.

> *Publicity remains a powerful, relevant marketing tool, but two things underpin success: the newsworthiness of the story and how well-written your press release is.*

WHAT IS A PRESS RELEASE?

Assuming what a press release is, and what it's for, can blinker us –
limiting our approach to publicity.

You will learn that a press release:
- is most successful when based around genuine, impactful news.
- is a powerful vehicle for great, news-related, marketing storytelling.
- must be written to publication standards.

Surely we know what a press release is and what it's for? You'd think so – yet many press releases are written as advertisements, offers or articles.

What's more, times change – and so has publicity.

Yesterday's press release isn't like today's. The communications media is different. Influencers are different. The way news spreads is different. Marketing is different. About the only thing that's the same is most people call it a *press release* (and we'll come to that later).

It's no bad thing to get back to basics and ask: what is a press release?

A PRESS RELEASE IS AN ANNOUNCEMENT

A press release *announces* something: news which has both relevance to, and impacts on, its target audience.

The combination of *relevance* and *impact* makes a story newsworthy, with the focus firmly on what affects the reader.

For example, many companies announce new hires via press releases. While a new hire is important *within* a company, it has little relevance to *outsiders*. If you're about to buy a television from a chain store, do you care who its national sales director is? Of course not. Unless it is a senior appointment for a well-known brand, such stories seldom do well in mainstream outlets (although they can get some coverage in sector-specific media).

People care about what affects them. They're more interested when it's something new. Press releases should be announcements of new things (events, products, services, whatever) that aren't just important to you, they're important to others.

A PRESS RELEASE IS A PITCH

Although press releases go to many audiences, including directly to the public, a press release is essentially a pitch.

Your main objective is to get outlets and influencers to write about a topic – and a press release pitches that topic to them. This is an important consideration. As with any pitch, you're not trying to overload someone with the whole story. You're hawking the best bits, the most interesting, the most relevant. It's the trailer, not the movie. Other information can be prepared and provided, but not delivered in the press release itself.

A PRESS RELEASE IS FOR DISTRIBUTION

Press releases are written to be distributed and syndicated.

Traditionally, this would have been via the media, but today's press release can be circulated to a wider (and potentially more beneficial) network of recipients. This still includes the media, but also encompasses other influencers such as bloggers, specialists, industry commentators and more.

Many sector-specific news sources are run by industry specialists or enthusiasts rather than big media companies. This doesn't mean they are a less valid means of distribution: indeed, it's not unusual for an authoritative specialist to have a range of influence that rivals mainstream news sources.

While press releases are principally a primer for journalists, delivering the facts needed as the *basis* for a news story which they will write, many press releases are published as is. While the press release of yesteryear could get away with dry, factual prose, today's press release should be written with an equal eye to both the media *and* the final audience. It needs to be not just 'editor ready', but also 'reader ready' – so, if required, it can be published unchanged.

A PRESS RELEASE SHOULD BE ONE PUBLICITY TOOL OF MANY

Press releases are a powerful tool, but too much can be expected of them. Indeed, they are all too often the *only* thing used to make an announcement.

When you have a story to tell, a press release is just one way to tell it. It can be the *central tool*, but it shouldn't be sent into the cold, like a Spartan child, to succeed or fail alone. Better results come from using a range of media to tell the story in different ways. Infographics, images, documents, videos – all of these can make publicity far more successful. They help you reach a wider audience, to connect with different communities. While that may sound like 'more work' it's what the most publicity-savvy companies do.

A PRESS RELEASE IS NOT AN OFFER

Many press releases are compromised because they're used in place of other marketing media which would be far more relevant for that message. An example of this might be to promote a special offer: say, 50% off a service for a period of time. This might seem like 'news which you want to announce', but it would be far more effective to use an advertisement or mailer – because it's not news: it's an offer.

When promoting something, challenge yourself by asking:
- is a press release the best way to do this?
- would something else do the job better?

It's tempting to think: well, what's the harm? If it gets our name out, surely sending a press release is better than doing nothing?

Sending out a lot of offer-based or sales-focused releases can be counterproductive. Instead of building market awareness for your values, you create a reputation for being a bargain-basement trader. This can be harmful to your brand. Since you distribute press releases via third parties, you don't just have to worry about what your customers might think; you also have to worry about what outlets and influencers think. Even when they don't get published, a constant flow of deals and offers will negatively affect your reputation with influencers.

Outlets will only place a story when it benefits them in some way. Their goals are to satisfy their audience, increase their readership, or have more people talk about that story on social media. They want your *news*, not your offers. When you build the wrong kind of reputation with media outlets, it becomes progressively harder to get good, real, stories placed.

Once earned, a poor reputation is hard to shift. It also means you're unlikely to be asked to comment on news stories other than your own – and providing an independent view on another story can be great publicity. When big stories break, the media wants to quote specialists, experts – people who know their market in depth, in terms of something other than price. They don't ask street traders.

A PRESS RELEASE IS NOT AN ARTICLE

Sometimes you'd like to get your views out to the market; to perhaps associate yourself with new legislation, a product or service that somebody else has launched, or an emerging trend. A press release seems a quick and easy way to do this – but it only works when you're *adding* something to a debate which is, in itself, news.

All is not lost: outlets often want editorial and commentary from specialists. You could still get an article placed – instead of a press release. Contact a journalist or editor and pitch your idea *before you write anything*. You'll quickly find out if your idea has merit and, if it has, they may ask you to write something.

An article isn't an easy ride. You need facts or research to substantiate your position, plus interviews with people who have opposing views. You must be a better than competent writer, with a nose for uncovering facts. You have to be objective and sometimes argue a position that's the opposite of your own. Most of all, unlike a press release, an article is usually published in one place – because the outlet will almost always require exclusivity (although it will often be syndicated – and you may be able to also use it on your website).

Writing articles can be an excellent part of a strong publicity strategy.

They allow you to explore topics with a depth you can't match within a press release. When you have something *important* to say, something which is *not news*, they can be a better vehicle than a press release.

HOW 'PUBLICATION-READY' SHOULD A PRESS RELEASE BE?

While many outlets will use press releases as the basis for stories which they subsequently write, this isn't always the case. Many outlets use press releases with little or no alteration.

 If editors can't use your press release as is, it's more likely to be discarded than corrected. Editors, website owners and bloggers are all busy. Make life easy for them by writing releases which are as publication-ready as possible.

This puts the responsibility on you to be a better writer. If your stories aren't well-written, there's far less of a chance that they'll get placed. True, outlets wanting to write their own version of a story will do so anyway, but your story has to captivate them first – which means it still needs to be written well.

A press release is primarily used to announce something which is genuinely newsworthy. It shouldn't be a quickly deployed substitute for other marketing activities. Write in such a way that your story is immediately ready for publication.

WHY IS IT CALLED A PRESS RELEASE?

Since the mainstream printed media – the press – is likely only a small part of the audience you wish to reach, is it helpful to continue calling your media pitches press releases?

You will learn that a press release:
- has become far more than a means by which to reach the media.
- has contemporary purposes that are not understood by everyone.
- may have an archaic designation, but it's one with which we should probably stick.

Much of our language is tied to the past. We still 'dial' telephone numbers, despite phones now having keypads and touchscreens. We carry wives over the 'threshold', despite no longer using thresh (straw) as a floor covering. Hotels offer 'room and board' despite dining tables not being called 'boards' for several centuries. We still use horsepower as a means of measurement.

So it is with 'press release'.

It's a title created years ago, when the document's purpose was to inform the press. At the time, this pretty much constituted the entire media.

The first modern press release was written by Ivy Lee, who worked with the Pennsylvania Railroad. In 1906, a West Jersey and Seashore Railroad train fell off a swing bridge. 53 people drowned. That's bad news indeed. Not wanting newspapers to be full of speculation, misinformation and suppositions, Lee created a document which was distributed to journalists and photographers, inviting them to the scene so they'd get a consistent take on the story and be able to ask questions directly of the company.

This laid the foundations for the now common practice of informing the media of a news event via a single mechanism.

Even in the 1950s, when radio dominated and television was on the rise, the term *press release* was becoming archaic. We clung to it in the 1960s and 1970s when television came to the fore. The rise of the Internet didn't see it being renamed either. It's just one of those things, like dialling a telephone number, that perhaps we're stuck with.

If the name 'press release' has a flaw, it's that it can imply a primary purpose which is no longer true, since 'the press' is but a small part of its potential distribution. Today, there are better, more accurate, terms.

You could, perhaps, consider using:

- media release.
- news announcement.
- news release.
- publicity release.

In many ways, these better reflect today's use of our news announcement document, yet 'press release' remains the most common term. Is this a problem? Not really, providing there is a shared and accurate understanding of its use.

It's possible that the term 'press release' can set an expectation that the primary purpose of your document (and therefore your publicity) is to *engage with the press* – which *can* be problematic. Stakeholders may not understand why you put as much, or more, effort into reaching other kinds of influencers. They may feel let down (despite its success otherwise) if *the press itself* doesn't take up a story.

It's important that stakeholders properly understand your publicity strategy. They should know that *the press* is just one part of a vast media soup; that other outlets can boast as much – or more – influence as the mainstream press. It may be called a press release, but its reach is far bigger.

In the end, what counts most is not *what you call it*, but *what you do with it*.

Of the suggestions we've offered, *news release* is a term that's gaining ground. You certainly wouldn't be misunderstood by stakeholders if that's the one which you decide to use.

Press release is a well-known, comfortable phrase: stick with it if that's easiest. Or, if you feel it doesn't entirely represent your publicity distribution, don't be afraid to substitute it for something which works better for you.

Within this book, we do still often refer to *press releases*. That's just our choice. While arguably an anachronism, it's still the term most people both use and readily understand. It's so entrenched that it's likely to survive, regardless of how the media changes.

You may well make a different choice. That's fine.

> *Don't get hung up on what you call your publicity documents –*
> *but do correctly set distribution expectations with stakeholders,*
> *so that everyone understands their purpose.*

HOW PUBLICITY HAS CHANGED

Being able to reach an audience through less formal influencers means that public relations can finally deliver on the promise inherent within its epithet: it's about creating a relationship with the public.

You will learn that publicity:
- is now both formal and informal.
- has a greater reach and delivers greater benefits than ever before.
- can enable you to more directly reach your target audience.

Publicity isn't what it was.

Originally, you (or your agency) wrote a press release with the aim of getting it into the media; only by doing so could it reach the public.

Communications flowed one way – and monologues do not build relationships. In that context, if ever any phrase was a misnomer, that phrase was *public relations*.

To make matters worse, to be published in the media, you had to write things in which *the media* were interested. You couldn't write directly for your audience, even if you knew exactly what they wanted to hear. You wrote for an arbiter. It's a relationship with a chaperone – an interpreter go-between with the power of consent and the power to censor.

The media still has an indispensable role to play in a solid publicity strategy. But it's no longer the sole gatekeeper to the public.

A modern publicity strategy has a far broader audience, the most important of which are your market's influencers.

REACHING INFLUENCERS

An independent outlet may be more valuable in terms of influence than a mainstream news service, because (unless it is specifically for your sector) only a fraction of a mainstream readership will likely be your target audience. An influencer's reach may not match the sheer numbers of a mainstream outlet, but the relevance of the audience can count for more. Influence is more important than readership numbers.

This isn't the only thing to differentiate influencers from the media. An influencer may also be a peer consumer of your product or service – someone with direct knowledge and experience of what you (and perhaps your competitors) do. The influencer has authority. The influencer is trusted.

There's another fundamental difference between an influencer and the media. You can more readily form a close relationship with an influencer. It's easier to create a two-way flow of information – not just between the two of you, but also between you and an influencer's audience.

A well-placed campaign into an influencer's community can reach more people – and have more impact – than getting coverage in a mainstream outlet. It may not stroke the ego as successfully, but it can be far better publicity.

Influencers include:

- industry specialists.
- event organisers.
- market analysts.
- online magazines and specialist media.
- professional bodies and membership bodies.
- forums and industry groups.

That's not to say you should leave the mainstream media behind – far from it, the mainstream media can be essential to your publicity activities. But try not to think of distribution in such narrow terms.

Other organisations within your sphere of influence should also be kept up-to-date with your company's activities. These include:

- current and potential customers.
- suppliers and partners.
- peer companies across your industry.

We previously referred to the press as 'gatekeepers' of your relationship with the public. Many of these other influencers are also gatekeepers. Including them in your publicity distribution can enable you to achieve a far wider reach and, while not part of the formal media, their modus operandi is still broadly the same. You reach your ultimate audience through their grace, so this still isn't a direct relationship. This is where social media comes in.

GOING SOCIAL

Social media is seen by many as miracle marketing. It's cheap: in fact, other than time expended (unless you are sponsoring/promoting posts), it is often perceived to be without cost. There's no need to buy advertising space, employ a publicity professional, an e-mailer, or pay for postage.

However, the physical costs of marketing are far from being the only costs. When you consider the time and effort spent creating a strategy, developing the proposition, engaging with the audience and measuring the results of marketing, the physical costs can, by comparison, be trivial. If a social media strategy is planned, executed and measured with equal rigour as other marketing media, those creative, management and administrative costs still exist. It's only a free ride if it's unplanned, ad hoc, unmanaged and unmeasured.

While social media connects you directly with the customer, it doesn't obviate the need to use other publicity channels. Plus, for an effective social media presence, you still need to generate content – stories, images, videos and so on.

USE PUBLICITY TO BUILD A SOCIAL FOLLOWING

Publicity can be a valuable tool in helping your organisation build a significant social media following. If social media is a megaphone for your voice, publicity lets you reach thousands of other influencers, each with their own megaphone, each talking to people with whom you want to connect. Using social media *instead* of other forms of publicity isn't as effective as using them together.

There's a process for doing this: a publicity and marketing model called PESO. PESO stands for 'paid, earned, shared, owned' – which refers to the different types of media channels an organisation would wish to reach. PESO, which we cover a little later in this book, helps organisations to implement more cohesive publicity campaigns.

Originally, a single press release could enable you to address an audience via a printed publication. Today, it can do so much more. You can reach the world, through many channels, all from the same starting point: the press release.

Today's publicity strategies embrace far broader types of media than before. What remains constant is publicity's central purpose: to announce something, to tell captivating stories, stories that inspire others to share your news. The press release remains a terrific single starting point for this.

ARE PRESS RELEASES STILL RELEVANT?

In a world where news is increasingly influenced by social media, is a press release still a useful publicity tool?

You will learn that press releases:
- can be your primary announcement mechanism to the outside world.
- provide a practical and measurable focal point for your campaigns.
- are a great launching-off point for other activities.

Given the rise of social media, it's fair to question whether press releases are still a relevant part of the marketing mix.

While the term 'press release' may in some ways be anachronistic, that doesn't mean the press release has had its day. Indeed, press releases still have a powerful role to play. In many ways, there's never been a better time to use press releases: they can get your news out faster than ever before and reach a far wider audience both quickly and easily.

WHY NOT JUST USE SOCIAL MEDIA?

Social media is essential. You should be using it. But one approach doesn't obviate the benefits of another. You should be doing both.

You can reach lots of people with a press release who would likely miss a social media update – and vice versa.

Consider the following:
- What's the coverage of your social media?
- How many people follow you?
- Does the media follow you?
- Do industry specialists, commentators and analysts?
- Do all of your customers and potential customers? Your business partners? Industry websites or publications? Industry bodies? Local or national newspapers? Business partners? Suppliers? Industry events organisers?
- Of those who do follow you, how many will see your every update before they are pushed down their timeline, to disappear almost instantly in a tide of other updates?

Social media updates go primarily to your connected network, although re-tweets, shares and promoted posts do extend your reach. A press release can go way beyond your connected network – plus, it can be used to drive people to your social networks, to help build them further.

Press releases and social media updates work in very different ways and each has its own pros and cons. A social media update can't be anywhere near as long as a press release, nor carry a significant amount of detail. A press release can't be as fun, snappy, dynamic nor as conversational as a social media update. They each use a radically different vocabulary. They each demand an almost opposing creative approach.

Both are needed to get a story out; they both work in different ways but should be created at the same time. Your social updates can be more fun, carry more emotion, be used to specifically engage around conversational concepts – and so on.

When you want to give people 'the whole story' from within social media updates, a more complete news story is a great destination.

It's not a binary choice. Do both.

DO PRESS RELEASES WORK?

Some people say that, "Press releases don't work any more." What this most often means is that press releases haven't worked *for them* and, rather than question the quality of their press releases, they conclude that the medium is at fault.

In reality, a press release doesn't fail because it is an inherently lame marketing tool: it's typically because it's either poorly written, or the story just isn't newsworthy enough.

If your story is strong, the release is well-written, and you're reaching a good, targeted distribution list then it *will* have an impact.

Press releases work when:

- the story is newsworthy.
- they're well-written.
- they form part of a bigger campaign.
- they're supported by other content, such as infographics and videos.
- they're distributed properly.

And, as with other forms of marketing, you get *far* more back from publicity when activities are part of a sustained, consistent marketing plan that's rolled out over time.

Press releases remain an excellent way to announce news, direct interest from social media campaigns – and they work superbly in concert with other marketing activities.

PLANNING BEYOND THE PRESS RELEASE

Using a publicity planning model helps you to deliver more successful campaigns.

You will learn that:

- planning helps you to reach far more people with your story, via different channels.
- you will get better results from each channel by using that channel's most effective media.
- not all stories work as big campaigns, but, with planning, you can more quickly recognise which will and which won't.

A useful – and powerful – model for getting the most from publicity is PESO. PESO stands for 'paid, earned, shared, owned' – four groups of marketing channels which provide an efficient way of organising campaigns. It was developed by American public relations expert, and author of *Spin Sucks*, Gini Dietrich. Although relatively new, many publicity firms and publicists have adopted PESO. PESO helps people to think about, and plan, publicity as it should be done – embracing all media.

PAID MEDIA

This is media for which you pay – good examples might be advertising (offline, online, radio, television, billboards, pay-per-click and advertising in social media), direct mail, sales promotion, sponsored posts, brand/event sponsoring and so on. With paid media, you typically have total control over content.

EARNED MEDIA

Earned media is coverage you 'earn' on third-party websites, outlets and other channels. This might be traditionally thought of as media relations or publicity. It's what others say about your company – when the media or influencers write about your products and services. With earned media, you typically have little control over your content other than priming it with a press release, similar story pitch or perhaps by sending out review products.

SHARED MEDIA

Like earned media, shared media reflects third parties gifting you coverage

– but specifically on social media. Shared media includes posts on Facebook, Instagram, LinkedIn, Pinterest, Twitter and so on. As with earned media, you have little control over the life of shared media.

OWNED MEDIA

This is content which you create and publish on venues over which you have control – such as your website, blog, Twitter account, LinkedIn account and so on. Content can include videos, podcasts, webinars, employee or customer stories, reviews and so on.

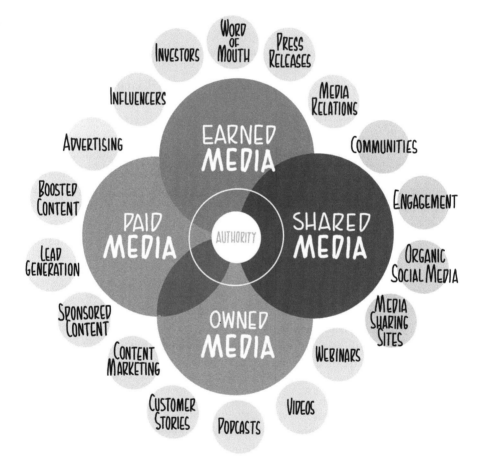

Our simplified take on the PESO model, from Spin Sucks. We highly recommend investigating PESO and becoming familiar with the far more complete, original diagram.

IT'S ALL ABOUT BALANCE

A great benefit of PESO is that it encourages you to think about the best way to manage broader publicity campaigns. Rather than the starting point being, "let's get a press release out", PESO pushes you to more carefully consider the quality of the story, because you must plan for different outlets and audiences.

Let's look at how to apply PESO to a typical campaign – when a company is launching a new product or service.

A TYPICAL PESO CAMPAIGN

It's a given that we will require some form of advertising and promotion: *paid media*.

The campaign needs *owned media*, such as a white paper on the benefits/savings of using the new product/service; perhaps some demonstration videos and blog posts.

To engage with the media, we need a press release, story pitch, event invitation, trial products (and of course the media has access to all of the owned media too). The press picks up on the campaign: *earned media*.

Content from the paid, earned and owned channels ripples across social media, perhaps using content created just for that channel: *shared media*.

It's easy to see why using PESO can result in more effective campaigns. It's balanced and thorough. It encourages people to think across all channels and prepare a campaign accordingly. Almost always, it beats, hands down, simply using a press release. It also beats using any one tool: when you rely solely on any single advertising, marketing or publicity tool, campaigns have gaps.

ONE CHANNEL GOOD; MORE CHANNELS BETTER

Some organisations concentrate efforts on one PESO channel. It's certainly easier to focus on owned media, for example, because it's entirely within your control. It feels less risky. But this misses the benefits of paid media, earned media and shared media – which can significantly extend your reach. Likewise, shared media delivers reach – but what do you share if you are neither generating original content nor engendering earned content such as media articles?

You don't have to hit all four PESO channels every time. Not every press release has to be a multimedia campaign. Sometimes, a press release *will* suffice. But only by using a methodology such as PESO can you properly plan truly compelling publicity campaigns.

THE ELEPHANT IN THE ROOM

While applying the PESO model is an excellent way to achieve more compelling publicity, it undeniably spawns more work. As Judy Shapiro said in Ad Age, "The most lethal arrow to aim at PESO's heart is squashing any illusion that PESO will ever result in a cost reduction for marketers." (Source: Ad Age)

Well, unless they're of poorer quality, 'more things' do usually cost 'more money'. Doing less, simply because it's cheaper, is a false economy.

Ideally, cost shouldn't be the primary concern when planning media: value and effectiveness should be. Even when you remove items from a campaign because of costs, it's still useful to explore the *best* way to do something, since then you can be realistic about the resulting compromise.

Of course, cost is always a factor, especially for smaller businesses, which may feel disadvantaged – that only large marketing departments have the resources to create the content needed for PESO campaigns. This isn't true: a professionally produced video, for example, will almost always outshine one from a smartphone – but plenty of people run successful YouTube channels using pretty modest gear and without professional skills. In some ways, smaller businesses can perform *better* – not only can they typically get things done faster, consumers are also more forgiving of their home-brewed production values.

PESO isn't so much about *what* you spend as it is about *where* you spend it.

NO MEDIA CHANNEL IS FREE

It's important to dispense with the idea that publicity and social media are free. All media has costs. While you don't *have to* pay for Twitter, LinkedIn or Facebook channels, they still take time to manage, itself a cost – and it also costs to create good quality content. This is true whether content is created within the organisation or via an agency.

Most stories benefit from a boost. An infographic, a white paper, a video – these, and other content, can elevate your story and extend your campaign. PESO helps you to plan the media or content that might work best for your story.

ASSESSING THE STORY

PESO helps organisations to think about publicity as being more than simply press releases. When a news story is suggested, the PESO model can be used to test the strength and value of the story as much as it can to ascertain which media and channels to use. It can help you to decide not only between the best ways to communicate your story, but also if the story is good enough to run with.

A CAMPAIGN TEMPLATE

It can help to prepare a 'template of activities' that includes not only the press release, but also other items typically required.

For example, a campaign plan might include:
- a press release.
- a story pitch to the media.
- a photograph (pack shot, headshot etc).
- an infographic.
- social media posts.
- blog posts.

Such a plan can include what your company thinks is the right way to approach your most usual campaigns (otherwise, the list would include *everything*). But with an agreed general approach, you're more aware of the gap when you remove things, and the benefits when you add them – rather than justifying why you need to create more than a press release.

PESO is a more evolved and complete way of looking at how marketing can work today. It provides a useful, easy-to-use process for planning more effective publicity and marketing.

PULLING THINGS TOGETHER

It's not unusual that a press release is one of the last items considered when planning a marketing campaign. But what if you brought it right to the heart of your thinking?

You will learn that:
- a press release can be an effective tool for creating sharper marketing messages.
- a press release provides an accessible vehicle for stakeholders to express their thoughts and agree on important messages.

All marketing campaigns need planning. Even the smallest campaigns benefit from some upfront thought and a defined structure. Press releases can provide a simple, practical vehicle for pulling together ideas on a marketing topic.

Great press releases are a concise distillation of thought – all of the essential information of a campaign. With a little push, they can even form a campaign manifesto – and provide a simple, practical vehicle for pulling together ideas.

When planning campaigns, you'll consider many things. What is the campaign about? What's the one, central message you want customers to retain or act upon? What are your goals? What are the key benefits to customers?

Where a press release is part of a broader campaign, information will be made available in different forms, such as presentations, videos, brochures, case studies and so on. Quite often, organisations create these items anyway, pulling from them the bits needed for press releases.

Consider turning this process on its head and putting a press release at the heart of the creative process: using its distilled thoughts to create fuller messages for other media. In terms of execution, the press release remains the same. But its new role exploits the unique sharpness of thinking press releases need to convey a message both powerfully and in an economically worded way. As a core part of the planning process, its keenly honed proposition is a great starting point from which to build the complete campaign.

A MORE COMPLETE CAMPAIGN

Using a press release as a campaign planning tool enables us to sharpen our message to its purest form. While doing this, we can think about the different audiences we want to reach. What makes them tick? What's important to them? What's the best kind of media to engage them?

Likely, we'll use the PESO model to help us plan.

As we draft our press release, we broaden our thinking to the wider campaign.

Does a particular point or benefit suggest the need for a separate press release for the media and a less formal one for customers? Would key benefits be better communicated to social channels via an infographic? Would a customer case study underpin the news story well? Would customers be interested in reading about specific elements of the news story in more detail, perhaps as a white paper? Would the story's key points be better covered in a video? Should a special offer run alongside the publicity campaign?

Our press release has a new, stronger purpose.

Not only have we created a better press release with a sharper story, we have also created a campaign planning document, complete with key messages.

Working in this way enables you to engage with stakeholders on a practical rather than theoretical level, with something they can help to shape and understand, getting their input in a more focused way. In a sense, the press release can become the definitive account of the campaign message. It has a sharpness which can get lost in a bigger, more conceptual planning process.

While any kind of writing can help you to structure your thoughts (and there's nothing 'special' about a press release in this context) press releases need to be created anyway. There's no additional effort. It's simply more efficient.

By using a press release to plan a campaign, we're more rigorously considering the media that best supports each message – for each audience.

Using press releases as planning tools can help maintain focus on what's important. Bringing the press release to the centre of your thinking can deliver clarity of thought, sharpness and consistency across the rest of your campaign.

NEWS HAPPENS, OR YOU MAKE IT HAPPEN

Don't hang around waiting for news to happen before reacting to it: news will happen, so prepare for it. And when news doesn't just present itself, make it happen.

Topics for press releases:
- can present themselves without warning, but you can prepare for them.
- are likely more plentiful than you expect.
- can be proactively created around content people want.

It's not unusual for organisations to struggle for publicity ideas. This is understandable. 'Business as usual' may not always seem interesting to you. Busy at the coalface, you can easily forget that your business can be interesting to others.

NEWS, WHEN IT HAPPENS

There are *things which happen* to your organisation, and *things which you make happen*. Both are a mainstay of publicity. They're important moments in time, of interest to others; stories you can tell the world.

Events *which happen* typically include:
- awards: giving, receiving and sponsoring.
- business milestones: important ones, such as your one millionth customer.
- business rebranding.
- business wins, such as a significant new contract.
- celebrity or public figure appearances.
- company anniversaries.
- company reorganisations.
- crowdfunding campaigns.
- customer advisory groups being set up or reporting results.
- customer giveaways.
- ecological improvements.
- employment creation.
- endorsements: received or given.
- event sponsorship or support.
- financial or stock updates.
- internships, apprenticeships or scholarships.

- investments.
- market expansion: by sector or geography.
- mergers and acquisitions.
- new hires, for senior or critical roles.
- new teams, or business units being established.
- partnering programmes or new partnerships.
- patent awards.
- premises changes and moves.
- public speaking/speaking at an event.
- response to a major event.
- seminars and webinars.
- service delivery changes.
- social interaction: successes and examples of fun interaction.
- social responsibility activities or charitable work.
- training, certification or credentials achieved.

All of these can be great topics for a press release and, in some cases, a bigger publicity campaign.

MAKING NEWS

You don't have to *wait* for something newsworthy to come along: you can *make* something happen. By doing so, publicity can be a scheduled part of your overall marketing strategy.

Press release topics which can drive proactive campaigns include:
- case studies.
- commenting contentiously on major events.
- content: e-books, podcasts, tutorials, training courses and videos.
- customer interviews.
- debunking a common myth or providing proof that accepted thinking is wrong.
- expert opinion.
- helpful tips.
- inspirational stories: how customers have overcome challenges.
- local business support.
- new uses for products.
- political support and affiliation.
- predictions of products, services or markets for the coming year.
- requesting people/media outlets to review your products or services.
- revealing scams.
- surveys or polls: gathering and publishing data and analysis.
- taking a stand on an issue.
- trend analysis.
- what is selling best and why.

It's true that several of the topics in each of these two lists could also sit comfortably in the other. For example, seminars and webinars could – when organised by yourself – be part of created campaigns, things you 'make happen'. The same applies to event sponsorships, celebrity appearances and public speaking.

Many of these topics involve creating content that is both timely and of value. For example, 'surveys and polls'. This can be a powerful way of generating publicity. A survey which is reasonably detailed, and provides information that isn't available anywhere else, can create several publicity opportunities – when the survey is launched, during the survey period and when the data is published. It provides scope for numerous press releases – from revealing facts to commenting on trends.

Think about the kinds of publicity activities which your company could undertake. Think big. Think about things which could put you at the centre of your sector. Think about something which delivers what people want: great, unique stories.

TAP INTO EVENTS

Because news is about *the now*, writing press releases can sometimes be reactive. Anything that can move this process towards being proactive is a good thing, as it gives you time to create more rounded campaigns.

One way of planning a more effective publicity schedule is to create a calendar which is pre-populated with the main events of the coming year. Tony Blair's Labour government did this successfully, with something they called The Grid.

The Grid was a weekly diary, filled with events; not just political events, but any event – from football matches to carnivals. Why? News doesn't take place in a vacuum: it's always part of surrounding events.

Knowing what these events are helps you plan the best time to launch campaigns, and identify events which can in some way contribute to your campaigns' messages.

For example, a good time to announce expansion into an overseas market might be when your country is playing against that country in a sporting event. This creates a story with greater resonance – because that country is already in the news.

Announcing that your company is taking on a new stream of apprentices or interns makes bigger waves during a national apprenticeship week. You might plan to reward your one millionth customer with tickets to a blockbuster film premiere.

You may have topics for which you want to develop a recognised position, perhaps something like 'women in IT'; a subject that aligns with your company's values. It's more effective to release stories about this during international equality week or to celebrate the birthday of a famous campaigner. Although you can't predict *every* opportunity, a marketing grid can help identify many instances where you can create greater impact.

BE ON THE LOOKOUT FOR NEWS

Try to be a publicity-focused company. Have a company-wide process which feeds potential news into the marketing department (or to the relevant person). All too often, great things happen but they're not exploited because word isn't passed up the line. It can be harder than you'd expect to escalate news stories, especially in larger companies. To work well, it should be something that's embedded in the company's culture, expected, encouraged. A reward for flagging potential news stories can be a great incentive.

Likewise, be on the lookout for things in the news with which your company can become involved or on which it can comment. Sometimes it's easier to join a conversation than to start one.

PUBLICITY ISN'T JUST ABOUT PRESS RELEASES

This book's focus is on writing press releases, but of course, publicity can – and should – go way beyond that. Publicity stunts can be a powerful way to gain coverage in the media and grab the imagination of the public. They are a real-world (or virtual-world) manifestation of your campaign.

One of the first organised publicity stunts was devised by Edward Bernays. Often recognised as the father of public relations (and modern propaganda) in the 1920s, Bernays believed that news, not advertising, was the best way to get a promotional message to the public.

Before the 1920s, it was not common for women to smoke, especially in public. In America, they could only smoke in designated areas. During the 1929 Easter Parade in New York City, Bernays hired models to hold lit Lucky Strike cigarettes as 'symbols of freedom'. Bernays took the phrase 'torches of freedom' from psychoanalyst A.A. Brill to help drive this point home. This staged 'news event' resulted in a seachange in both cigarette consumption by women and its social acceptability.

Publicity stunts remain a vital part of publicity, limited only by budget and imagination. Here are some examples:

- To promote the film, *Ant-Man*, 100 ant-sized cinema tickets were hidden around London.
- To launch the updated version of the children's television series, *Thunderbirds*, a life-size Thunderbird 4 was sailed up the River Thames in London.
- In 2012, a stunt conceived by Red Bull saw Felix Baumgartner become the first unpowered person to break the sound barrier. Baumgartner jumped from a balloon twenty-three miles above the Earth, resulting in eight million live views on YouTube.
- The famous photograph of Marilyn Monroe's skirt billowing above a

grating wasn't caused by a passing train as is commonly thought. A wind machine below the grating lay ready for exactly the right moment when photographers and journalists had gathered for the star's promotion of *The Seven-Year Itch*.

- It's hard to get bigger than the world's best-known bicycle race, the Tour de France – originally devised as a publicity stunt by Henri Desgrange, to raise the profile of the publication *L'Auto*.

Interestingly, the creators of publicity stunts would originally go to great lengths to make them seem like real events. Today, the opposite is true – publicists are open about what they do and encourage public interaction and involvement in campaigns.

Publicity stunts can be fun and engaging, but they should be grounded in something meaningful; something that's part of an overall campaign and inspired the story's focus. The best publicity stunts generate surprise – or educate or entertain. Our examples are audacious, but anyone can undertake stunts on almost any budget.

Great publicity stunts provide enormous fuel for press releases: they point people to something with which they can get involved.

A secondary story can be told about how a stunt is created – a behind-the-scenes view. For example, for the remake of the film *Carrie*, a short documentary about how MGM and Screen Gems created a terrifying telekinesis prank in a New York cafe garnered over 71 million views on YouTube, greatly amplifying the film's publicity.

WORKING WITH PUBLICITY PROFESSIONALS

Public relations professionals can add a massive amount of value to your publicity activities, whether it's organising a marketing grid, working out topics for press releases, or arranging publicity stunts. They have a wealth of expertise – real-world knowledge of what works and what doesn't, which can make a huge difference to your publicity activities.

When you don't work with a public relations professional, you're less likely to know what's possible – as with any specialist skill. They're more adept at working towards specific publicity goals, such as perception management. They can be invaluable when managing a publicity crisis. They are ideas people. They can lead stakeholders away from the wrong goals and that tiresome 'press release a month' cycle that serves only itself. They can help you to get results.

MANAGING A CRISIS

It doesn't take a genius to realise that the saying 'there's no such thing as bad publicity' is questionable. Bad publicity can be the worst kind of nightmare. It's something from which companies and individuals alike can struggle to recover.

When things go trotters up, public opinion can turn rapidly against you –

and will need managing. Publicity can help you to do this. The key thing in such situations is to be authentic and honest: excuses are usually unmistakable for what they are, and being defensive escalates negativity.

Most companies don't ever have to deal with a publicity crisis. Those which do typically don't have to do it often. In such circumstances, a publicity professional can be of invaluable help. Here's the catch-22: if you engage a professional to help when you're already in trouble, it can be too late. You would need to secure someone's services rapidly for them to be of real help. If you hire a professional, it's best to avoid making statements yourself, even to buy time. Don't run the risk of making the situation worse. Public relations professionals have far more experience of dealing with a crisis. They will have a contact network to enable them to get a response out. They'll know what works and what will make things worse.

Should you choose to handle things yourself, you need to act quickly, but don't knee-jerk. Plan your approach as an unfolding campaign: be prompt, but don't trip up over yourself just to get things out.

Fully take on board the reasons for the crisis. Accept that others' views of your organisation may be valid or, when they're not valid, they are still widespread beliefs. You should not belittle them, brush them aside or be confrontational about them.

Be authentic. Don't treat responses as a publicity campaign or repair job. Work out what the morally right action is and get your message out in a way which isn't overly self-serving.

If you're in the wrong, it may be better to say so right away. This can defuse a situation almost instantly – and it's likely what you'll ultimately end up doing.

Think about resolving others' grievances, not creating a win for you.

Press releases can't, in themselves, solve a publicity crisis – that requires other direct, decisive action. Press releases then communicate this to the wider world. Without real action, press releases are empty talk and can have the opposite result to the desired outcome.

Publicity is far more successful when you're in control, working proactively. A company-wide process to feed news to the publicity team, selecting the most newsworthy stories and creating news can transform the results you get from publicity.

THE GOAL IS PUBLICITY

When there's news to announce, many companies' default reaction is to write a press release. But that might not be the best way to get your news out.

You will learn that circulating a press release:
- isn't always the best way to get your message out.
- shouldn't be the end goal: *publicity* is the end goal.
- using press releases for all of your publicity can inhibit some opportunities.

One of the great benefits of writing a press release is that it's efficient. You compose one document, which you send to many places. Just as when seeds are scattered, not every story takes hold wherever it lands, but that's the trade-off for efficiency. Typically that's fine.

THE GOAL IS PUBLICITY
It's important to keep in mind that your goal *is not* to 'send out press releases', it's to *get publicity*. A press release is not the only way of going about this.

When a potential story is identified, always ask yourself if a press release is the best way to make the most of that story. As we've said, writing a press release is highly efficient – *for you*. But is it always the best thing for the media?

HOW THE MEDIA VIEWS PRESS RELEASES
Think about a press release from the media's perspective. It's a standard document, sent to a wide circulation. By definition, it's not an exclusive story. Right at the moment of distribution, your news story can be published across the Internet. For speed, the media may run the story as is; if they write it up into something bigger and better, they run the risk of being slow off the mark, behind the curve with a story that their competitors are already covering. As far as the media is concerned, a press release is a double-edged sword: convenient it may be, but it means they don't get the jump on their competitors. There are times when it may be better to sacrifice efficiency for a quality exclusive.

PRESS RELEASES AREN'T THE ONLY WAY
Commercially, media outlets need website visitors, subscriptions/sales and advertising revenue. What generates these is content, preferably unique content. In other words, either running exclusive news stories or getting a head start on the rest of the media. It may mean an *exclusive take* on the story, perhaps an

insider interview or a scoop product review. An exclusive doesn't preclude the story from having a wider publication; the media very often reports on news covered on other websites. If it's news, the fact that the competition got to the story first won't stop another outlet carrying it.

TALK TO THE MEDIA

Perhaps you have an exceptional news story and want to create more of a splash. Pick up the phone and talk to a preferred outlet. Have an informal chat about the story, in the context that it's 'something that's about to come up' and see how you can work together.

If the story is feeble, your contact will tell you. You may get some pointers on how to make it fly, or you may be advised to bin it. Either way, you've been saved a lot of time. Don't be precious about the press release – work with your contact to find the best way to make the most of the story.

MORE THAN A NEWS STORY?

People in the media not only have a great eye for a strong story, but also know how best to present it. Be open-minded.

Rather than run a news story, they might suggest you write an article or provide an expert opinion piece. They might suggest that you run some research and wrap the story around that. They might suggest talking to a customer and writing a case study. They might advise you to write an advertorial. They might want to pick up the story themselves and write it from a totally different angle.

A couple of points worth considering.

Some people feel that advertorials lack credibility – but most outlets find that well-written advertorials draw a decent readership. Good outlets know how to design and position these so they don't smack too much of advertising. Research by Reader's Digest found that advertising copy written to look and feel like an article drew 81% more sales than the same copy made to look like a traditional advertisement (source: Chron).

Then there's concern about cost. Advertorials generally come with a charge or a quid pro quo, but, where this is suggested, you can usually trust an outlet's advice. Seldom will a media professional recommend a paid-for option simply to switch you from a free news story. If it's a great news story, then she/he will run it as such. No media professional would risk losing a great story just for a bit of direct income. If you don't trust your media contact's objectivity, then you're talking to the wrong person or outlet. It's in media professionals' interest to steer you towards the best way of presenting your story. They want to generate the most website traffic or best coverage. They share your motives.

MAKING THE MOST OF THE STORY

Explore what can make the story work well; not just text, but also supporting media such as images, infographics and videos. Work with your contact to deliver what she/he wants.

If you decide to create a bigger article, ask how the outlet will promote it: on the website, on social media and so on. Will it be a lead story? The benefits of a good story are mutual – this is a conversation the outlet will want to have.

CREATE SOMETHING FOR THAT AUDIENCE

By working with a specific outlet, you can hone a story for that outlet's audience: something that a general press release seldom allows. Find out about that audience. What makes them tick? What's their preferred type of story/content? What challenges them? What are they generally for and against? Your contact will know this – and reading through some of the outlet's content will help further. You can create calls to action specific to that outlet, perhaps with an exclusive value-added download or offer – something else that you simply can't do within a press release.

QUALITY NOT QUANTITY

By targeting a specific audience, you reach those to whom your story is most relevant. It's far better to have an audience of a few thousand people who are keenly interested in your message than a million who couldn't care less. Relevance drives engagement better than numbers.

SUPPORT THE STORY WITH A GENERAL RELEASE

There's no reason why you can't supplement a targeted approach with a general campaign – almost certainly using a press release – to the wider media. The key thing to keep in mind is that you should be transparent with the outlet with which you're primarily working. They should know how you'll promote the story outside of their forum and when that will happen. This won't be challenging for them: they'll expect it. But it's best to keep everything in plain sight to avoid either surprising or upsetting them.

GET YOURSELF BEHIND THE STORY

As with any campaign, get your whole company behind the story. Make the most of it. Find ways to drive people to the primary outlet using e-mailers, social media updates/shares and more. Why to that website and not your own? Well, if readers are interested in visiting your website, *they will come* – but it's best that they first read the story on impartial soil. Help to create success for the outlet. If the article does well, then you'll open the doors for future collaborations; perhaps more ambitious ones.

The best way to give outlets or influencers exactly what they want is simply to ask: and then provide it.

PREPARATION

WORKING WITH STAKEHOLDERS

Stakeholders are your customers. You service their needs.
To do this successfully, you need strong, positive relationships
underpinned by shared goals.

You will learn that:
- you are responsible for stakeholders' expectations.
- you should help stakeholders understand publicity today.
- meeting stakeholders' needs means informing those needs, not just saying yes to everything.
- working in a structured way creates the most positive working relationships and the best outcomes.

As the person preparing news stories for your organisation, you'll likely work with stakeholders. Sometimes, this can be a challenge. Stakeholders are often not marketing professionals. They can be anyone – from your line manager to the chief executive; they can be managers of other business divisions/units; they can be trustees; they can be peers or superiors. If you work for an agency, or are freelance, then they're customers in the accepted sense – clients. It doesn't matter who they are. They're your customers. They expect you to deliver *for them*.

THE OVERHEAD OF BEING AT ODDS

It's especially challenging if you and your stakeholders are not on the same page when it comes to publicity and marketing. This isn't a question of who's right and who's wrong, it's just that you'll each have different expectations, assumptions and goals.

Because publicity isn't their primary remit or profession, stakeholders may have unrealistic expectations: that publicity is quick, cheap and easy; that there is a magic switch you can flip to make stories 'go viral'. They may insist stories are placed in logistically unrealistic or ineffective outlets. They may believe a story is great when it's poor. They may drive an agenda that's counter to the company's marketing or content strategy. They may request a press release when an advertisement would be better. You get the picture.

If a story doesn't meet stakeholders' expectations – even for very understandable reasons – it will likely be you who gets the blame, not the story or the stakeholder. It's therefore essential that you work *with* stakeholders; that you have common goals and expectations.

MAKE THINGS BETTER

While you should serve them *as customers*, you should take the lead, drive relationships, and educate stakeholders. Contrary to Harry Gordon Selfridge's assertion, the customer is *not* always right. Where your expertise is greater, steer and guide stakeholders.

It's not *their job* to understand what you do. It's *your job* to help them learn.

Just as you are busy, so are they. They have their own jobs to get on with, and publicity is a small part of their day. They won't be as invested in it as you. They may have fixed views or be difficult to educate. Be patient.

To manage expectations, establish them clearly upfront. Help stakeholders understand how the publicity landscape has changed; that:

- influencers such as bloggers and commentators can be at least as valuable as big-name newspapers or mainstream media outlets.
- publicity should also reach others of influence, such as professional bodies, researchers and so on.
- publicity now not only flows out through media gatekeepers, but also connects directly with the public.
- social media isn't a magic ride to success, unless there is great content for others to share or interact with.

Most of all, explain how a weak story *always* gets weak results, however much dynamite you lay under it.

BRING PEOPLE ALONG WITH YOU

If stakeholders are a touch hidebound, discovering that old publicity processes are no longer valid can sometimes undermine their confidence – in both press releases and publicity.

Rather than dwell on what's been notionally 'lost' because media influencers have changed, focus conversations on positives: the infinitely more varied publicity opportunities created by an evolving influencer landscape.

Help stakeholders to gain an updated understanding of distribution. Explain that it's not that 'mainstream media is now less influential', but rather that there are now many, many more avenues of influence with which to work. Help them to see the way these communities can add real value to your publicity.

Help stakeholders to understand:

- the organisation's overall marketing strategy and content strategy – and why every publicity activity, every news story, should ideally support those.
- the organisation's brand values and proposition.
- how you differ from your competitors; explore both the ways in which you seek to emulate competitors and the ways in which you seek to distance yourself from them.
- what your customers are really interested in and what really drives them to you – and to companies like yours.

Talk to them about cost. Undo the assumption, should it exist, that publicity is cheap. Marketing costs are frequently measured as production costs, which *are* relatively low for press releases, even when you factor in distribution. But there's still a cost to creating the idea, affirming its value, researching the approach, managing media relationships, planning the associated campaign or creating a campaign page on your website. In real terms, publicity can carry comparable costs to other forms of marketing – it's just the costs are in different places.

AGREE ON OUTCOMES

Agree goals. Challenge behaviours where press releases are fired out as quick responses, without planning, to a mindset where building a campaign (however modest) for news stories hugely improves their success.

When a press release topic is suggested, test the proposed story against your agreed goals, to help decide whether you're being wrongly tempted by opportunity, or if the 'drift' from your goals is acceptable. Goals shouldn't be prescriptive; deviate from them when events suggest but use them as a touchstone for every campaign. If stakeholders continually want something different, then perhaps your goals need reviewing – either to update them or to refresh minds and reaffirm your approach. Help stakeholders get buy-in and feedback from other parts of the business for their publicity activities.

IS IT NEWS?

Perhaps the biggest challenge, and the most important one to overcome, is helping stakeholders to understand when something *is news* and when something *isn't*; that weak press releases get poor results. It can't be stressed enough that when a story isn't good enough, it isn't good enough. If a story is likely to bomb, then it's better to have fostered a relationship where this can be discussed openly and positively. You may still decide to run with the story, but at least your expectations are aligned – and no one will be either disappointed or angry if the story doesn't do well.

Agree how you measure progress and results. Tracking how publicity is working can be complex and involve aggregating several sets of measurements, such as website analytics, social shares, growth in social media followers/likes, reach/mentions on other websites, evaluation downloads, customer enquiries and so on. You may also consider using software that's specifically designed to measure publicity activities. (You'll find examples of measurement processes and software in the chapter *Measuring results*.)

CHOOSE A SPOKESPERSON

Agree who will be the spokesperson cited within press releases. It's best that this is one person – and that the person is both informed and eloquent. The chosen person should have excellent knowledge of your products and services. She or he should be savvy: while the media don't typically try to wrong-foot people when interviewing them about press releases, it can happen. Also, the spokesperson should be fully bought-into the roadmap and not be pursuing another agenda. Sometimes, indeed often, you may be the spokesperson. As a marketer, rather than a practitioner, you may be perceived as lacking in-depth subject-matter expertise – this may be true; an interviewer could ask questions which aren't easy for a non-practitioner to answer. Someone who is in a customer-facing role, rather than from a marketing function, can be a better choice. Just as it's your responsibility to coach stakeholders, it's also your role to help the spokesperson perform well: don't leave her or him to it and hope for the best.

Without creating goals, within a positive working relationship, you can find that stakeholders pull you in different directions – setting expectations which don't match those of the business.

DIFFICULT STAKEHOLDERS

You may have a difficult stakeholder; someone who insists that you do something even when you know it won't work. These people are few and far between, but remember: just saying "yes" to every request isn't working *with them*. Nor will it ultimately please them. It's rare that you can't coach difficult stakeholders to share a common understanding: they're usually difficult simply because they're busy or don't fully grasp today's publicity landscape. Grow positive relationships, even if it's challenging at times. Being at odds with stakeholders is unproductive for everyone.

It's uncomfortable, but often true, that the clarity of a news story is typically in inverse proportion to the number of stakeholders. Each stakeholder may have different objectives – and managing these can be a real struggle. Your creative goal is to keep as close to 'one press release = one message' as you can, but your professional goal is to be as inclusive as possible and to satisfy each stakeholder. It's tough. The best route forward is to take on board stakeholders' needs early on (rather than in review) so that you can consider what will support the chosen message and what muddies it. Then, work with stakeholders to get them to see their needs in context, being clear with each of them about the core message and how their input might best help. The phrases, "That's a really powerful message, but this isn't the best vehicle for it," or, "That's definitely something we need to say but I'm concerned that it will get lost," can work wonders when pressed into including something that undoes an otherwise sound press release.

HELP STAKEHOLDERS EMBRACE MEANINGFUL GOALS

You may have been in a situation where a stakeholder says, "We've just landed a new customer; we need to get a press release out today." Fair enough, this is sometimes what needs to happen. It's a role publicity can perform well.

But when an organisation's *entire* publicity output (or a significant percentage of it) comprises of knee-jerk responses, then most resulting news stories won't have a particularly great impact. Why? Because they're written without a defined outcome, other than to let people know what's happened.

Press releases should achieve something beyond this – therefore, it's important to define the desired outcome and *write towards it*.

To assign a specific goal to a press release inevitably means giving greater scrutiny to the story. It forces you to ask that most searching of publicity questions: *is the story genuinely newsworthy?*

If the underlying story isn't that solid to begin with, then the likelihood of achieving a *specific, measurable* outcome isn't great.

Yes, the story may still be worth running to raise awareness – but what if stakeholders want to achieve something more specific? If press releases don't generate a clear-cut and direct response, it's not uncommon for stakeholders to 'blame publicity' rather than question the strength of their stories. Stakeholders often believe their stories to be more newsworthy than they are.

Ask stakeholders (and yourself), "What do we expect from this story?" In other words, what's the goal?

It's a tough question, but it makes stakeholders think. It creates a platform for discussion. It forces real consideration of the story's merits – and how it might be written and distributed. It makes publicity more goal-orientated, enabling you to both set realistic expectations and agree on outcomes. More than anything, it puts you in the driving seat, taking control of the story rather than accepting that it has to be batted out on a whim.

Let's wind back to where the stakeholder said, "We've just landed a new customer; we need to get a press release out."

Rather than, "I'm on it!" your response can now be, "That's great. What do we want as a result of this?" This isn't a truculent question. The resulting conversation shapes how you manage this story.

This challenge can initially flummox stakeholders, who may rarely consider specific outcomes from a press release.

If the response is that a press release will just communicate something that the market needs to know, then fine. As we said, generating awareness isn't a shabby goal – and at least now you have a common understanding. But if the answer is something more specific – media coverage, website hits or sales, social shares and so on – then *the quality of the story* can be assessed by its ability to meet those goals.

Perhaps you respond with, "As it stands, the story just isn't strong enough to do that," as a launching-off point for exploring the story's merits.

This professional response can help keep stakeholders' feet on the ground.

If the story isn't solid enough, can't easily be made stronger or needs to go out quickly, then lowering expectations is a sensible thing to do.

To achieve *anything*, your story has to be, first and foremost, *newsworthy*.

Help stakeholders to see that press releases are a starting point and not an outcome. Create conversations which help you to properly plan publicity, so that higher expectations can be more confidently met: "Let's talk about the kind of news story we'll need to run to achieve that."

Once you broaden the discussion, it's possible you'll move beyond planning a press release into planning a campaign. Why? The most likely reason is that if a defined goal is high, then a press release on its own won't be enough. This is fine: a press release is still a useful vehicle around which to organise your thoughts and launch a campaign within which it will be a core component.

While working with stakeholders can sometimes be a challenge, it's essential. If you don't work together, you'll find yourself knocked from pillar to post, delivering ineffective publicity – and getting the blame for its shortcomings.

ALIGNING TO A CONTENT STRATEGY

A content strategy provides a creative framework for marketing communications. It ensures press releases have defined, achievable goals which support an organisation's overall strategy and direction.

You will learn that:
- a content strategy provides publicity with structure and purpose.
- content-marketing strategies typically solve customers' problems rather than just 'sell hard' to them.
- without a defined content strategy, publicity can be aimless and ineffective.

Like other forms of marketing communications, press releases work best when aligned with an organisation's content strategy.

Those working within larger organisations may likely be aware of their organisation's content strategy. Those who work in smaller organisations, or are owners of small businesses, may either not be aware of the term – or may be aware of it, but not have a content strategy.

WHAT IS A CONTENT STRATEGY?

A content strategy defines how to plan, create, manage and measure marketing content. The phrase is perhaps most often associated with website content, but it can embrace any form of marketing media.

A key content-marketing goal is to respond to what drives customers – the issues they have, the problems they are trying to solve – and why they should come to you.

Consider this example: a company which sells cameras. The *company's* commercial goal is to sell cameras and associated paraphernalia. But the *customer's* goal is not to buy cameras. It is to *take photographs*. Understanding a customer's real needs is the heart of a content strategy. Successful content strategies (including for publicity) help customers scratch their itches, not pander to your commercial goals.

Why is this important? Well, even the keenest photographer will only buy a new camera perhaps once every five years. That's 1 day in every 1,825 days. As an expensive purchase, you can expect customers to undertake some research, say, 30 minutes a day for a couple of weeks. A potential customer is looking to buy for just 7 hours out of 43,800 – less than 0.02% of the time. Different products and services have different buying/research/interest cycles, but it's always true that people are in 'buying mode' for a fraction of the time in which they're interested in something.

According to Chet Holmes' buyers' pyramid, just 3% of people are typically in 'buying mode' (ready to buy now). 6%–7% are 'open to buying' so could be persuaded, with the right pitch. But 30% of people are not thinking about buying, 30% 'don't think' they are interested and 30% 'know' they are not interested.

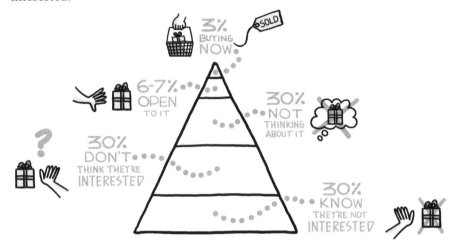

Source: Chet Holmes International

'Traditional marketing' targets customers when they are ready to buy, using website product pages, brochures and so on. *Which means that up to 97% of the time, marketing is ignored.* Since content marketing is about helping customers rather than selling to them, it can connect with the buyer up to 100% of the time. It enables you to build a relationship, so, when people are ready to buy, they are far more predisposed to buy *from you.*

In our example, a photography company might blog about new products, have demonstration videos explaining how to light shots, use software, describe the differences between lens types, demonstrate aperture use, and so on. This kind of content is *always* of interest to photography enthusiasts – not just the 3% of the time they're looking to buy. They search for it, absorb it, bookmark it, share it and engage in conversations about it.

Our examples could be accurately described as 'free training'. Some of the best content marketing has genuine commercial value, in the same way that a book might. This is a fundamental difference between content marketing and traditional marketing: content marketing can have an asset value, whereas traditional marketing is almost always a transient cost.

It's fair to say that our example is favourable: if you're keen on photography, then you're hungry for information. While true, it's not the buyers' enthusiasm which is the key motivator – they can be driven by a problem as much as a passion. Let's look at another example. Admittedly, very few people would be wildly enthusiastic about piping; so, if you sell piping, you're unlikely to tap into a market of ardent fans. Yet the principle is the same. People buy because of an itch, a problem, a need. Sure, your traditional marketing should list piping by diameter, length, material, and so on, with a price. But your content marketing would be about the problems each of these pipes solve, alternative products, fixing methods, how they are sealed, what happens when the seal goes wrong, and so on. Casual buyers don't think about pipes unless they're buying, but plumbers, joiners, builders and DIY enthusiasts will. And when casual buyers search online to solve a problem, you can be the one with the answers – not just the one with the pipes.

In sales and marketing, price is important – but so is trust. Building trust creates a predisposition to buy.

Content marketing doesn't replace sales-orientated marketing. You'll still need brochures, advertising, product pages and so on, but your marketing now not only casts a far wider net – but also, importantly, tries to connect with people at times *other than when they are buying*.

WHAT'S THE PAYBACK?

Is content marketing *yet more work* to land the same number of sales? No. There's strong, consistent evidence to show that content marketing increases the number of customers in your sales funnel and can influence their buying decisions. For example, the Content Marketing Institute found that: "80% of business decision-makers prefer to get company information in a series of articles versus an advertisement" (source: Content Marketing Institute). Custom Content Council found that: "74% of companies indicate that content marketing is increasing their marketing teams' lead quality and quantity" (source: Custom Content Council).

EMBRACING THE CONTENT STRATEGY

For the publicist, working within the organisation's content strategy ensures that publicity measurably supports its goals, brand, mission and values in a way which has been predefined and agreed.

A content strategy also encompasses a company's 'tone of voice', its stance on various sector issues, products (even those from competitors), solutions and so on. It not only helps you to focus content on customers' problems or interests, it also helps position why your solutions differ from those of your competitors.

A content strategy helps you to write in a more self-aware way. You know what to talk about, the tone of voice to use, what the organisation's goals are and so on.

A content strategy can be a 100-page manual or a single statement on a piece of paper which says, "We want to talk about x". It doesn't have to be grand, but it should be defined.

If a content strategy doesn't exist, there's a solid argument for creating one. Even a modest strategy is a strategy. It provides direction.

Without a content strategy, it's harder to find the right context and structure for news stories.

Press releases are more effective when linked to content which supports the company's strategic goals. Without a content strategy, such content is unlikely to exist, so press releases can be expected to do too much on their own, or they can become 'all about offers' linking back to sales pages. News stories can do more than get people to buy – they can help build relationships, manage perceptions and more.

Even sales-led press releases should support your content strategy, sending people not just to offer-response forms but also to valuable, interesting content.

EXTENDING THE MESSAGE BEYOND THE NEWS STORY

It's beneficial to provide links to content that's of value, helping you dovetail publicity into the company's content strategy. It's efficient for readers when you link back to a landing page which aggregates several pieces of content, putting everything helpfully in one place in an organised way.

When you point people to more information, ensure the press release still stands alone. It should always contain the full announcement. Rather than being a fractured piece of the story, additional information should provide extra value.

Link to content which creates a win for customers; things which solve real problems, which are educational, informative and perhaps even entertaining. You can also link to things which don't sit comfortably within a press release, such as opinion pieces.

LET THE CONTENT STRATEGY CHALLENGE YOUR THINKING

Working within a content strategy considerably aids the publicity-writing process, because it forces you to answer simple but incisive questions. What are you writing about? What do you make content about? What fits in with your values? What are your customers' problems or goals? Why do they buy from you?

It encourages you to actively address your customers' real needs and, in doing so, more accurately work out who they are and how to reach them.

Think about the following:

- How does a news story directly support your company's content strategy and business goals?
- How does a news story address a defined customer problem, challenge, question or issue?
- Why would somebody want to share the press release/story?

- How is what you are saying unique or different?
- How well do your company's values come across in the press release?

Should a content strategy not exist and there's no corporate desire to create one, then it's worth considering creating one for your own benefit, even if it stretches no further than your publicity activities. Doing so provides a meaningful, customer-relevant structure for your work.

> *It's not so much that publicity doesn't work without a content strategy, more that it doesn't work as well, or as predictably. A content strategy is something a publicist should hook into, or help to create.*

TWO AUDIENCES; DIFFERENT GOALS

Setting goals for news stories is important – but when doing so, bear in mind that press releases have two audiences: news outlets and the public.

You will learn that:
- for publicity to meet expectations, it's important to set meaningful goals.
- you should define desired outcomes for your campaigns for both news outlets and the public.
- there are lots of possible goals; choose those most meaningful to you.

Always remember, you write a press release for two audiences:
- news outlets and other influencers.
- the public.

Your goals for each aren't identical.

SETTING GOALS FOR THE MEDIA

Getting a news story 'published' may seem like an obvious goal, but is it a good enough metric? For example, anyone can blast out a story to newswires – and, tick! News outlets have carried the story! What's missing? Why isn't this a good enough metric?

A newswire is paid and not earned media. It's advertising, not publicity; a launching-off point, not an endgame. We need to move the story into earned media for our metrics to go beyond the newswire.

Set goals for *earned* media: for news outlets.

Goals beyond basic syndication are harder to achieve. It's not called *earned media* without reason. It's important that your stories are strong and are supported with engaging, shareable media. News outlets want, more than anything, impactful, well-written stories that feed and grow their readership.

The best way to find out the kind of stories an outlet wants (or whether a story you're working on is good enough) is to ask. Pick up the phone, talk to the editors and ask what *they need* to make more of the story. You can't do this with every story, but you can with a choice few. The answers you get might be surprising: that a story might be a winner with some research to back it up, or a video to demonstrate something 'live', or product evaluations as an exclusive giveaway and so on. You might discover what will transform a so-so story into one with far stronger legs.

Getting stories published takes work – and not all of that work involves writing. Goals you might set for outlets could include:

- building relationships with key outlets, so that you become known personally – and can call on them to discuss stories and campaigns.
- becoming a trusted source.
- making it easy for outlets to deal with you, by providing what they want.
- becoming recognised as a source of good, strong news stories.
- helping outlets generate traffic for themselves.
- working towards them asking you for stories, or to contribute to stories they are writing.
- becoming part of their connected and active network.
- becoming familiar with you, so that you're not just another e-mail in their inbox.

SETTING GOALS FOR THE PUBLIC

When setting goals, keep in mind that a press release is an announcement, not an advertisement.

Use publicity not just to make sales, but rather to do things that other marketing media can't – such as influencing opinion, building trust and sparking interaction.

If your primary objective is to make a sale or promote an offer, a press release is likely not the most effective means of achieving it. When stakeholders are primarily focused on sales outcomes, guide them towards more suitable communications tools – such as advertising and mailing campaigns.

Guide stakeholders towards more relevant goals. Talk about:

- a shift in market perception.
- a shift in the type of business you do, or how you do business.
- acquiring people into your content-marketing process.
- enquiries/sales/sign-ups.
- files downloaded.
- influencers engaged.
- market perceptions and awareness.
- media coverage.
- new backlinks to your website.
- other online coverage.
- social shares.
- syndication success.
- website hits.

IT'S PRETTY MUCH ALL ABOUT THE PUBLIC

Although you're writing for two audiences, the focus of your press release should always be the public. Write a press release as a finished story.

News outlets will alter a story if they need to, but many will welcome being able to run it as is.

KEEP ON PLAN

Align your goals to those of your company and work within its content strategy. Avoid tricks and gimmicks intended to create a buzz for its own sake – these may get shares and likes, but typically won't contribute to your marketing strategy.

YOU NEED GOALS YOU CAN MEASURE

The methods used to measure publicity affect your ability to set goals: after all, if you can't measure it, how can you set it as a goal?

There are many tools available to help you measure results. Some are free; some are not. (We touch on measurement tools and processes in the chapter *Measuring results*.)

While it's possible to achieve an adequate degree of measurement with free tools, more sophisticated, dedicated publicity analytics software will enable you to set more precise and relevant goals, and measure them with greater ease. They can also help you to be more ambitious in terms of what you measure.

Each organisation may wish to set goals which are meaningful to itself or to each campaign – and measure progress against these, in its own ways. Measure what's important to you – but having at least *some* form of measurement provides a platform around which you discuss and set meaningful goals.

Setting meaningful goals helps you to avoid writing reactive press releases, which usually vanish without a trace – and help you to build a more successful publicity strategy.

SEARCH OPTIMISATION

Optimising press releases for search engines is vital for them to be found online.

You will learn that search optimisation:
- is not hard to master.
- is best done by following official search-engine guidelines.
- does not involve tricks.
- can, if done poorly, significantly damage your search results.

Search-engine optimisation (SEO) is neither especially difficult, nor does it consist of ruses known only to a select few. Indeed, Google and other search engines publish extensive guidelines, to help content creators and website owners.

While, at a technical level, the way in which search engines work *is* pretty complex, it's not something you need to worry about. You don't need to know every last detail about how an engine works in order to competently drive a car.

CONCENTRATE ON CONTENT

You don't need to worry much about algorithms, that's the search engines' business. Focus your efforts on:
- creating great, unique content.
- using, naturally within your text, words most likely used by others when searching for topics mentioned in the press release.

THE SCOPE OF THIS CHAPTER

SEO is a *huge* subject.

We address the topic purely from a publicity writer's perspective. We're here to help you optimise press releases, not become an SEO expert – because *you don't need to be one* in order to optimise press releases well.

We focus on Google's core principles, which, despite ever-changing algorithms, have remained consistent for years.

Stick with these and you won't go far wrong.

We also highlight things you should avoid, because SEO has many traps for the unwary.

GOOGLE, BING, YAHOO AND MORE

We frequently refer to 'Google' rather than all, or other, search engines.

Google is the clear leader in online search, and has been for years; its nearest competitor, Bing, has a small fraction of its market share – so we mostly talk about Google. However, while other search engines may work differently, they're not so dissimilar that our advice isn't also relevant to them.

FOCUS ON THE STORY

It is often believed that because Google frequently adjusts its algorithms, that SEO and copywriting must also change. The reality is that algorithm changes only penalise content that has been trying to cheat, or is simply poor. To avoid getting hit by algorithm changes, focus on what Google wants: really good stories and quality content. Not only has this always worked, such content has never been penalised later because of algorithm changes.

WHY OPTIMISE A PRESS RELEASE?

News stories have three main search-engine objectives:
- to be easily discoverable when people search.
- to lead people back to your website.
- to contribute to the popularity of your website.

RELEVANCE AND POPULARITY

Let's look at how Google works. When someone searches, Google tries to return those pages which it considers the 'best' matches.

In simplistic terms 'best' is based on how *relevant* a page is to the search and how *popular* it is on the Web.

For a website to have *relevance*, it should contain the words you've typed – or synonyms of those words – and be about the same topic.

It doesn't take the smartest person in the world to spot a problem: for every search, there will be hundreds, thousands or millions of possible pages. How on Earth does Google know which ones to choose and how to rank them?

THE POPULARITY PAYOFF

This is where *popularity* comes in. From the most *relevant* items, Google presents the most *popular*. As per the classic Venn diagram, it's where relevance and popularity overlap that you find the best chance of getting the strongest results.

For the most part, this works pretty well – but, of course, the reality isn't that simple.

Google's search results use algorithms which consider hundreds of factors – it's not just that 'the words match' plus 'the most popular website'. Sophisticated algorithms assess website pages for several hundred factors. Each factor differs in value – and only search engines know what these relative values are and how their algorithms work. Because of this, it's not always clear, on a particular page or website, which factors are more important than others. It's hard to know what to change to get higher in the search results. This can be difficult for website owners to understand: they can be frustrated when their website isn't on the first page for a particular search. They want to know *why* they're not at the top.

The straight but brutal answer to that question is: "Why *should* it be at the top? Why does it *deserve* to be there?"

Since it's impossible for *every page* to be at the top, the majority of pages are always lower down. Mathematics is funny like that, but it doesn't stop website owners obsessing about the top spot.

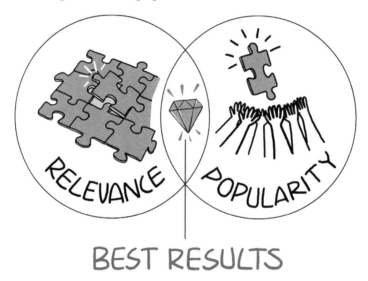

HOW RELEVANCE AND POPULARITY SHIFT

Let's consider an obvious search query: 'The White House'. This is almost certainly going to return whitehouse.gov – not because Google magically *knows* that you want *The* White House website, but because it's by far and away the most likely result – a combination of relevance and popularity.

Relevance or popularity can change in a couple of ways.

Let's assume you want a different White House, perhaps a White House Restaurant. Adding that final word, 'restaurant', changes the results of the search. If that doesn't locate what you're seeking, you can further narrow down the search by adding a location, for example: 'White House Restaurant London'. The seat of the United States' government is no longer at the top of the search results – because its relevance has diminished relative to the search term used.

There's another way this could happen. Let's say a massive event took place at a *different* White House: perhaps a terrorist attack or celebrity wedding at a White House Hotel. For the duration of that news event, it's possible that whitehouse.gov wouldn't be the most popular website for the search term 'White House'.

Here's an example of this.

British voice-over Emma Clarke hit the news a few years ago when she posted some humorous audio tracks on her website. Emma is one of the voices of the London Underground; every day, commuters hear her saying "mind the gap" and other announcements. The audio tracks were spoof London Tube announcements, created by Emma. Emma's public relations agency sent out a press release; the story was picked up by the media, who asked Transport for London to comment. Transport for London wasn't amused with Emma's brand of humour – and said so. The story went national. Then it went global. Within 24 hours, Emma Clarke's website received over one million hits – and, if you typed just 'Emma' into Google, the only search results above Emma Clarke's were for Spice Girl Emma Bunton.

This is how popularity can dramatically affect search results.

The news died down and, a few weeks later, she no longer ranked highly for the search term 'Emma'. Relevance and popularity had shifted back, though, for a while, they were slightly higher in her favour. Over more time, the balance reset.

RELEVANCE: WHAT ARE KEYWORDS?

Despite the slightly technical-sounding name, keywords aren't in any way magical. They're simply the words most likely to be used when people search for your content. For news stories to be found online, they should include the most relevant keywords.

Working out which keywords to use doesn't require much more than common sense and a little research.

Bear in mind that most people search using a lower register of grammar than they would use within formal communications, marketing copy or even when conversing with professional peers.

While your company might provide 'automotive components' or 'automotive consumables', most people would consider that you make 'car parts' (or 'automobile parts' in the USA) – but they'd be unlikely to search for that. Their searches would be quite specific, based on actual needs: 'spark plugs', 'brake pads' and so on.

If you run a training company, you might consider yourself a provider of 'learning services', but your customers will almost certainly want a 'training course' and they'd be more likely to search for a course on a particular subject, such as 'team leadership training'.

In our examples, 'spark plugs', 'brake pads', 'training course' and 'team leadership' are keywords.

They're simple words, not obscure ones. Business leaders and marketing teams like to use grandiose terms to differentiate their company, but to be found online, writers should – as much as possible – adopt the vocabulary of searchers.

Many SEO 'issues' are fixed by removing jargon and writing in a more approachable way. A beneficial side effect is that your copy will connect better with readers, who are typically turned off by jargon and posturing text.

UNDERSTANDING WHICH WORDS TO USE

A useful way to validate which keywords to use is to enlist the help of a tool such as Google Trends (google.com/trends). Google Trends lets you compare the volume of searches for a series of keywords. You can drill down via geography (important for our car/automobile example) and by time range (because terminology does change over time).

A learning provider might compare 'learning' and 'training' directly (at the time of writing, 'training' is about 35%–40% more popular than 'learning').

The context of use is important: if someone is searching for learning/training in a generic sense, or for a course, then we'd suggest using 'training'. But if you sell e-learning or a 'learning management system', you can't substitute one word for the other.

Be careful about results from Google Trends, because some terms' higher popularity can be because of searches which don't relate to your industry/sector. An example of this is 'recruitment-to-recruitment' (companies which recruit for recruitment companies). In the recruitment sector, recruitment-to-recruitment is more often known as 'rec to rec', 'rec2rec' and even 'r2r'. Google Trends tells us which of these terms people search for the most ('rec to rec') – but it can confuse us with the high volume of searches for 'r2r'. At first glance, it seems vital that we also optimise for 'r2r', but in fact, that term is *also* used by several *other* industries. If we optimised for 'r2r' as well as 'rec to rec', we could dilute, or even undermine, our efforts. We could lose ground for our most important keyword in an attempt to cover all of the bases.

NOT JUST KEYWORDS, BUT PHRASES, TOO

The term 'keyword' is a slight misnomer, because we're at least as interested in *phrases* as we are in *words*. If you consider the keyword 'car', it's hopelessly broad. Optimising on 'car' alone could never carry a press release to the top of Google. The good news is that, when searching, people are instinctively aware of this, and automatically include other words which might help deliver more relevant results, such as 'car servicing'. This phrase is better, but still too broad to be of much help to the searcher. Again, people tend to use additional words which are specific to their needs. A real-world search might be 'car servicing Audi Manchester', which would deliver pretty accurate results.

This is an important concept for writers of press releases, as there is little point in optimising for short, often vanity-driven, search phrases. Even if you get to the top of the search results for such phrases, it won't help your business – because people are almost always searching for something more specific.

INCLUDE SYNONYMS

Many keywords have natural synonyms. While people have traditionally thought about search optimisation in terms of exact words/phrases, search engines are now far more sophisticated. Using synonyms as a natural part of your writing doesn't just add variety, it helps search engines more fully assess your document – and is also one of the things which Google uses to evaluate the quality of content.

OPTIMISE FOR ONE TOPIC

At typically around 300–400 words, a press release is a short document, focused on a single subject. Search optimisation should follow the same singular thinking. Optimising for lots of topics, with many keywords, dilutes optimisation effectiveness. Focus optimisation on the main topic of the press release – do what's most important, rather than trying to do everything.

WORDS WITHOUT VALUE

Some words have little or no search-engine value, such as 'solutions', simply because their meaning is so broad. While we may need to use those words, a more direct alternative may be an improvement – not only from a search optimisation perspective, but also to improve readability. For example, the phrase 'training course' is far more accessible to readers, and has more search-engine value, than 'training solution'.

HOW TO INCLUDE KEYWORDS

Use natural, informal language. Don't shoehorn keywords into place. It's how people search and how they prefer to read. If it helps, read press releases aloud to help identify and remove any stilted language.

Don't use keywords as a cheat. You are *not* trying to rig the results; you are *trying harder* to be found when people search.

Try to include a subset of your main key phrases into the press release's headline and synopsis, as search engines typically place greater importance on keywords found within page headings, paragraph headings and introductory paragraphs.

Inserting keywords into the heading and synopsis can be a challenge: search optimisation isn't your only goal – or even the primary one.

The strength of your news story comes first, always. Never put search optimisation before the needs of the reader. Search engines want to deliver great, unique content. Your job is to provide that.

There isn't a fixed rule for the number of times your keywords/phrases should appear in the main body of the press release: between 2-3 times at the least and 4-5 times at the most is usually considered sufficient by search optimisation professionals. Always err towards a lower number, as too many repetitions of the same phrase within a 300-word press release can not only be tedious for the reader, but it can also increase the likelihood of search engines flagging it as spam.

For the same reasons, keywords/phrases should be spread out throughout the document and not recur within close proximity of each other.

WHAT IS PAGE RANK?

Much of Google's early success sprang from an innovation called page rank. Then, the search engine was called Backrub; this name alludes to page rank's workings.

Page rank gave each *page* on the Web a 'popularity score'. When one page linked to another, Google took the link as evidence of popularity – like a vote. The *giving* page passed on a percentage of its page rank score to the *receiving* page. If the giving page had a bigger score (because *it* had more links to it) the value of page rank passed on would be higher.

Page rank used a logarithmic scale. Imagine a staircase, where each step is double the height of the preceding one. That's page rank. It's exponentially harder to get from step 3 to 4 than from step 2 to 3 and so on. Therefore, very few websites ranked as 7, 8, 9 or 10. Most websites ranked between 1 and 5.

Since a *percentage* of page rank was passed from giving to receiving pages, it was (and still is) far better to receive links from high-ranking ones. A single link from a Web page with a page rank of 7 could be of far greater SEO value than many, many more links from Web pages with page ranks of 1.

Notice that we're talking about page rank in the past tense. This is because, for SEO purposes, we can now mostly discount page rank.

Google's John Mueller said in 2014, "I wouldn't use page rank or links as a metric. We last updated page rank more than a year ago (as far as I recall) and have no plans to do further updates. Think about what you want users to do on your site, and consider an appropriate metric for that."

LINKS STILL MATTER

However, page rank (or at least the data behind it) is likely still a part of Google's algorithms, so inbound links from news stories still contribute to the popularity of your website.

Interestingly, Google filed a patent in 2014 which confirms that online activity such as mentions of a brand constitute 'implied links' to the brand's website and can add authority to it. Many SEO professionals believe that this is already a part of how Google works. In a world where social media is a good measure of popularity, this makes sense – social media posts by others don't often link directly to the mentioned website, even when the brand is cited – but Google wants to take these brand mentions into account. Conversations on social media are all becoming part of a more complex (and complete) measure of popularity.

HOW BAD SEO NEARLY KILLED GOOD PRESS RELEASES

Let's rewind the clock a little and examine something that came close to fatally undermining press releases' usefulness. This backstory is important in understanding what *not* to do with press releases.

As people began to understand more clearly how page rank worked, many realised that generating news is a powerful way of increasing a website's page rank score. This is as it should be: a new story appears on several news websites; they link back to you; your website not only gets more traffic but also receives a Google popularity burst.

There was an obvious way to rig the system. News stories could be placed on newswires, themselves often high-ranking websites. This in itself isn't an issue: a newswire is a valuable service, delivering news to influencers with whom you don't have a relationship. But, since they are earning money from the transaction, these links are *paid for*, not *earned*. Although against Google's guidelines, the 'news' nature of the content seemed to offer some protection – and so, for a while, posting news stories became reliable and easy SEO.

Less ethical search optimisers pumped out valueless news stories, usually via free newswires. It was search-engine magic. From a single press release, a company could get hundreds of inbound links. This created an explosion of junk news.

This wasn't just bad for Google, it was also bad for public relations, undermining the credibility of the press release by turning it into a dirty SEO tool.

Good news stories drowned in a sea of nonsense. Many people lost faith in publicity. Others began to see press releases as little more than an SEO tool.

GOOGLE STEPS IN

Google waded in to sort out the mess. It did so without mercy.

From Google's perspective, there were several issues to resolve:

- The inbound links from newswires were bought, not earned.
- Inbound links from press releases were 'over-optimised' for SEO.
- The same press release might appear several times in its search results pages.
- A growing proportion of press releases were poorly written, constructed for SEO only and valueless to humans.

SEO VALUE OF INBOUND LINKS FROM NEWSWIRES KILLED

Google has long warned against using *any* paid-for links, saying that content should earn them.

Google made an explicit clarification: that press releases are not, in themselves, news – and because newswires charge for their service (whether directly or via advertising) any links they host are *always* considered *paid-for*.

Google made sweeping algorithm changes to address websites which bought links. It penalised, hard, websites with high percentages of bought inbound links – including links from newswires. Many companies fell off Google as a result of this.

To comply with Google's guidelines, and to continue to provide a useful service, good newswires add a hidden 'nofollow' attribute to links within press releases. This tells Google to not pass any popularity ranking to the receiving website, though the link still works for humans. That way, press releases still get distributed, can still be picked up (or republished) by outlets but newswires are not *in themselves* contributing to a website's Google popularity score. Since outlets take the story without any payment, any links they publish can legitimately pass on a popularity ranking.

Some less ethical newswires continued to trade unaltered, but their customers' websites were steadily down-ranked. With no SEO value, and since the news from most of these seldom reached outlets and other influencers, their value proposition evaporated.

Good newswires remain a valuable and often vital distribution tool, extending the reach of your press releases.

Since Google has stated that links inside press releases should contain the nofollow attribute, it's vital that newswires you use must adhere to this standard. If they don't, your website will pay the penalty.

WEEDING OUT OVER-OPTIMISED LINKS

In 2013, Google updated its webmaster guidelines to explicitly ban: "Links with optimised anchor text in articles or press releases distributed on other sites." By "optimised anchor text" Google means aggressively optimising links with keywords, for example, creating links such as [low-cost cars] and [car servicing London]. Within a sentence, these links might look like: '*ABC Motor Company sells [low-cost cars] and is a specialist in [car servicing in London]*'. Google considers these links to be over-optimised and you should avoid this approach.

Google's guidelines are quite specific, pointing to the links themselves as being the offending items, rather than the press release or the hosting website.

HOW TO INCLUDE LINKS

Since it's good for usability to make links descriptive, writers should be careful that they don't unwittingly over-optimise link text. Links such as [find out more] are descriptive and could not be considered over-optimised. However, they could be more useful for readers. It's considered poor usability to phrase links as 'click here'; it's better to describe what is on the other side of the link.

For example, 'people can [read the annual report]'. This 'promise and deliver' method of naming links is a foundation of good website usability.

Whether you place links inside the body of the press release, or at the end ('for more information...') depends on the context of the link. Typically, the latter is fine and, since a good press release is about a single topic, one link is usually enough. You may legitimately need to add more links where you cite research, or for specific downloads – but more than two or three links can overwhelm readers; by giving people too many options you can create choice paralysis.

Littering links throughout a press release is distracting, makes the story look like an advertisement, increasing the chance that Google will flag it as spam.

When you absolutely need your press release to contain several links, consider instead directing people to a campaign-specific landing page, via a single link – to a page that aggregates information, resources and actions (such as a contact form) in one place. This is safer search optimisation and more useful for humans.

THE FIGHT AGAINST DUPLICATE CONTENT

A press release is a means to an end: when outlets receive it, they either write a story *based* on it or use part of it as a subsection of a bigger story.

Even when rewritten a hundred times, the stories are always different. Each has a place and value in the search engine results pages, so you get SEO benefits from each.

However, when published as is many times, a press release is duplicate content. Google avoids showing people lots of versions of the same thing, regardless of its value, so only one version will typically appear in the search-engine results. Which is fair enough. Who wants to see dozens of versions of the same thing?

Many outlets are busy, and it's not unusual for them to cut and paste a story rather than rewrite it. When this happens several times with the same press release, it becomes duplicate content.

Since Google works hard to avoid presenting duplicate content in its search engine results, it's highly unlikely that you'd see more than one instance of an identical press release on the same search page.

Google's actions against duplicate content have led many to believe that it can result in websites being entirely blacklisted.

However, according to Google, the idea of an SEO hard penalty for duplicate content is largely a myth. Google's Susan Moskwa said, "Let's put this to bed once and for all, folks: there's no such thing as a 'duplicate content penalty'. At least, not in the way most people mean when they say that." (Source: Google)

What happens is that Google presents one version of an article (or press release) to those searching. It works out which is the 'best' and weeds out the rest – this is often the originating source, but it can be the most popular website hosting that content.

You don't get to decide which version of your story comes first in the search results, Google does. If your news story is on a high-ranking outlet, then it may well be that Google displays that, instead of the one on your website. Other than for your ego, this is not a bad thing: your story is ranking higher than it would if *only* placed on your website.

Some newswires try to help search engines identify the 'canonical' (primary) version of the story by citing a source reference at the bottom of the story, such as "this news story first appeared on [websitename]", "this news story first published on [websitename]" or "this news story originated on [websitename]". Be aware that this isn't a defined standard; it's more a useful practice.

THE QUALITY OF CONTENT

Eliminating poor quality content from search results pages was perhaps Google's hardest punch against SEO press releases. Via its algorithms, Google has increasingly turned the screws on poorly written, news-empty, SEO-focused content that no one wants to see. This has been highly successful – to the point where little content of this nature now appears in the search engine results.

GOOGLE WINS; PUBLICITY WINS

While Google's actions hit a lot of websites hard, they're fair.

Google has consistently said that people should focus on creating great content – and let SEO look after itself: "Create unique, relevant content that can naturally gain popularity in the Internet community." (Source: Google)

Great news naturally attracts backlinks and delivers SEO value. The best results come from press releases which inspire independently written stories or when outlets publish edited versions.

The quality of the news story matters. An uninteresting story won't warrant an outlet either editing your press release or writing their own version of it.

GET BETTER SEO – AND COVERAGE – BY WRITING MULTIPLE STORIES

Many companies see a press release as the sole tool to get news stories out. And it can be. But it's worth considering how we can sidestep the SEO impact of duplicate content by drafting variants of a story.

These aren't 'the same release with the odd word changed', they are entirely rewritten versions of the story. One might be the standard release for the media. Another would be for your own website's news section. Another might be for informal influencers. Oh, no! Three times the work! No one likes additional work, but this isn't without payoff.

This is good publicity practice. You *should* write the story in a different way for each of these audiences. They each want different things from it. Press release distribution software company Prezly says that additional versions of the same story, written for specific audiences, generate significantly better results for all of its clients.

GIVE OTHERS REASONS TO LINK TO YOUR WEBSITE

To encourage others to link to your website, consider creating useful and unique content that people will *want* to share, and provide links to these from your news story. These can include how-to videos, useful tools, downloads, free software, templates or more detailed information. There has to be a *reason* for outlets to create a link; they must feel that it would be genuinely useful for their readers. Such content delivers powerful search optimisation, with as much chance, if not more, of being shared and linked to than the originating press release.

OPTIMISE SOCIAL MEDIA POSTS

Social media is a vital part of publicity and essential for search engine success.

There has been some debate about whether search engines use social signals as ranking factors. Google says not – but things aren't that simple. Google's Matt Cutts said in 2015: "Facebook and Twitter pages are treated like any other pages in our Web index so if something occurs on Twitter or occurs on Facebook and we're able to crawl it, we can return that in our search results." He went on to say that there is no current process to convert numbers of followers (social popularity) into ranking signals.

Social posts do end up in the search results, drive traffic to your website and encourage other actions that also deliver SEO. But the magic comes mostly from others reacting to you – from the conversations you create, not the updates you broadcast.

It's common for companies to post social media updates about a news story, linked to the press release – often with just the headline, or the headline prefaced by something like: 'new press release'. This isn't enough. Just as your news story needs to be interesting, so do the social media posts leading to it. Also, just as you need to think about SEO when writing a press release, the same is true of social media updates.

A news story gets better traction on social media when you add something – a photograph, meme-type image, infographic or video – these can not only encourage others to share it but also allow you to pick up on points within the story in interesting or amusing ways.

Additional media shouldn't be a bolt-on, but rather a core part of the story, telling it differently, in a way that engenders sharing. Think of the story as a conversation; look for ways to get people talking and interacting. In the past, publicists controlled the message; today, customers control it. Social media enables them to praise, damn, joke, sass back, create memes, troll, loop in other brands – and more. Find ways to make this happen and to keep it positive.

Is there a way you can get others to join in? For example, if you're launching a new product, can you run a competition for the best picture of someone using that product?

Is there a way you can seek out customers on social media and thank them, or even reward them, for their loyalty?

It's worth repeating the two most important SEO fundamentals for publicity writers.

1: play with a straight bat

Get into any conversation about SEO, and it's likely some experts will offer advice on shortcuts and tricks. Let's unpick three words there: experts, shortcuts and tricks. First, experts. While Google and other search engines publish extensive guidelines to help website owners, their algorithms are almost entirely secret: so, unless they work for Google or Microsoft, most SEO experts can only guess at them. Therefore, always take the word 'expert' with a pinch of salt. When it comes to shortcuts and tricks, the bottom line is: avoid them. You don't need them. Even if they work now, chances are they'll compromise your search results in the future. Be honest with your SEO. As we said before, optimisation is about improving findability, not rigging results.

2: the story always comes first

There's no denying that optimisation can create wording changes in a press release. If a change renders a smooth story clunky, makes it repetitive or arduous to read, then backtrack on your changes. Always put the story first. Good SEO will almost always follow.

WANT TO LEARN MORE ABOUT SEO?

If you want to grow your SEO skills, there are almost endless resources available. Start with those developed and delivered by Google, because you can't beat advice from the horse's mouth. Go to: Google Search Console (search. google.com/search-console), Google Analytics (analytics.google.com/analytics/ academy) and Google's Digital Garage (learndigital.withgoogle.com).

Getting the essentials of search optimisation right isn't too difficult –
and is usually more than enough for press releases to be found online.

COMPETITOR RESEARCH

Without studying competitors' publicity, it's almost impossible to be sure that your press releases are different enough to stand out.

You will learn that:
- knowing your competitors is vital for effective publicity.
- understanding competitors' publicity strengths is not the same as understanding their commercial strengths.
- publicity competitors may not yet be commercial competitors.

"*If you know your enemies and know yourself, you will not be imperilled in a hundred battles ... if you do not know your enemies nor yourself, you will be imperilled in every single battle.*"

Setting aside the reflected glory of quoting Sun Tzu (544–496 BC) with the ease that only Wikipedia can deliver, great strategists have always leaned on knowledge when planning: knowledge of themselves and, of equal importance, knowledge of their enemies. Our competitors aren't *enemies* in the military sense, but you are fighting against them for the same things – share of customers' minds, hearts and wallets.

It's a battle to be taken seriously. Publicists should always be aware of what competitors are saying and doing.

Not only does the public judge your publicity against that of your competitors, so do the outlets and influencers – those hard-to-please but highly important gatekeepers to the public's eyeballs and ears.

Most companies want others to perceive them as different from their competitors: better, typically, but incomparable, almost certainly. This is essential with publicity; you don't want to say the same things as your competitors. Observing how your competitors speak helps you build your own unique voice.

Such research is ongoing. You might start with an in-depth competitor analysis, but – at some level – it's something you should do all of the time.

Assessing a company via its publicity output is an interesting exercise. The reality of an organisation, and what it says about itself, are two different things. A small company which perhaps you don't consider to be a business threat can be a real threat in publicity terms. Many smaller companies grab market share by first grabbing mind share.

Research requires interpretation: not all of your evidence will be empirical. After all, you're studying companies' rosiest views of themselves. This isn't so much about commercial strengths and weaknesses but rather their marketing prowess, or lack thereof. It's imprudent to be sceptical about the publicity of a competitor you happen to know is commercially weak. Others may well take what they say seriously – and so should you, for that very reason.

WHAT TO LOOK FOR?

You're looking to understand how self-aware (in marketing terms) your competitors are: the ones who are thinking deeply about their publicity and the ones who are just phoning it in.

Try to discover what works for them, and why. Don't make assumptions about their publicity's effectiveness. A competitor may publish a seemingly compelling news story which brought envious fists down on your boardroom table, but how did it *really* perform? You can track this relatively quickly, using Google and other search engines. Copy and paste the headline, or perhaps a snippet from the release, into a search engine. This will quickly show you how many outlets republished the story. You can set these up as Google Alerts (google.com/alerts), too.

Tools such as Mention (mention.com), Social Mention (socialmention.com) and SharedCount (sharedcount.com) track social shares of keywords, in a similar way to using Google Alerts. Tools such as Cision (cision.com) and Onclusive (onclusive.com), which provide extremely comprehensive analytics for publicity, can also be incredibly powerful competitor-research tools.

This kind of tracking helps to separate the reality of a press release's actual success from the paranoia and assumptions expressed by others. It tells you what *genuinely* works for your competitors, rather than you guessing or assuming what works.

Study what they're saying and doing.

- How much of it is new, or different, and in what way?
- How frequent are their press releases?
- How well-syndicated are they?
- Are they using paid newswires and, if so, which ones?
- How well are their stories shared and commented on?
- Are the comments positive?
- How well-written are the stories?
- How do they employ search-engine optimisation: is it good, bad or over-egged?
- What do their stories link to: do they create landing pages for campaigns (pages which aggregate useful content to support the campaign, downloads, multimedia and calls to action)?
- How do they use social media: how well do they *interact* over Facebook, Twitter, LinkedIn, Instagram and so on?

In some cases, only your professional judgement can assess others' publicity output, but in many cases, there are tools available. For example, you can partially judge how well-written something is by using a tool such as The Readability Test Tool (webpagefx.com/tools/read-able/).

While not perfect, it can provide helpful information on writing style.

Just as small companies can be tough publicity competitors, some large companies can coast: don't assume what they do works, just because they are big. Some companies are so big they could send out crayon-written press releases on toilet paper, and they'd still get published. Some companies have products that are so great, or so essential, that even poor publicity can work for them.

Assess competitors' stories on their own merits and isolate this from what you know (or assume) about them. How genuinely newsworthy are the stories? Which are strong and which are weak – and why?

You don't have to limit research to competitors. What can you learn from partners, suppliers, peers and industry bodies?

Perhaps redefine which companies you see as competitors. Don't just think about direct competitors. Supermarkets don't just compete with supermarkets; they also have to compete with radically different businesses, such as petrol companies (where supermarkets have filling stations at the store) and online retailers. Supermarkets know they don't only compete to sell stuff that's on the shelves, they compete for people's income. If you're a commercial training company, your competitors aren't just other training companies. They are other *information and services providers.* For example: book publishers, business consultancies, conference organisers, government departments, educational institutions, social networks and groups – and so on. They may not sell the same things as you, but they want to eat from your table.

Such companies become competitors because they understand the buying motives of your customers. They look to solve the same problems you solve, just not in the way that you solve them.

You may not see these competitors coming. You can not only learn from their publicity but also spot commercial challenges.

Studying competitors' publicity can help you to write better, stronger news stories. It can help you to plan more complete campaigns. Create more successful landing pages. Become more influential on social media.

Learn from your competitors; use that knowledge to become different, a voice that stands out – one which can outmanoeuvre competitors, by acting on what is true rather than what is assumed.

Knowing competitors is vital if your publicity is to be unique, effective and market-leading. Without competitor research, a publicity strategy can be undone by misplaced concerns, complacency or guesswork.

WRITING

IS IT NEWS?

There are two main reasons why press releases fail: the story isn't newsworthy enough; although the story is potentially newsworthy, the writer didn't pinpoint what could have made it interesting.

You will learn that:
- press releases should be newsworthy.
- not everything a company does is news.
- identifying the newsworthiness of a story is a publicist's core skill.

News: noun. Newly received or noteworthy information, especially about recent events.

Sorry to take you back to school, but the definition does bear repeating.

Your goal when writing a press release will typically be to generate news. A press release in itself isn't news: it's an announcement of something that you think is newsworthy.

WHAT MAKES ONE STORY NEWSWORTHY WHEN ANOTHER ISN'T?

News is, by definition, something that's new. (The word comes from the late Middle English plural of new, a translation of the Old French noveles or medieval Latin nova, meaning 'new things'.)

But being *new* doesn't automatically make something newsworthy.

When a few bricks crumble in a building, it's not news. When a building collapses, it is. Events such as this – disasters, accidents, political events, economic changes, shifts in government policy, sports matches, arts or culture performances, technology changes – are often automatically news. We are interested in them because they affect us in some way.

We don't need press releases for these kinds of events. When they happen, the media jumps on them without encouragement.

Businesses write press releases to generate media coverage, for their story to *become news*. But many press releases simply aren't newsworthy enough to warrant coverage.

IS IT NEWS?

Deciding whether or not something is newsworthy requires objectivity. We need to consider the story from an outside perspective.

Typical press release topics which aren't – in themselves – newsworthy include:

- a new hire.
- a new service.
- an offer.
- attending a trade show.
- winning an award.

"But those are news!" some people cry. Well, it's not uncommon for such topics to be perceived, *within organisations*, as newsworthy. Sorry to burst your bubble, but they seldom are.

The new hire: hiring someone new may be important to you and your company, but is rarely even remotely of interest to outsiders.

The new service: this may be exciting to you, but it's hardly ever – whatever you think – exciting to others.

The offer: the right place for an offer is an advertisement, not a press release.

The trade show: what exactly is news about 'XXX company to display at XXX Show'? 'Man gets on bus' is the same level of newsworthiness. "Ah," you might say, "but this is the industry's biggest event, and we're one of the sector's major players; therefore it *is* news." Not buying it. For this really to be news, you'd have to be a *major* brand – and typically there would also need to be something unique about the exhibition.

These events are simply business as usual. They are not news.

Moreover, what makes press releases like this any different from those of your competitors? News outlets will pass them over. The public will be disinterested. They have little or no impact.

Let's look at the final item on the list. Winning an award can be significant, but it has to be something like 'Leonardo DiCaprio wins Oscar' or 'Gerry Anderson awarded MBE' to be *important enough on its own*. But, let's face it, Leonardo DiCaprio walking down the street is news. The late Gerry Anderson shaped entertainment for children, so, when he was awarded the MBE in 2001, the event alone had an impact. Many other accolades, especially industry awards, aren't always newsworthy enough to carry a story. It may be better to lead with why the award was won. For instance, if a recruitment agency is named 'recruitment company of the year', then a headline such as 'GHI Jobs awarded recruitment company of the year' is fine but functional. For a more exciting headline, especially for it to resonate with a wider audience, it would be better to focus on why GHI Jobs won the award – for example, '280% ROI lands GHI Jobs recruiter of the year award'. This shift in focus upgrades the story from utilitarian to compelling.

WHAT MAKES SOMETHING NEWS?

To be news – and newsworthy – something must have *a real impact on the outside world*. Something of consequence. Something that affects people. Something that changes the landscape. The new in news isn't just the fact that it's happened now. It's also that it's new – that it's *change*.

It's the impact on the outside world which counts most. Hiring someone or exhibiting at a trade show takes time, a lot of planning and a good deal of money, so, within an organisation, these have an impact and therefore feel like news. But unless they have a real impact on others outside of your company, then they're just not, in themselves, that interesting.

Which brings us to the second issue: properly identifying the heart of the story.

WHAT CAN WE DO TO MAKE STORIES MORE NEWSWORTHY?

We cited five topics as not, in themselves, being news. This was a bit of a cheat. How? Well, often, such topics can be news. It's a question of finding, within the story, the thing which makes it newsworthy. In other words – *what's the real story?*

Attending a conference or exhibition isn't news, but using that venue to launch something new gives the story legs. 'XXX to launch new mousetrap at XXX' is, without doubt, more newsworthy than 'XXX to display at XXX'.

A new hire isn't interesting, sometimes even if it's a new MD/CEO. But ask yourself: why are you hiring? If it's just a straight replacement, then move along: nothing new to see here. But what if you are expanding into new territories? If you're pushing a particular growth strategy? That absolutely *could* be news.

A new product or service in itself isn't news – but the problem it solves can be. Does it save time or money? Does it make something obsolete? Is it a game-changer? These topics make the story far more newsworthy. Rather than your press release saying 'XYZ Company to launch ABC Product', focus on the product's impact: 'ABC Product cuts time wasted in half'.

An industry award is a far stronger news story when you focus on the reasons *behind the award*. Was something changed? What was the impact? In other words, winning an award is not news in itself, but the reason for winning it could well make it newsworthy.

A supermarket opening twenty new stores enjoys media coverage because it means more jobs or that it is *entering new regions*, not simply because it's opening new stores.

The news is about how something *impacts upon the world*.

THE IMPORTANCE OF OBJECTIVITY

When assessing whether something is news and how to make the most of that story, objectivity is vital. Outsiders won't typically view your company with anything like the same degree of importance you do.

Many will view your news with a degree of cynicism, so it's vital that it's genuinely newsworthy. That it's factual and objective. That you find 'the story within the story'.

Write your press release as if it were a real news story; don't think about what you are promoting but concentrate on writing about what it means to the reader. Put the news first; let other benefits follow through naturally, don't force them in.

PASSING THE NEWSWORTHINESS TESTS

These two questions: "Is it news?" and "What's the real story here?" are the entrance examination for all press releases. They are questions which demand honest answers. If the answers don't measure up, *it's not news*, no matter how hard you spin it.

THE HARM OF LESS NEWSWORTHY STORIES

Distributing a press release about something that isn't news can damage your reputation with outlets and influencers (they'll tire of you tediously peddling 'business as usual' as news). It can dent your status with customers and prospects, who may think you have little of value to say. And it causes damage internally: stakeholders are more likely to feel a press release bombed because it wasn't well-written or well-placed, rather than accept the story wasn't up to much.

It can be hard to be dispassionate about your own news stories. It can be harder to get stakeholders to understand why something which might excite them won't create much of a ripple out in the market.

When a story's not newsworthy, it's better to be honest and upfront with stakeholders than waste time on it.

Where a story fails both of these tests, it would be far better to kick it into the long grass. Spend your time on something more productive, such as writing a press release that is far more likely to succeed.

Some types of organisation are automatically more newsworthy than others: charities, social enterprises and so on. People are typically interested in what these kinds of organisations are doing and will more readily share updates. Other businesses, usually large or influential ones, enjoy such an elevated status that almost everything they do is news.

But for most businesses, publicity is harder. They need to make sure their news *really is* news. Putting out a large number of uninteresting press releases does little more than create noise.

WHAT ABOUT WHEN A STORY DOESN'T SEEM TO HAVE ANY IMPACT ON OTHERS?

There are instances when you'll want to send out a press release, but you're struggling to find the impact on others. Great examples of this include a book by a new author, a record by a new band or a painting by a new artist.

If the creative is well-known, then there's little issue: a new book by Stephen King is always newsworthy. But what if you're a new author – or an author with just a few books published – and you've yet to hit the big time?

There's no argument for saying that the impact of the book ("horror book written to scare readers") is newsworthy. It isn't. But you may well be involved in a promotional activity which is. Some examples include book signings, sending free books – as a thank you – to the library you used as a child, participation in genre events and so on. These make the basis for a good news story. As ever, the news isn't that you would be hosting a book signing, but what this means for readers – signed books, photographs, readings, questions and answers, discounts and so on.

TO GET YOU STARTED

Asking "is it news?" and finding the best way to approach a story isn't always easy. To help you along, the chapter Handling common news topics contains prompts for writing press releases on almost fifty different topics.

Newsworthy stories focus on what's important to the reader, not to the writer: on the impact of events, not the events themselves.

KEEP THE READER IN MIND

While press releases are a vehicle for promotion,
they should do this in a way that is relevant to the reader.

You will learn that:
- news stories which are structured around how others are affected by the announcement are more successful.
- people are more interested in their own needs than a company's importance.
- boastful press releases don't engage readers.

For a press release to resonate with readers, it should focus on what's important to them.

And yet, many press releases are introspective, sometimes to the point of narcissism. They squander much of their word count eulogising the company, its products and its services.

On the face of it, this doesn't seem to be greatly at odds with the role of a press release, which, let's admit it, is *to promote*. It's therefore understandable why some publicity writers take this approach. Understandable, but still a mistake.

IT'S NOT ALL ABOUT YOU

At the most basic emotional level, people simply don't like those who can't stop going on about themselves. You'll empathise with this if you've ever been on a date with someone who is self-absorbed, or sat next to an immodest guest at a dinner party. Unless that person is Batman, listening to someone endlessly hold forth about her or his exploits is tedious. It also creates the impression you're not interested in others.

So it is with press releases.

Let's look at an example: perhaps your company is about to launch a new product (or a service) in a market where you're already a leader.

A release expounding a 'fantastic new product' from a 'world-leading company' comes across as merely boastful.

To tell *your story* more effectively, make it meaningful to readers. Write it with them in mind.

In our example product launch, we should consider why this is important to others. What is the new product? What problems does it solve? What are the benefits of using it? What do people gain? In short, *what's in it for them*? Putting yourself in their shoes, thinking how they think, writing about what's important to them, is what makes a press release relevant to others.

People won't buy your product because you're a 'world leader', because it's 'new' or because you've claimed it's 'fantastic'. They need to know what it's going to do for them; why they should open their wallet for it. You have to excite them. If it lets them do something for a tenth of the price of other products, then it's exciting. If it lets them do something they couldn't do before, it's exciting. If it takes a tedious everyday task and automates it, it's exciting.

The same thinking applies even when positioning your own company. World leader in a particular sector you might be, but what does this *mean* to customers? Is it genuinely significant to them or is it just posturing? Perhaps written to provide the 'comfort' that clients are dealing with a world leader, it nonetheless doesn't connect directly with the individual because it's a statement about mass; about an entire market. You may well want readers to understand that your company is a world leader, but continually telling them outright is a clumsy way to go about it. You have to prove, in prose, why you are a leader, not just state it. You need to show, rather than tell.

A more reader-focused approach would be to say why *individuals* choose your company, how they've *directly* benefited from your products/services and over what period.

A press release entitled 'XYZ Company to present at DX World' may well be factual, but it assumes the mere fact of the company being at the show is both newsworthy and of relevance to the reader. Neither is likely. Better to include what you are presenting, why this is important to others and how they will benefit. This makes the story far more interesting. It connects what you're doing with what customers want.

 Putting yourself into the reader's shoes forces you to challenge the real value of a story. Testing a story cynically is a great thing to do. Asking yourself tough questions such as, "What will people *really* think when we say this?" and, "What do people stand to gain from this?" can help you to structure a story in a far more reader-relevant way.

It can be difficult when explaining this external viewpoint to stakeholders, who may be insistent that customers should be told again and again how good you are – and don't understand why saying so outright isn't the best way to get the message across.

MARKETING LANGUAGE, BE GONE

The language used during the marketing planning process often filters through to press releases and other marketing deliverables. It's usual for such language to be marketing-focused and perhaps even pompous. This isn't the way your customers think or talk. Phrases such as 'dominating the market' can creep in. You may want to dominate the market, but individuals don't like to be thought of as part of a target market, let alone as someone to be dominated.

They want you to help them, not annex them. Marketing and business language, terminology and phrases belong in internal documents.

LET THE READER DIRECT YOUR WRITING

Putting the reader at the heart of the press release shapes your writing in the most fundamental way possible. It helps you to understand what the key point of the story should be, what to say in the headline to grab people's attention, how to lead them into the main story from the synopsis, and how to shape the calls to action.

It also helps at a nuts-and-bolts level: using the readers' vocabulary, rather than your sector's, creating a story which is far more accessible and better optimised for search engines.

If there *is* a place for telling people how good your company is, then it's within the boilerplate, outside the main body of the press release. However, since this is typically aimed at news outlets as contextual information, any claims made should remain factual rather than boastful.

Continually telling people how great you are isn't an effective way to get that message across. For people to believe it, they should see how your company, and its products and services, can solve their problems. They should see what's in it for them. What you do is as important as what you say.

SETTING NEWS IN CONTEXT

News doesn't happen in isolation. It's part of events: local, national and worldwide. Setting news stories in context helps make them more relevant.

You will learn that:
- context gives news stories meaning.
- without context, press releases can lack substance.
- how people, companies and places are affected by change makes a story newsworthy.

When writing a press release, it's natural to focus on the organisation it features.

But your organisation isn't the centre of the universe. Customers don't orbit your company as if it were the only source of gravity. Competitors don't bow to your might. Time doesn't stand still for you. You're part of a real world, part of communities and events.

To ignore the outside world means you could underplay things which make your story newsworthy: your company's impact on others, or the world's impact on your business.

Let's say you're launching a new product. Your focus (of course) is on the new product; after all, you've spent ages developing it; your customers may be waiting for it. But your product exists in a wider context. No one creates products for their own sake; they're designed to fulfil a need. Ask yourself: why are you releasing it now? What did your customers do or say that drove the development of the product? How will they use the product? What problem does it solve, or opportunity does it open up?

These are all excellent questions, but there's a wider context still: what's going on in the outside world? The world where industry events, political events and social activities take place. The world where legislation is changing. The world where people are protesting. The world of financial change.

How does your product launch sit within this outside world? Can citing this change the significance of the press release?

Perhaps your product is a new software package, a revolutionary application that can bring fuzzy images into focus, quickly and cheaply. The inward–looking part of the story is that you've created a software package that, with a couple of clicks, can rescue an extremely blurred photo. Yes, that is news, but how the new product affects the outside world is an even bigger story. It's not a story of a new product. It's a story of how millions of people can now rescue otherwise useless images; how cameras no longer have to be costly for photos to be sharp. It's about how expensive lenses and focusing systems are no longer needed because your software fixes images from *any camera*. It's about how photographs taken by amateurs will now look pin sharp – even if they were running when taking the shot.

The product's news is big, but the real impact is massive. The story becomes so much stronger when set in context.

Journalists tend to write in this way. They work out from the epicentre of the story and focus on the effects, using context to give the story meaning and gravity.

Companies write press releases about new business wins because this is exciting to them, but when written without real-world context they generate little attention. Context transforms a story like this. What are you going to deliver as part of the contract? What does that mean to your customers, and perhaps for their clients? How does this affect the market? What's going on in your sector – does this buck a trend, accelerate a trend or create a new one? How does this affect those countries in which you operate? Did a legislation change push customers towards needing your kind of product? Why did they buy from you? What were their other choices? What are other companies doing? What impact does your product have on the world, and vice versa?

Even though a press release is written to promote a company or client, it shouldn't endlessly push things from that perspective. That's not how the outside world sees your product. Set your press releases in context, in the real world: part of events and a part of the lives that readers live.

Introspective writing downgrades even strong stories into self-serving advertisements that lack newsworthiness. For press releases to resonate, they should show how the news affects the outside world.

LANGUAGE STYLE

Press releases should be factual, but there's no need for them to be dry. However, when spicing up prose, don't turn a press release into something it isn't: you're not writing an advertisement.

You will learn that:
- press releases should always be grounded in facts.
- over-exuberant language can undermine your story.
- news stories are viewed from 'outside', so are always written in the third person.

One of the joys (and pains) of writing is that language provides an almost boundless palette of words from which to draw.

This does make the notion of 'creating rules' for a particular form of writing something of a challenge. Writing is a subtle, creative art. There is, always, more than one way to express an opinion, describe a product, or chronicle an event. One way isn't right and others wrong. They're just different. Literature, journalism, marketing – indeed all forms of writing – are all the richer for it.

Part of the fun of writing is exploring vocabulary; finding those subtly different ways of saying something.

The publicity writer's creative framework is certainly a comparatively narrow one. The central conceit of a press release is that the content is fact; solid news. The reason we say this is a 'conceit' is simply that a press release isn't, of course, solid news – it's news with a promotional agenda. Nevertheless, we should accept we're writing *news*. More than anything else, this should govern our writing style. A press release may well be a vehicle bound by an unspoken conceit, but our writing style should not reveal this conceit: it should never become an advertisement, a brochure or a poster. It should be news; it *must* be news. This is the framework within which publicists work. Narrow? Yes. Confined? No. You are limited only by your own creativity and the newsworthiness of the story.

FACTS FIRST

Always build a story around facts.

It often helps to create a quick list of the who, why, what, where and when of the story. Filling in the *facts* for each of these enables you to create an unvarnished outline for the story: what's real and what's important.

It is undeniably the role of a press release to paint a company, its products and services, in a favourable light – but press releases fail miserably when they are all spin and no substance. They fool no one. Facts make a story newsworthy and compelling. We explore using 'who, why, what, where, when' (and often 'how') in more detail in the chapter *The heart of the story*.

FINDING YOUR TONE OF VOICE

You should write factually, but there's no need to be stilted and unemotional. While a formal approach to publicity writing used to be not just common but *de rigueur*, this is no longer the case.

One reason for this is that press releases were originally used to inform mainstream media – an agency would write a press release, but a journalist wrote the story.

While this remains true, today's publishing landscape is significantly different. It's now common for many outlets to publish a press release either entirely as written, or largely as written. This may not happen much with bigger mainstream media, but it does happen. Indeed, by volume, press releases which are used more or less as they are submitted comprise a considerable percentage of what we might call 'the news'.

This has an important implication for writers: you should write much more *like* a journalist; you should write the final story.

True, a journalist would likely write the story differently; perhaps more forcefully, more critically or with more humour. Journalists each have an individual writing style – and every publication has its own house style. Journalists can be more 'out there' than you should be. Balance your writing between the old, formal-facts style of a press release and that of a finished news story. A press release should stand on its own two feet, for outlets which wish to publish it without change, but it should also work for those who will rewrite it entirely.

This isn't an insurmountable challenge; it's simply something you should be aware of when writing. It does mean you need to be a more self-aware writer.

You have to question your work. Can the story be published without change? Does it read like a finished article? Does it provide the hooks and facts needed for journalists to write their own stories?

A factor governing whether you write entirely factually or create something close to a finished article is the company for which you are writing. If you're writing for a well-known, popular brand (such as Adobe, JCB or Virgin Airlines), then it's far more likely that *whatever you do* is news. Most stories will almost certainly be picked up by the media, so more formal, factual releases are just fine – even if they're something of a creative cop-out. For less well-known brands, the writing *must* be more creative; the story much stronger.

Just as not all companies have equal publicity traction, so not all news stories are equal. Some news stories are so compelling that even the smallest business would have no trouble catching the world's attention. The problem is, how do you know in advance which stories are winners and which aren't? You can't. Better to write them all as well as you can.

If it's dry, then it's dull. It won't engage with the bigger media outlets, and the small ones won't be able to use it as is. They'll both probably bin it.

THIRD PERSON, FIRST CHOICE

Write press releases in the third person. This is the nature of the vehicle and it's a good thing. It naturally inhibits the writer from using the kind of colourful language which can undermine a press release.

First person, second person and third person refer to the use of personal pronouns – and can be considered a 'point of view' – in that each individual has a different grammatical perspective when referring to herself/himself or others. The news is always viewed from the outside, so you always deliver it in the third person – the 'outside perspective'.

This means that you write about *the* company, *the* product or *the* service. *It*, when referring to a thing (such as a product or business); *her*, *she*, *him*, *he* when referring to a person.

You're not hamstrung by this. When quoting someone, it is fine for *them* to speak in the first person. First-person personal pronouns include *I*, *we*, *me*, *us*, *my*, *mine*, *our* and *ours*. As an example, a quotation from a person from within the company might say, "I believe this initiative sets us apart in the market." Within a quotation, this use of the first-person perspective is not only fine, it is also expected.

It's not likely that you would employ the second-person viewpoint. This uses the pronouns *you*, *your* and *yours,* which means you are directly addressing the reader. This doesn't work within the prose of a press release, although there are some circumstances where it *might* work within a quote (as in this example: "A customer said to me, 'improve your service'. So I said, 'we will'."). Typically, though, it doesn't.

First person, second person and third person are common enough in marketing materials. You could comfortably talk about solving customers' issues as 'solving your problems', for example. However, within a press release, you do not directly address the customer – as with movies, there is a fourth wall (a space which separates the audience from the performance), which we don't want to break. When we do so, it is typically within the confines of a quote.

Since press releases should be grounded in fact, a first-person quote is a handy way to present opinion. This can be within the news story, to support the main narrative – or it can be in the headline, forming the news story itself. For example, if a leading educationalist believes that the way we teach in schools is wrong, then this could be, in itself, news, despite it being an opinion. '"I believe that today's learning model is broken," says education guru,' for example.

AVOID HYPERBOLES AND SUPERLATIVES

While we want to make a story engaging, we can go too far. A news story which claims that a new product is 'astonishing' or 'amazing' within the central prose undermines its credibility (though, as we've said, it would be fine for a spokesperson to say this). The language of a press release should be calm and measured; it shouldn't go overboard. Keep close to the facts and their impact, without emotional interpretation.

SHORT SENTENCES

In his book, *Indlish (The Book for Every English-Speaking Indian)*, Jyoti Sanyal says: "Based on several studies, press associations in the USA have laid down a readability table. Their survey shows readers find sentences of 8 words or fewer, very easy to read; 11 words, easy; 14 words, fairly easy; 17 words, standard; 21 words, fairly difficult; 25 words, difficult and 29 words or more, very difficult."

This is sound advice.

Try to write in sentences of 15–20 words *or fewer*. This serves two purposes. First, it keeps your mind on track. Say what's needed to make a point, briefly, then move on. Second, it's better for readers, who can get bored or fatigued trying to hold long paragraphs of text in their heads.

NEVER EXCLAIM

Avoid exclamation marks entirely, even within quotes. You won't typically see one of these in a leading news publication or media outlet. They discredit your message, and undermine the objectiveness of your story.

Grammatically speaking, an exclamation mark is something of a blunt instrument. Look! I'm shouting! Exclamation marks are often the grammatical equivalent of laughing too loudly at your own jokes. Many writers even feel that the exclamation mark has had its day, and that a sentence shouldn't need it for the reader to realise that someone has exclaimed.

AVOID (OR SUBSTANTIATE) COMPARATIVE CLAIMS

The media would not typically want to give a product or company undue credence or publish an unbalanced view. So, if you claim a product is the best in your market, it's essential that you support this with evidence. (Remember: we can use opinion within a quote to sidestep this need: "We believe that our product is now the best in the market," said Joe Johnson.) Statements such as 'market-leading', 'best in class' and so on should be substantiated. An editor or journalist won't take the time needed to contact you for evidence; she or he will likely delete the claim or even drag the entire press release to the bin. They can't get behind unconfirmed claims.

THINK GLOBALLY

We're writing this book in English, for an English-speaking audience. You may well be doing the same with your press releases. However, since news now almost always reaches (or is available to) a global audience, colloquialisms should be avoided if possible.

As an example, we Brits are global enough citizens to know what a flashlight is, and Americans typically know that Brits call it a torch, but its use could still be a stumbling block, slowing readers down. Try to avoid words which have different meanings in other countries. It's not just specific words either, but also common expressions. In the UK, the phrase 'belt and braces' means 'fully prepared' or 'double-protection'; in North America this phrase conveys little meaning because Americans wear suspenders, not braces, to hold up trousers (whereas in the UK, suspenders are items of ladies' lingerie).

TRY NOT TO ASSUME KNOWLEDGE; AVOID JARGON

All industries have their own jargon and specialist knowledge. You may work within such an industry and need to write press releases for specialist products or services. Be aware that while this vocabulary might be common to you, it will typically be less well understood by customers. Don't assume customers have your knowledge; write for a lower denominator and make sure you explain everything clearly. Avoid abbreviations, acronyms, jargon and buzzwords where possible. The simple act of having to expand an acronym, for example, is a visual stumbling block for the reader. Try to keep these out, where possible.

YOU'RE TELLING A STORY

While a press release should be grounded in fact, it can still be exciting. You're telling a story, not listing facts. You may feel boxed in because you should avoid hyperboles, superlatives and so on, but many professional writers would, in any event, consider those out-of-bounds. Think about the press release as a story and try to create a journey for the reader. We talk about this in the chapter *the heart of the story*, but it's worth noting that 'writing a story' does affect your language style – and it's something you should embrace. The traditional three-step structure of setting up the story with a challenge (the beginning), explaining how you overcame the problem (the middle) before outlining the outcome (the ending) is still a good one. Using a defined structure makes writing easier, and it's also more satisfying for readers.

WRITE WITH HEART

Just as singing isn't simply a question of perfunctorily hitting the right notes, writing is more than just stringing words together. It's storytelling. It should have heart. Nowhere on your computer keyboard will you find a function key to 'add heart' – it's something you learn, and something (by definition) you feel. If you don't feel it, those reading won't feel it either. You might think that our list of don'ts – no exclamation marks, no hyperbole, no sensation – makes it difficult or impossible to write with heart. It isn't. Open yourself up to what your story means, understand its impact and don't be afraid to write with feeling. If you overdo it, pare it back in the edit.

READ IT OUT LOUD, LISTEN TO THE FLOW

You may feel self-conscious doing this, but reading a press release out loud is an excellent way to spot language that's pompous, clumsy, in the wrong voice, unstructured, missing something, etcetera. Give it a try. You won't have to do this forever – doing it for a while will train your mind to review text in that way automatically. It can be a tremendous help in finding a natural flow to your writing.

WRITE YOUR STORY IN MORE THAN ONE WAY

Although press releases are most often written once and then sent to everyone, many companies write different versions of their stories. While this creates a little more work, it is extremely effective. It lets you talk more directly to each specific audience about what is important to that audience. If you consider (just as two examples) the needs of influencers and shareholders, they are radically different. What you write might be fine for one of these groups but will fail with the other. Writing press releases to match specific audiences also lets you adapt the language style accordingly – in our examples, influencers could receive a far more informal press release slanted towards upcoming changes, compared to shareholders who will be more concerned with facts and performance.

While press releases should be grounded in facts, they should never be uninteresting or dull. Tell a story. Make it relevant. Take readers on a journey.

STRUCTURING AND FORMATTING A PRESS RELEASE

*Working within a defined structure makes you more productive
and your writing more compelling. For press releases,
most of that structure is predetermined.*

You will learn that:
- there is an accepted framework for press releases, to which you should broadly adhere.
- by giving your press release a story-like structure, you can communicate key points in a far more engaging and successful way.

There are two ways to think about the structure of a press release. The first is practical: how you organise information on the page. The second is creative: how you build a compelling story. Let's look at these in turn.

THE PRESS RELEASE TEMPLATE

While there are no hard and fast rules as to how a press release is structured, there is an accepted format, which includes:
- the headline.
- the sub-headline (optional and sometimes superfluous).
- the date (or dateline).
- the synopsis (or introduction).
- the body (or main text).
- the closing mark (or end mark).
- the boilerplate.
- contact information.
- word count.

The headline is used to both summarise your news and to grab attention.

The sub-headline is a kind of secondary headline which gives a different spin on the story or explains it in a different context. Using one doesn't obviate the need for a synopsis: they each do different things. You should avoid the sub-headline repeating information which is in the headline. Not all websites and newswires cater for a sub-headline, so you can't count on everyone using it.

The date (or **dateline**) is the intended distribution date of the press release, which is usually the current date, or a future date (if a press release is embargoed). The dateline may also include the words 'for immediate release' and incorporate the geographic source of the release (usually town and country) and intended distribution: this might be global, national or regional. However, since most news is distributed via the Internet, geographic restrictions are unrealistic. If you include an instruction to embargo a press release until a specific date or time, be aware that journalists aren't obligated to honour this, although they typically do.

The synopsis (or **introduction**) provides a crystal clear précis of the news story, what you might consider to be the key facts: the who, why, what, where, when and how. It shouldn't be a first paragraph of, or a lead-in paragraph to, the press release's main body text. Lead paragraphs *flow into* and are *a part of* the body text; a synopsis stands alone while inviting people to read on.

The body or **main text** is the content of your news story. It includes all of the story's information, facts, quotations and so on.

The closing mark (or **end mark**) tells the media that the press release (not including the boilerplate, which comes after the end mark) has ended. A common end mark in North America is "-30-" while "###" (three octothorps, without spaces between) is an alternative. (It's not known for sure how these conventions originated, but a popular theory is that they were handed down from Western Union telegraph standards dating back to the American Civil War; X marked the end of a sentence, XX the end of a paragraph and XXX the end of a dispatch. XXX is 30 in Roman numerals.)

It's also common to use the word 'ends', 'story ends' or 'news ends'. Many press releases don't carry an end mark, relying on the heading of any subsequent supporting information to inform the reader of structure (for example, "About XYZ Company"). Doing this is typically fine, if not best practice, but it's unlikely you'll be judged on it.

The boilerplate is a standard paragraph which provides supporting information about your company.

Contact information is for the media: it's the person/people who journalists should contact to pick up the story. It's not aimed at the public and shouldn't be a sales number. If you include sales calls to action, do so in the body of the press release.

The word count includes the heading, synopsis and body of the press release. It should exclude boilerplate information, contact details and supporting text.

HOW MANY WORDS ARE TOO MANY?

There's no set rule as to how long a press release should be, but around 300-400 words is usually about right. Online, you will find lots of differing advice on this. This isn't surprising. Many news stories can be conveyed in fewer words while others (such as a scientific discovery, pharmaceutical announcement or even a company's year-end results) may justify more detail.

It's usual, though by no means essential, to limit a press release to a single page (either A4 or letter). Any story should be 'as long as it needs to be' and a press release is no exception, but once you've filled a second page, that story had better be a corker. Being concise is *always* better than being verbose.

LINE SPACING TO MAKE READING EASIER

Text should be either double-spaced or spaced at 1.5 lines: this additional line spacing makes it easier to read. Double-spaced is a traditionally quoted standard but it comes from an era when typewriters just couldn't space 1.5 lines – and double-spaced text isn't significantly easier to read than text with 1.5-line spacing. Never single-space a press release.

FONT SIZES AND TYPEFACES

Text should be at least 11pt in size. It's common for some formatting guides to quote 12pt, but 11pt is generally fine; indeed, 12pt can seem overlarge. It's likely that many people wouldn't notice if the text is 10pt, but you are safest with 11pt or 12pt.

There isn't a standard font for press release use, but you're safe with the usual suspects: Arial, Helvetica, Tahoma, Trebuchet and Verdana, for those preferring sans-serif fonts, and Georgia, Times and Times New Roman for those who prefer serif fonts. More modern fonts such as Tahoma tend to have narrower bodies and larger lower-case letters so can look bigger than traditional fonts of the same size.

People are interested in your story, not its appearance, so there's no need for fancy formatting or multiple fonts. Using these can make you look an amateur.

PAGE MARGINS

The page should have reasonably wide margins. This is no longer to do with journalists making notes in the margins, although that used to be the case. When people read, their eyes track along each line of text from beginning to end, before moving to the start of the line below. Shorter line lengths help the reader to automatically locate the correct line below rather than accidentally starting to read the wrong line. This makes reading faster (it's one reason why newspapers use narrow columns).

FILE FORMATS

The traditionally accepted format in which to supply a press release is as a Microsoft Word document.

Using a cloud-based document service such as Microsoft 365, Google Docs or Apple's Pages on iCloud is increasingly common, but do make sure that journalists won't need to create a login for a service they wouldn't otherwise use. In this respect, one of the advantages of Google Docs is that most people have a Google account – but bear in mind that their work e-mail address may very well be different from their Google account e-mail address. It's important to check the document's sharing permissions – so that people can only view and not change the text, which is clearly fraught with risk. You can also provide documents via a link to an online storage service, such as Dropbox.

Don't provide news stories in PDF format; it takes a lot more work to copy and paste text from PDF files, because the copied text can often include unwanted formatting, such as hard line breaks, which can be a pain to remove or fix.

Journalists don't like e-mails which say just 'press release, see attached' with an empty e-mail body and the news story as an attachment. Why? Because they get dozens or hundreds of press releases a day and the additional work opening up documents is a tiresome overhead. Therefore, include the full press release in the body of your e-mail as well as an attachment. It's a good idea to use the press release headline (or a salient part of it) within the e-mail's title, so that a journalist can find it more easily later; you have no idea how many e-mails they receive titled just 'press release' or 'press release from XYZ Company'.

A golden rule is to avoid making it a chore for outlets to deal with your press release. It's important that people don't have to jump over even minor hurdles to do their job.

ORDERING YOUR THOUGHTS

The structure of a press release template may be quite ordered, but the way you *tell news stories* is largely up to you. Think of your news story as a journey. At the outset, people know nothing about that journey; by the end, they should know everything. As the writer of the press release, you've already been on that journey, so you know the story's key facts. Your challenge is to present those facts in the most meaningful order, creating an unfolding story that leads people in one direction, to a logical conclusion. A typical press release journey first identifies a problem or opportunity, then highlights the impact of this on the world or a particular community. It then leads into how the problem was resolved or the opportunity seized, and the likely impact (or benefits) of this. Woven throughout, supporting information such as customer statements or independent facts/research reinforce the story. Finally, it leads people toward an action which benefits them (and, of course, you).

USING OUTLINING TO STRUCTURE THOUGHTS

Many people write as part of their job but aren't professional writers. They tend to write without a strong level of self-awareness, sitting down to write without first giving the topic great consideration. That doesn't in itself make the writing 'bad' but it often means that it will be less structured; less complete; less rewarding to the reader; less effective. It's more of a brain-dump than a story. When a professional tackles a plot point, she or he is *consciously* thinking about what the reader should feel. Writers achieve an emotional response by engineering it; making it happen – not by hoping it will.

Outlining is an essential tool to help you understand the readers' journey.

Think about what you have to say and what you wish to achieve, then plot out the points that will take people through the story. What do they need to know first? What next? Let one point lead into another, so there is a direction to the story. Be flexible as you plan – be prepared to shuffle the order of points – always considering whether something might be more powerful if disclosed sooner or later. Be ready to remove key points entirely – professional writers say that they sometimes have to 'kill their darlings'. However attached to something a writer is, the greater good of the piece must prevail. Writing press releases can be tough: you have to cover a lot of ground, quickly, using relatively few words. Ruthlessness is a powerful ally.

If your news is about a service that solves a problem, start the main body of the press release by first describing the problem, then the service, and finally how the service solves the problem. How the problem is solved will usually become the key point in the headline, because that's the thing which makes the story newsworthy. Your synopsis, like a trailer for a film, presents the story's most important facts in a self-contained way. Both the heading and the synopsis lead people into the main body of the press release – since this is written as a self-contained story, it's fine to repeat information from both the headline and synopsis. The main body of the press release is where you take readers on a journey, in this case from problem identified to problem solved. In fiction, this writing model is known as 'conflict to resolution'. (It's true that the headline and synopsis give away the ending. A press release isn't fiction; doing so is a necessity of the medium.)

The key points of your outline are like stepping stones. They're needed to get from one side of the river to the other, but it doesn't pay to dwell on them. Keep your press release moving; try to avoid getting bogged down, labouring any of the points. Learn to recognise when this happens and be objective (and merciless) about remedying it.

WRITE FOR YOUR AUDIENCE

Industry peers have a strong understanding of the processes and terminology of your sector. Specialists and analysts will have an even better grasp of these – and will likely know more about what customers think and what competitors are doing. Customers (and potential customers) don't have this depth of knowledge – they commonly use terminology that's less specialist. And of course, different customers have different levels of understanding. A buyer may well understand some, or even much, of the terminology you use, but others – even decision-makers, budget-holders and influencers – may not. Likewise, the media will contain people who have a good understanding of your sector and those who do not. Your writing must cater for these differences within the readership. It's all very well saying 'our message is intended for the buyer' but the reality is that you reach buyers not just directly but through many different kinds of readers. You can't assume *any* level of foreknowledge – and you should avoid patronising those who possess it.

Think carefully and inclusively about your potential readership. Look at your distribution lists and imagine the journey your document may take. Think about what people may and may not know.

KEEP IT REAL

Try to keep your news story in the present as much as possible. The news is about *now*. For example, when desktop publishing came along the big news was that it put great design and layout into everyone's hands. It meant marketing could be done in-house, with production values matching those from professional designers. That was the news, not the massive shift from publishing's roots back in the 1400s when William Caxton and Aldus Manutius lay the first foundations of modern publishing. The big picture may be fascinating or make a great documentary, but it's seldom news. Keeping your story in the now keeps it relevant.

STRUCTURED STORYTELLING

Old advice is often good advice. That's why it has survived. The storytelling structure of the beginning, middle and end may not be essential (or even the best way to tell a tale), but for a press release, it's a pretty solid framework. Think about what you need to say, what you'd like people to know, what you want to achieve – all of those key points – and work out where they fit in that tried and tested beginning, middle and end structure. Then take people on that journey. Associated Press recommends a broadcast guideline that's also useful when structuring press releases:

- Lead (the story's essential facts)
- Backup (build on the facts)
- Details (additional facts)
- Background (giving the story context)

Working within this framework, let's explore how a financial business could launch a new service which audits data. We'll also use the 'who, why, what, where, when' framework. We can lead in with 'new data audit approach to cut costs, simplify compliance'. The *backup* expands on this, 'XYZ Company launches new service, which enables insurance providers to audit data more accurately and in a fraction of the time currently taken.' We then provide the *details*: *who* has developed this and *who* it is for, *why* this is an issue and *why* it improves things, *what* it costs now and *what* it will cost when adopted, *how* much time and money can be saved, and *when* it will be available. (It isn't mandatory to include each of the who, why, what, where, when and hows.)

STRUCTURE IS ESSENTIAL

However you do it, structuring news stories in advance is vital if you want to avoid them meandering around verbosely, without covering all of the facts.

FOLLOWING GUIDELINES

Many newswires or news distribution services provide style guides. Although these are broadly consistent, they do differ (sometimes surprisingly so), and it's impossible for a writer to research and adhere to them *all*. That said, if you're regularly using specific newswires, then it's *essential* to read, and act on, both their style guides and their advice on press release structure/writing. A good (if exhaustive) reference is the Associated Press Stylebook (apstylebook.com) – although this is aimed more firmly at journalists than publicists.

It's worth making the point that 'rules' often aren't rigidly applied or even always that important: your story is more likely to be bounced for being dull than it is for breaking a style guide.

Remember that it always helps to make life easier for the media; if your press release adheres to the right standards and relevant style guides, then journalists and editors won't have to spend time reworking it.

ENCOURAGE SOCIAL MEDIA UPDATES

News outlets have busy social media channels. Give outlets what they need to promote your story on those channels.

A press release isn't intrinsically social media friendly. Unless you provide them, outlets will need to spend time composing any tweets and updates, finding and resizing graphics – and hunting for your hashtags and @names. Create these for outlets and send them the press release. Save them the time and effort.

While it's tempting to copy and paste parts of the press release to get the job done quickly, the reality is that's not the best way to present a story on social media. For example, seldom does a press release's headline translate naturally into a tweet.

The nature of social media means it's better to be less formal with your message or even introduce a little fun. Provide alternatives – long and short sentences – so the outlet can choose what works for them. If you supply images and videos, be sure these are the correct size and format.

There's no guarantee these will be used, but you'd surely be creating them for yourself anyway? Send them along and help the outlet to get your story out.

Learning to write with greater self-consciousness and structure can elevate the quality of your writing and the effectiveness of your publicity. It requires that you both think ahead and continually challenge yourself.

WRITING COMPELLING HEADLINES

A headline can make or break a press release. For people to read further, it must sell the whole story, at a glance. For people to find your story online, you must also optimise it for search engines.

You will learn how to write a headline that:
- grabs the readers' attention, using the fewest possible words.
- delivers all of the story's essential information.
- helps your story be found quickly by search engines.

SPEND TIME ON THE HEADLINE

The headline of a press release has to work very hard. Journalists, editors and influencers are busy people; they are bombarded with hundreds of news stories every day, and can typically pursue only a few. They're good at spotting what is and isn't news – and are both efficient and ruthless at passing over stories which won't deliver the goods to their audience.

Setting aside the media, the rest of your audience won't read your press release unless the headline is compelling. The headline counts. Ensure you spend enough time on it to do the rest of the story justice.

There's no hard and fast rule as to how long you should spend writing a headline, but consider this: a copywriter is likely to spend as long on an advertisement's headline as *on the copy itself* (within some agencies, the headlines are even written by a different team). That's how much it matters. Typically, a press release isn't as well-crafted as an advertisement, but you should still set aside a decent chunk of time to write it: perhaps 20% of your writing time. *It's that important.* Make it a task in itself.

WHAT IS THE STORY ABOUT?

Don't tap out the first headline that comes into your head. First, write: what is this story about? Underneath, list key points as bullets, but only direct answers to this question. Don't deviate; you can embellish later. Your bullets are neither headlines nor text for the final release; you are only establishing the story's main facts. Now, write: *who cares?* For a story to resonate with readers, it has to have some impact on them. If one of your bullets says, "We've grown by 65% in 12 months", this is something *you care about* but *isn't relevant to readers.* What drove the growth? How does it benefit customers? Why should others care about this story? Sit back and review your notes. However many bullets you've written, the headline will be the *one, single* thing you want people to take away from the story – the main thing about which they care.

START WITH THE MOST IMPORTANT INFORMATION FIRST

The headline should convey the key point of the story. Note the singular: point. Not points. Every story should have just one key point – and the headline should communicate that key point *clearly*. Within the main text you will have room to include supporting points – but, in the headline, you do not.

News is often about something happening. A new product or service. A new key employee. A change of strategy. An award won. A customer success story. These kinds of things are typically exciting to *you*, so it's tempting to make this the point of the headline. This is often a mistake. Why? Because, in themselves, these are often not newsworthy. You might think they're a big deal, but will others? Unless you are doing something genuinely massive (such as, say, launching a new version of Windows, which is – fair enough – news in itself) the news is *the impact* of that thing happening.

Consider these headlines:

- Joe Hill to join MyCompany
- MyCompany hires Joe Hill

These headlines tell us two things:

- Joe Hill is hired
- MyCompany is hiring him

Unless Joe Hill is a newsworthy person, then this is *not* the 'point' of the story; therefore, it's a weak headline. It may deliver key facts, but it doesn't draw readers into the story. It's dull – and a boring headline signals to readers that a boring story will likely follow.

The *real* story is how this recruit affects things; why the hire is taking place; what's driving it; what the result will be. If Joe Hill is replacing Jane Field simply because she left, then – let's face it – that's not news. No amount of clever copywriting will make it news: journalists can spot lipstick on a pig.

But if the hire is because of some other factor, then it's more likely to be news.

Consider these alternative headlines:

- Joe Hill to take MyCompany into Asian markets
- MyCompany hires specialist Joe Hill to drive sales of widgets
- MyCompany targets double–figure growth: hires Joe Hill

These headlines don't just deliver more information; they raise questions which pique curiosity. Why the Asian markets? Why the focus on widgets? Why does MyCompany think it can grow sales by so much?

In addition to telling us that Joe Hill was hired, these headlines deliver one other essential piece of information: *why* he was hired.

Why he was hired is really the key point of the press release. Therefore, it should be the key point of the headline – providing the hook for people to want to read on.

The key point is the most important aspect of the story *from the readers' perspective*. Another example of a typical headline might be: "XYZ Training to introduce child safeguarding course" – which seems fair enough. It tells us the name of the company and about the training course being introduced. But is this the most important aspect of the story? Why has the course been introduced? What will be the impact of its introduction? A more compelling headline would be: "New safeguarding course aims to reduce child abuse." From the readers' perspective, the reduction of child abuse is far more important than either the course itself (which for you is a new business opportunity, but for them is a means to an end) or the company delivering it. If you wish to include the business name, then something like "XYZ Training's new safeguarding course aims to improve child safety" adds just two words.

LEAD PEOPLE IN

A headline performs a challenging balancing act. It should primarily encourage people to read the rest of the press release, pulling them into the story. For those who don't want to read the whole release, the headline should impart the story's key point. Ideally, everyone should go away having understood the core of the story from the headline alone, whether they read the entire release or not.

According to David Ogilvy, often called 'the father of advertising', "On average, 5 times as many people read the headline as read the body copy. When you have written your headline, you have spent 80 cents out of your dollar. If you haven't done some selling in your headline, you have wasted 80% of your client's money."

The balancing act is to avoid providing so much information that the need to read the story is rendered redundant. We should pique people's curiosity to get them to go further. Telling people about *the impact* of something can generate more interest than telling them about *the thing itself*.

But what if we *really* wanted to get people thinking?

Consider these examples:

- MyCompany hires new sales head Joe Hill to exploit demand from Asian markets
- MyCompany hires Joe Hill to target growing demand for widgets across Asia
- Widgets to drive double-figure growth under new sales head Joe Hill

In these examples, we've established the 'why behind the why'. We now know that MyCompany hasn't hired Joe Hill on a whim. There's a business imperative: demand for widgets in Asia. We want to know more. The headline leads us on.

But something else has happened. We've discovered that hiring Joe Hill isn't actually the news. Therefore, it's time to ask whether his name adds value to the headline. Unless Joe Hill is reasonably well known, attaching his name to the press release *headline* might not add that much weight to the story. Although we haven't done so, we could further strengthen the headline by *removing* his name.

Consider these examples:

- MyCompany to exploit demand from Asian markets: new investment in sales
- MyCompany to target growing demand for widgets in Asia: experienced sales head joins
- Widgets to drive double-figure growth at MyCompany under new sales head

The choice of whether to include Joe Hill's name in the headline is down to one thing: does its inclusion make the story more newsworthy?

KEEP IT SHORT

The next challenge is to keep the headline short. There's no hard and fast rule which decrees the length of a headline. But short headlines score in many ways.

People's time is tight. You don't want to make reading the headline feel like a chore. Once you're over a dozen words, a headline becomes visually off-putting. A great headline can be read quickly and understood at a glance.

Headlines are syndicated on search engines such as Google and hopefully on other websites. Wherever your news story travels, a shorter headline always works better.

Bin redundant words. Make every word not only count, but also work as hard as possible. Try shuffling words around to see which version of the headline works best. Consider this headline: 'MyCompany hires specialist Joe Hill to drive sales of widgets'. It could also work as: 'MyCompany hires widget specialist Joe Hill to drive sales' (we removed 'of' and made it clear that Joe Hill is a specialist in widgets, not just sales).

Think about amplification on social networks. How will yours perform on LinkedIn, Facebook and Twitter – especially Twitter, where there is a character limit? A long headline isn't just a chore to read, it gives you less space to expand on the story.

To shorten a headline, use punctuation such as a colon or dash. We've already used one in our examples, for instance: 'MyCompany targets double-figure growth: hires Joe Hill'. In this, the colon removes the need for additional words which not only wouldn't add value, but would also make the headline more pedestrian. Consider how less exciting the headline is when we replace the colon with the word 'and': 'MyCompany targets double-figure growth and hires Joe Hill'. The headline goes from strong to lame. A headline does not have to be an immaculately constructed sentence. It's perfectly valid to connect two statements, using a colon. Fewer words: more impact.

You don't have to use a colon – it can be a dash.

KEEP IT FACTUAL

A certain amount of descriptive colour is expected – and useful – in a press release, but even modest hype has little place in the headline. If and when other outlets carry your story, they may choose to beef up the headline. They might even add conjecture. That's their job, not yours. Think about one of our sample headlines: 'MyCompany targets double-figure growth: hires Joe Hill'. It's entirely factual. But write it as 'MyCompany to double sales by hiring Joe Hill' then it's conjecture. Avoid this: it is a red flag to journalists, and it triggers scepticism in readers.

If your headline seems dull, consider the following before you start throwing adjectives and superlatives at it:

- Is the headline dull because the story is dull? If your story is a dud, bin it.
- Perhaps you approached the story from the wrong angle. If you gave the story a different twist, could that create a natural opening for a different headline?

Avoid using less accessible words. For example, instead of 'immediately' use 'now'; instead of 'demonstrate' use 'show'. Simplified language does not downgrade your headline: it makes it both faster and easier to read. Using shorter words also reduces character count, which is better for tweets (and most social media updates). Most importantly though, natural language helps make stories more believable.

OPTIMISING HEADLINES FOR SEARCH ENGINES

A headline should also accommodate the needs of your non-human readers: search engines.

The good news is that if you followed the advice given so far, then your headlines will already be a long way along the road to working well with search engines. This is because search engines don't work in a mysterious way. They're designed to be used by humans. Since their job is to deliver what we ask for, we just need to understand how people search. A headline that's good for humans is good for Google.

There's a view that writing for search engines stifles creativity and leads to the repetitive use of a lot of keywords. This is outdated nonsense. There is no contradiction between writing for search engines and writing for people.

- The use of keywords *is* important. But they don't have to be used excessively to succeed; intelligent use in natural prose is typically enough.
- Conveying the main point of the story *always* trumps trying to be smart with search optimisation. If keywords compromise the headline, let them

go (or perhaps move them to the main body of the press release).

- Be wary of creativity trumping clarity. You're writing a press release. It's not an article or an advertisement, where the headline should be creative. You're trying to impart information quickly, not win a writing award. Creative headlines can undermine an otherwise excellent press release.

Writing a headline in the most obvious way often provides the most effective solution. Take these two headlines:

- Oscar nominee loses life: crashes Porsche Spyder on Route 466
- James Dean, 24, dies in car crash

While the first of the two headlines isn't *that* creative, the desire to embellish renders the headline all but meaningless to people. It's also valueless to search engines – because it's missing the most important keywords: 'James Dean', 'dies' and 'car crash'. Yes, there is an unnecessary fact in the second headline (at least from an SEO perspective) that he was 24. While this may have little search-engine value, it's emotive: possibly the most emotive part of the story. It sets the context for the senselessness of the loss; it has people asking, "Was he really only 24?" The *impact* of a headline should not be hampered by pandering to search engines.

Not only is this headline good at the time the event was news, it also has great search-engine value over the long term. When people search on James Dean, especially his death, they will easily find this story. This is important: people readily think about news as being the here and now, but great press releases can continue to add both search optimisation and publicity value for years.

As we said before: people typically search using a low grammatical register, consisting of common words – pretty much the way they would speak. Nowhere are posturing, inflated words more unwelcome than within a headline. They are off-putting to the reader and almost valueless for search optimisation.

Search engines typically place more value on keywords which are towards the start of the headline. (Interestingly, usability and eye-tracking studies also show that people glance almost immediately to the start of a headline on a page, sometimes not even reading the entire headline before clicking away to a different page.)

Think not just about words you wish to include but also those you should exclude. If words don't have search-engine value, then challenge whether you need them at all. You can't strip out everything except keywords – the headline wouldn't make sense – but you can whittle a headline down to something that is as lean as possible. Where keywords are needed, try to place them towards the start of the headline, but don't obsess about this. The needs of human readers *always* trump those of search optimisation.

You should consider potential keywords when writing *any* part of a press release, but they are particularly useful for the headline – because Google gives greater importance to keywords in the heading of a page and the HTML 'page title' (the title is the text you see at the top bar of the browser). For news stories, the headline and the page titles are almost always the same, or similar. The page title might also include the name of the outlet carrying the press release – so, a press release headline 'MyCompany hires widget specialist Joe Hill to drive sales' may well become the page title 'MyCompany hires widget specialist Joe Hill to drive sales – Newssite name'.

You can't influence the HTML page title other than via the story's headline.

INCORPORATING BRANDS INTO THE HEADLINE

It can be a good idea to include brands within your headlines, whether this is your company's name or a product's name. This is important not only for brand exposure, but also for search-engine optimisation. When people search for your company's name, or product, this increases the chances of them finding the press release.

However, a company's name eats into the headline's precious word count and strongly influences the way the headline is written. Although companies often expect to see their name in a press release heading, only use it where it adds value – as a fact that's relevant to the news – or if space allows. For example: 'Widget specialist hired to drive sales' doesn't have all of the relevant facts. Better to include the company name: 'MyCompany hires widget specialist to drive sales'. Conversely, there are times when the company's name just isn't needed, such as: 'Warner Brothers' James Dean, 24, dies in car crash'.

INCLUDE STATISTICS

When statistics drive a story, it can make a compelling headline: '45% of TV viewers hate their remote control'. This deploys the story's most important fact within the headline, rather than pursuing any promotional agenda.

USE ACTIVE VOICE

This is true not just of the headline, but also for the rest of the press release. Passive voice takes readers out of the action, rather than drawing them into it. Avoid 'be' verbs such as 'be', 'been' and 'being'. It's far better to say 'XYZ Company has upgraded its security systems' (active) than 'XYZ Company's security systems have been upgraded' (passive).

THE IDEAL LENGTH FOR A HEADLINE

A long headline has few virtues:
- It's more work to read.
- It's more work to understand.
- It's less grabbing of a reader's attention.
- It takes up more lines on a website (once a headline spreads over more than one line, reading it just feels like a chore).

- It could get truncated on other websites or search engines.
- It's far more likely to be edited by news outlets.

Consider this: the headlines on most news websites are typically no more than five to ten words long. There are variations and differences in editorial structure, but that's about average. Some news websites are even more economical with their headlines. For example, on the BBC News website, it's uncommon to see headlines of more than eight words – and just check out how well written they are. The BBC's guidelines call for headings of 55 characters or fewer; its news headlines are often a model of succinct, fact-bearing language (source: BBC). You should consider this an upper limit of what is acceptable. In comparison, many press release headlines are at least twice as long as this.

Long headlines can take up double the number of lines (or more) on mobile devices – and that's where most people pick up their news. Two lines on a website could be four or five on a mobile – more than enough to be off-putting.

Always return to this guiding principle: a headline should communicate only the main point of the press release. Don't embellish it with secondary points. Headlines are often too long because they are trying to include too much.

While some press release writing guides recommend specific word counts or character counts for headlines, this is something that's best left to your judgement. If you bust an arbitrary recommended length by one or two characters to sell the story in the best way, then no harm, no foul.

The length of the headline is important within search engines. According to a study by Schwartz MSL Research Group, around 80% of press release headlines are too long for Google (source: Schwartz MSL Research Group). Google displays roughly 65 characters in its search results pages, so a target length of not more than 70 characters is ideal when considering how your press release will look on Google (source: Schwartz MSL Research Group).

Whichever way you look at it, a long headline does you few favours. When you're considering what should go in a headline, remember that a shorter headline trumps many other factors, however worthy.

BE EYE-CATCHING, BUT NOT TOO CUTE

Using alliteration, assonance or consonance can create a more catchy headline. 'Substantial sales generate growth', for example. Don't overdo this – journalists and outlets have more latitude to be cute with headlines than you.

Likewise, you may often see headlines in the media which play with words for impact, perhaps offering double meaning. Let's say some particular insects are crawling into computer data centres and threatening the servers. A headline such as 'Giant spiders could break the Internet' is certainly interesting – but it's easy to overdo this and end up with something which trivialises your story or looks like a clickbait headline. An outlet may rewrite your story in that way, but that's their call. Be cautious if you take this approach: it may work better in other versions of your press release (perhaps to customers) or on social media than in a pitch to news outlets and influencers.

AVOID POLAR QUESTIONS

Generally, questions don't make great headlines. You're announcing something, not asking people to make a decision. But while occasionally they work, and they are used by the media, for publicity writers they're best avoided. This is especially true of polar questions – where there are only two possible answers, usually with opposite values, such as yes/no.

The publicity writer's job is to lead the reader in a specific direction and not give them an out. A polar question, by definition, gives a large percentage of the audience a reason to stop reading. 'Will AI dominate the home within a decade?' gives permission to part of the audience to say "no" to the article and leave without reading. A press release is not an article, it's a primer for the pump. Lead people. 'AI set to dominate homes within a decade' is more forceful and tells people immediately the direction of the story.

The general reason why writing headlines as questions is ineffective is sometimes known as *Betteridge's law of headlines*, in which: "any headline that ends in a question can be answered by the word *no*." Such a headline might be 'Does software increase productivity?'

We couldn't state it better than Ian Betteridge in his article from 2009: 'TechCrunch: Irresponsible Journalism' which says that, "The reason why journalists use that style of headline is that they know the story is probably bullshit, and don't actually have the sources and facts to back it up, but still want to run it."

WRITE THE HEADLINE LAST

Writing the headline first can box you into writing the story in less effective ways. Since writing a headline can take a lot of time, you could also lose your creative momentum. Write the story first – that way you know what the story is about, and therefore what the headline needs to say. You can also speed through the story, working on the headline as you edit the rest of the text.

*There are many ways to write a good headline, often providing subtly different ways to say the same thing. It's always possible to shuffle around the facts to improve a headline. The key things to remember are: a headline sells the story; it should be as compelling as possible; a headline must be short; a good headline conveys the story's main point; a headline must work for both humans and search engines – but **always** put humans first.*

THE SYNOPSIS: LEAD READERS INTO THE STORY

Like the headline, the synopsis has to do a lot of heavy lifting – with just a few words. Although its primary goal is to encourage people to read on, it should also impart enough information to enable those who go no further to understand the essence of the story.

You will learn how to write a synopsis that:
- encourages people to read the full press release.
- provides enough information so that those who don't read the entire story will nonetheless have a good grasp of what it's about.
- doesn't just repeat what is in the headline, but works *in unison* with it to deliver the story's key points.

We'd all like to believe that everyone who sees our news story will read it from beginning to end but, in reality, people are busy. They scan news websites quickly, glancing over the front page and reading only what's compelling.

This sets a pretty good framework for writing a synopsis. Our primary aim is to write a summary that will make people want to read the rest of the story. But we should also cater for those who read no further. The synopsis should work in concert with the headline, so that the two combined provide a good overview of the story for those who don't have time to read the whole press release.

HOW LONG SHOULD A SYNOPSIS BE?

As with the headline, brevity is vital. While there's no rule for the number of words to use, common sense tells us that a synopsis just a few lines long is more inviting to read than a massive paragraph.

Just as a large proportion of people will read only a story's headline, we must accept some may get no further than the synopsis. Therefore, it is important that the synopsis contains the story's key points.

That said, incorporating every important point in the synopsis may make it too long – something to be avoided. A shorter synopsis is always better than a longer one, so it's preferable to cut words rather than stuff in lots of facts. Within a synopsis, conciseness trumps detail.

Ask yourself: "What do I want people to take away from this story?" Ensure that the headline and the synopsis combined address that question. To do this, précis the story as succinctly as possible.

Consider also how a news story will look when syndicated: how it appears on other websites, especially search engines. Just as the headline is important in this context, so is the synopsis. When your story comes up in a Google search, the synopsis will typically sit under the headline. This has a significant influence on how long the synopsis should ideally be – since, on Google, that particular snippet of text is around two 'Google lines', or, perhaps 20–25 words. 20–25 words: *yes, you read that correctly.*

That's a pretty tight word count within which to deliver the story's most important facts. Plus, the nature of a search results page means that your story will likely appear alongside competing content – another reason to ensure that your synopsis is compelling.

If you do need to write a longer synopsis, the key facts still should be found within the first 20–25 words.

On mobile devices, where at least half of the news is read, we can't even count on the reader seeing 20–25 words. Your synopsis may be truncated further still. On some news apps, it may even not be used. There's little we can do about that.

EVERYTHING AN EDITOR NEEDS TO KNOW

Busy editors and content-curators do not have time to read every press release. They are newshounds who can quickly sniff out a good story from the scores they receive daily. They start with the headline; if that's compelling, they will then read the synopsis. Many horses fall at the first hurdle – and few make it past the second. The synopsis must tell the media professional everything she or he needs to know. It has to confirm that reading the whole release will be worthwhile.

SUPPORT THE HEADLINE, DON'T REPEAT IT

It's not uncommon to see a synopsis which repeats much of the headline. Avoid this: it's both a waste of space and of the reader's time. A synopsis should support and reinforce what's said in the headline, giving the reader more, not the same thing again. Some repetition may be unavoidable, or even desirable. For example, if you're writing a story with the headline '88 new jobs created in software development' it's fine to include, in the synopsis, a reference to that number – though you might change this to 'nearly 100' to provide a natural variety of words. In the same way, you might refer to 'nine years' in the headline and 'almost a decade' in the synopsis. Use this kind of repetition where it helps to create a more natural flow between the headline and the synopsis, or creates a bridge between the headline and the story, but avoid it if you can.

PITCH THE STORY

It's useful to see a synopsis as a sales pitch for the story, or as an 'elevator pitch'. For those who are unfamiliar with this term, imagine this: you get into an elevator – or, if you're in the UK, a lift – with someone who is potentially important to you. Perhaps that person can give you a new job, or become your biggest customer. You nod in polite greeting. The nod is returned, names are exchanged and then comes the question: "What do you do?" You now have a scant few seconds to pitch, with no idea if, or when, the opening elevator doors will cut you short.

That's what the synopsis has to do – pitch the story to readers. It has to be compelling enough for them to press the hold button, so you can finish talking, and preferably exchange business cards at the end.

Every word counts. If you don't grab the person's attention, the opportunity is gone, potentially never to be repeated.

BENEFITS NOT FEATURES

Remember that you grab people's attention most by making your story relevant to them. While your story needs to say that your company's new computer is twice as fast, it's more meaningful to demonstrate this by illustrating how a common task now takes half of the time.

IT'S ESSENTIAL THINKING

The synopsis is a distillation of the entire story: the press release in a nutshell. You can't write a captivating synopsis without having first identified the story's key facts, so it is far easier to write after you've finished the main body of the press release – or having outlined the story's main points.

DON'T CREATE A MYSTERY: DELIVER FACTS

Novelists get readers to stick with books by creating intrigue: keeping readers on their toes. They throw in a plot twist or two to wrong-foot readers – even the occasional red herring.

We're not writing novels. Withholding facts doesn't generate excitement. It does not lead people into a story. It's a waste of effort; misplaced creativity. Think about the elevator pitch. In a movie or novel, the elevator pitch might play out as a scene where the hero pitches to a potential sponsor: "Imagine that I could make you rich. Imagine that when this elevator door opens, it opens onto a whole new world – to a place beyond your dreams." Language such as this is great in a film or book. In real life, a potential sponsor would see you simply as a dreamer with nothing to deliver because, however eloquent, the words have no substance. It's the same with a synopsis.

Avoid hype. Concentrate on facts. If the facts don't sell the story, no amount of superlatives will help.

Let's think about key facts ascertained while writing our headline about Joe Hill.

- Joe Hill is a new hire
- Joe Hill is experienced
- MyCompany is hiring him
- He's being hired to help MyCompany expand into Asian markets
- MyCompany wants to sell more widgets in Asia
- MyCompany wants double-figure sales growth
- Demand is growing for widgets in Asia

While each headline has pros and cons, none has enough room for all of the key facts.

The natural place for those facts left over when you've written the headline is the synopsis. Write a 20–25-word paragraph which contains most of these, and you won't go far wrong.

Let's say we go with the headline, 'MyCompany targets double-figure growth: hires Joe Hill'. It follows that we will want the synopsis to include the demand for widgets in Asia as a key supporting fact, something like: 'Ambitious market expansion strategy and new leader of sales to help MyCompany harness growing demand for widgets across Asia.' Within just seven words for the headline and nineteen for the synopsis, we have delivered *all* of the key facts.

While there is some repetition (the company name), this is an acceptable device to help us communicate multiple facts and can be useful from a search optimisation perspective.

Consider these exemplary headlines and synopses from BBC News:

Italy quake: Norcia tremor destroys ancient buildings

Towns and villages in central Italy have been hit by an earthquake for the fourth time in three months.

Carney "tremendous" as BoE chief, says business secretary

Business secretary Greg Clark has said Mark Carney has done a "tremendous job" as governor of the Bank of England, following a report that Mr Carney might choose to step down in 2018.

The combined headlines and synopses deliver all of the essential facts. Each synopsis builds naturally on the headline – and leads the reader into the story. Those people who read no further still know all of the essentials. While there is some slight repetition between headline and synopsis, the repetition provides a more exact qualifier for words/phrases in the headline. In the first example, we see the location described differently, to build a richer picture – and provide more detail on the region's earthquake history. In the second example, the synopsis names Mark Carney in full, introduces his job title, names the Bank of England in full and delivers the name of the business secretary praising Carney's work.

These key facts enable readers to understand the most important part of the story without going further. They are models of brevity. The headlines are just seven or eight words, the synopses between nineteen and thirty-three. And the way in which they're written pulls readers in – they'll want to find out more.

While we chose the BBC for our examples, other top news websites broadly apply the same writing model. Here's the first story, this time covered by Sky News:

Italy's strongest earthquake in 36 years reduces towns to rubble

"There are no towns left," says one official, after Italy's most powerful quake in 36 years devastates entire communities.

A slightly longer headline, but by no means a wordy one, using the same process – the headline delivers the key facts, and the synopsis builds on the headline.

BIN THE BYLINE

A byline is a short phrase or paragraph which provides the name of the author, or other kinds of credits (hence the word byline, as in 'this article is by'). This is out of place on a typical press release. If you're a person of reasonable profile, asked to write an article for publication, then you'd likely include a byline. When you're submitting press releases to the world, it's not needed. Your contact details go at the end. Journalists use bylines, not publicists.

THE SUB-HEADLINE

Some newswires and media websites allow for a sub-headline. This shouldn't be confused with the synopsis. A sub-headline is a kind of secondary headline; it shouldn't repeat what is in the main headline but rather provides a different take on the news story, in headline format.

Where available, it can be useful. Take this headline, which we've previously identified as lame: 'MyCompany targets double-figure growth and hires Joe Hill'. We can split the two key pieces of information into a headline and sub-headline, with the headline being 'MyCompany targets double-figure growth' and the sub-headline being 'New hire Joe Hill to drive new markets'. This can revive a lame headline, making it more compelling. However, there's a problem.

Not all outlets use sub-headlines – and the nature of press release distribution means that you have no idea when they might, or might not, be used.

It's best not to rely on them: see them as something that's useful when available; something additional to the headline and synopsis.

Using a sub-headline can radically alter how you compose the headline – which is dangerous, since the sub-headline won't always be there to support it. Our example above works because there is both a headline (to describe the growth) and the sub-headline (to say what's driving it). It's better to incorporate both of these pieces of information within a single headline. If you add a sub-headline, the rest of the press release – and in particular the headline and synopsis – should function without it.

YOU CAN'T ALWAYS COUNT ON THE SYNOPSIS

Just as some outlets don't cater for a sub-headline, others don't cater for a synopsis – and you don't always know in advance which outlets will use it and which won't. This is seldom an issue because, where an outlet doesn't use a synopsis, it simply becomes the press release's first paragraph.

Style guides which omit the need for a synopsis still typically tell you to place all key facts in the first paragraph – which pretty much amounts to creating a synopsis anyway. Where you don't have the option to use a synopsis, formatting your first paragraph as bold or italics can help to distinguish its purpose.

A strong synopsis links the headline with the story, leads the reader in and, for those who are too busy to read the entire press release, conveys all of the story's key facts.

THE HEART OF THE STORY

Time spent planning and structuring your story will enable you to write with greater ease – and turn in something far more newsworthy.

You will learn that:
- ascertaining your story's key facts gives your news story a clear direction and purpose.
- structuring a press release around its key point delivers a more powerful story.
- with press releases, less is often more.
- writing for specific audiences pays off.
- a great press release tells a story that's meaningful to readers.

If the key failings of most weak press releases are not identifying the story and/or failing to bring it to the fore, then the fundamental weakness of inexperienced writers is to just sit down and type away. Good writing requires preparation and structure.

STRUCTURE FIRST

First, structure your press release in outline format. We talked about using outlines when writing the heading and synopsis; in practice, you'll only do this once – for the whole press release – and not separately for the headline, synopsis and main text.

An outline is essentially a bulleted list, where subordinate topics sit as indented items under superior ones. In outlining terminology, these are often called 'parent' and 'child' ideas, or nested topics. This allows you to quickly and easily structure thoughts and topics.

The first, and only, parent bullet is the main point of the press release: the single idea around which you will write. Underneath, secondary points *directly support* the main point. If something *competes* with the main point, toss it away or store it for a later release – press releases which try to convey more than one main idea usually die trying.

Finally, at the third level, you can flesh out ideas.

For example, let's look at our Joe Hill press release in outline format.
- Joe Hill
  - Hired
  - New investment
  - Attracting top talent to the team

- Widgets
  - Innovation
- Asia
  - New for the company
  - Challenges ahead
  - Joe Hill's experience
- Double-figure sales growth
  - Timescales
  - Partnership and channel opportunities

A popular alternative to outlining is mind mapping. Although the process is essentially the same, subtopics are branches, and subbranches, from the central topic. Imagine a simplified tree, drawn from above, and you won't go far wrong.

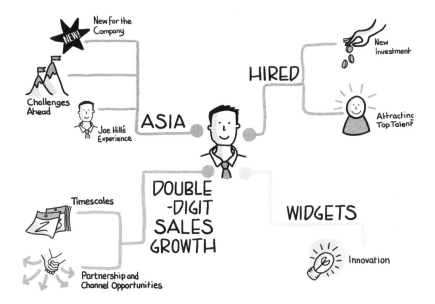

Although centuries old, mind mapping was popularised by British psychology author Tony Buzan; he introduced the term 'mind map' during his 1974 BBC TV series, *Use Your Head*. Its strength is that it is visual – it can incorporate colours, doodles and icons as readily as text.

Both outlining and mind mapping help keep a writer on track.

Fiction writers often describe themselves as either 'plotters' or 'pantsers'. The former plot out the narrative in advance, so that they know exactly where the story will go; the latter fly by the seat of their pants, seeing where the story takes them. For novelists, there are merits and drawbacks to each approach. *Publicity writers are not novelists* and should not be pantsers. You need to know where you are going. You don't want the story to have a life of its own. The only way to be in control is to plan – to work out, in advance, the story's key points. If you wait for them to occur to you while you are writing, you'll omit likely relevant topics and your writing will lack both structure and direction.

Another benefit of listing the facts is that it helps avoid repetition. Publicity writers should make each point and then move on to the next, always making progress and never boring people. Outlining the facts, and ticking them off as you write, is a real help.

FROM OUTLINE TO WRITING

As you move from the outline to the first draft, avoid embellishing the story's language – and don't succumb to the temptation of making your first draft your only draft. Think of writing more as a sculpture than a one-off performance: keep chipping away until it's just right. A press release is something you shape: start with the facts and then embellish around these. Add a little, then a bit more.

Press releases aren't novels. You don't need that much grammatical decoration. The danger, if you write as a pantser, is that you can't know how much embellishment is required – you haven't yet identified the key facts. You will almost certainly overstate unimportant facts, miss crucial points, obscure whatever facts exist and perhaps undermine the objectivity of the release.

Planning removes uncertainty and generates impetus. It can also save you *lots* of time.

WHO, WHY, WHAT, WHERE, WHEN AND HOW?

Many people find that ascertaining a story's 'who, why, what, where, when and how' is a quick, practical way to get a handle on the essential facts. This isn't a structural aid (in that you don't write a press release starting with 'who' and ending with 'how') but rather a means to identify what's important.

- **Who?** Who are the press release's main players? Think about your company, its leaders, the key people in this release (who could include a product team, for example, if it's a product launch), your customers, your competitors and so on. Mostly, think about those who your news will affect – especially who it will benefit.
- **Why?** Why is this news? What about it is different from other stories? Why is this happening now? Why would people sit up and take notice?
- **What?** What's new or has changed? If you're asked to write a story about something, and it isn't new, then it probably isn't really news. Find out about what's new, what's changed, what is changing or what will change.
- **Where?** Where is this happening? Is it relevant to a particular country, city or town – or even an event? Does it have wider geographical ramifications?
- **When?** When is this happening – or when did it happen? Did it happen at the same time as something else, because of something else – or did it cause other things to happen?

- **How?** How did the news come about? If you created a new product, what drove that – and how did you respond?

START BRIEF

Rather than trying to write the entire press release in one go, first, write a single paragraph that encapsulates the whole story. Don't focus on whether that is the headline, synopsis or the body of the press release, just test how contained you can make the story: distil it down to its essence. This paragraph may be used within the final story, or it may be discarded. Its purpose is to help you to understand the heart of the story and keep it firmly in your sights. Many novelists write chapters or scenes which they know won't be used in the final book; they're simply written to firm things up in the writer's mind.

ONE MESSAGE: KEEP ON POINT

We've said several times that a press release should have one key point, with everything else supporting it.

This can certainly be a challenge when there are many stakeholders with differing agendas. You may have stakeholders who feel that a press release delivers the maximum value by also covering this, this, this and that. The opposite is true: the more you ask a press release to do, the less effective it will be. Your key point is the single thing you *want the reader to come away with*. It's what you want them to know, remember and talk about. Agree this with stakeholders in advance, perhaps using your outline and single-paragraph story as discussion aids.

CONNECT WITH THE TARGET AUDIENCE

The only way for a press release to resonate with its target audience is to write with that audience in mind. The perspective from which you write your story should be that of the target audience. Recognising that your audience has specific interests, needs, pressures, desires and so on helps you to write in a more meaningful way. They're not an anonymous, amorphous group. They're real people.

Consider whether your target audience has preexisting knowledge of your company, its products or services. As an example, if you're writing a press release about a new type of camera, the target audience may well be photographic professionals or enthusiastic amateurs. The camera may have a groundbreaking ISO range, something which doesn't need any introduction to that audience – so you can write about it without too much qualification. Yet the same camera may well have a wider market: occasional photographers who want to press a single button to take what enthusiasts might consider snaps.

In a scenario such as this, you have three choices:

- You can try to make one press release work for all audiences.

- You can promote the new ISO range and then explain, in clear terms, what this means, what the benefits are.
- You might decide that the first two choices compromise both target markets and opt to write separate press releases (or significantly tweak one release) to connect better with each audience.

It doesn't pay to assume knowledge on the part of the reader, but equally, when writing for a particular market, you don't want to patronise them.

Thinking clearly about your audience helps you to pitch the story. Uncertainty about where you place a press release can result in a news story with little impact, because you're writing for everyone and anyone. Business readers, financial readers, local people, specialists in a specific sector or skill – these are all examples of target audiences with different needs, values and interests.

WHAT ARE THE BENEFITS TO OTHERS?

While your press release is *about you or your company*, it is a mistake for that to be your focus. If you're promoting a new product, is being a leader in a particular market, increased sales and more profit of interest to customers? Not really, that's the kind of thing which excites stakeholders. When you buy a television, do you care if you're buying it from *the* market leader? Or how many televisions they sell, where they sell them and how much money they make? No, you're interested in *what the television will do for you*. When evaluating a topic for a press release, list – say – five ways in which this delivers genuine benefits to customers: things which they previously didn't have, or couldn't have at the price. Incorporate the most relevant into your story, or shape your story around it.

ADD PROOF: ENSURE THAT YOUR STORY IS BELIEVABLE

Your press release may include claims. You should always substantiate these in some way. Some newswires don't allow stories with unsubstantiated claims, and most editors and journalists will strike them from the text, even if they carry the story. While it's common (though perhaps predictable) for companies to say they are 'a market leader' in a press release, it's beyond the pale to claim to be 'the market leader' without proof. If your new product saves time, say how much time, and why. Just saying it isn't proof: substantiation comes through measurement, research, a case study or feedback from customers.

WRITE ABOUT PEOPLE: MAKE IT REAL

News outlets like a human element in stories. Including people brings stories to life and gives them meaning. It enables others to connect more immediately with the story.

Think about the groups of people affected by your announcement.

How does the topic within the story impact on them?

Where possible, give specific examples rather than generalise. Consider the sheer volume of news coverage from the Vietnam war. Yet it was a single photograph of Phan Thi Kim Phuc, taken in 1972, which created one of the biggest shifts in perceptions of the war. The photo gave meaning to a story which had been ongoing since 1955, because it showed a real person, an affected human, not just a nameless crowd.

Use press releases to put a human face on your company, by including quotes from a spokesperson. However, try to avoid bland self-praise such as "We're delighted to be launching this product..." Well, of course you are! But how *interesting* is your delight? However compelling the story, your delight in it isn't something of interest. Use the quote to say something of value, something which directly supports the key point of the press release.

Get customers to give their perspective, perhaps referencing a contract or case study. Put a human face to the story. While it's hard to get customer quotes, it's worth it: they carry far more value than the easily obtained quotes from within your organisation.

Writing a press release is not so much an art, or science, as it is a means of construction. Once you establish the building blocks, putting them in place is not only relatively straightforward, it delivers superior results.

INCLUDING QUOTATIONS TO BUILD CREDIBILITY

Incorporating quotations allows you to inject emotion, viewpoint and conjecture into a press release – adding excitement to a story.

You will learn that quotations:
- enable you to express emotion within a press release.
- can boost the credibility of your news.

Quotations perform a useful role within publicity, which is why you'll find them within most press releases.

They enable you to use enthusiastic language that would be incongruous within an otherwise factual and evenly written story.

Quotes allow you to inject emotion. Passion and excitement, normally uncomfortable and jarring within a press release, sit well as part of a statement from a business leader or customer. When launching a new product or service, excitement is understandable; even superlatives (to a point) flow naturally within this context. Use quotes to provide both insight and emotion, not information. "Last year our turnover increased by 145%" is a waste of a quote, since facts sit more naturally within a press release's main text. It is better to report the facts and then use a quote to comment on them: "This is a significant increase in turnover, positioning us perfectly for next year."

ADDING EMOTION

Quotes enable you to underline an announcement with personality: not just the emotions of a single person, but even how an organisation 'feels' about something. A person might express herself or himself in this way: "I believe this is the most exciting development in our sector for decades," while you might express an organisation's views by saying, "XYZ Organisation believes that this is the most exciting development in our sector for decades."

A word of caution: don't push the expression of emotions too far. Keep them credible. Use words similar to those used in regular conversations.

Avoid extreme superlatives. Consider how your choice of words adds to, or detracts from, your story's credibility. To 'believe' something shows your faith and commitment. If you say that something is 'astonishing', then it should truly astonish, or you undermine credibility. (Let's face it, when was the last time you were genuinely astonished?) 'Great', 'terrific' or even 'exciting' sit well within normal speech, but shifting up a gear to 'wonderful' or 'magical' can compromise credibility. Some words, such as 'groundbreaking', 'revolutionary' or 'unique' can work well within either speech or the main text of a press release. If used in the latter, then they should always be substantiated, since then they're a claim, not a feeling. We can excuse them within speech, as they express a personal viewpoint. There's less need to make good on assertions.

Speech enables you to offer an opinion on something; to provide conjecture. In the main text of a press release you should *always* substantiate facts, but within speech, we can be more relaxed about things. For example, within speech, we don't always need to explicitly state exactly why a new service or product will transform an accepted process – the person just needs to say that they *believe* it will. That said, it always *helps* to substantiate claims, where you can: "because, to achieve X, people no longer have to do Y."

When quotes state a point of view, softly warn the reader that this is not a fact. Preface conjecture with something like, "we believe that …" or, "it's our hope that …" Both provide an adequate flag that what follows is an opinion, not solid fact.

GO AGAINST THE FLOW

Speech enables you to contradict accepted thinking. We each have differing opinions on many topics; there's no reason that a person speaking in a press release can't express an opinion that's challenging or controversial. Indeed, views such as these can form a potent part of the story, helping your company to make waves with new thinking; demonstrating that you are bold and prepared to disrupt established ways of doing things. In some cases, a contrary view can, in itself, be newsworthy, as long as it's credible – supported with logic, if not facts.

WHO SAYS WHAT?

Carefully consider from whom each quotation comes. The usual approach is to attribute quotes to senior people within the business. Mostly, this is fine and accepted, but sometimes the view of a specialist can be more credible. The choice of person shouldn't be random: develop an agenda to build up the profile of key people (leaders and specialists) within the media. Ensuring that quotations come from a handful of individuals – or fewer – will help achieve this goal. Be consistent about who is responsible for commenting on different types of information: financial results might come from one person, strategic views from another and product launches from another. This allows them to become your voice on a particular topic.

THIRD-PARTY QUOTES

Quotations from third parties are powerful. Delivering an independent view, they provide *evidence* which supports your announcement. Whether endorsements from customers or the professional affirmation of outside experts, these can elevate claims into something of greater substance. Such affirmation may be grounded in fact, or be a respected personal opinion.

As we said before, use third-party quotes to add insight and emotion, rather than facts. "Feedback from our teams on XYZ Company's new product is outstanding" is far better than "we've adopted XYZ Company's new product worldwide".

By their nature, it's considerably harder to obtain third-party quotes, but their greater value makes the effort worthwhile. Planning publicity in advance enables you to factor in the time taken to get quotes. If you only crank out press releases as reactions to recent events you just won't have the time to source third-party quotes. Networking with clients and industry experts can reap great rewards when the need for a quote arises.

News services are *far* more likely to carry a press release that includes quotations from third parties, especially ones which add weight to your publicity. Why? Because the effect of the announcement on the outside world is evident in the press release; the involvement of a third party adds substance to your story.

Quotations enable press releases to
more credibly express emotion, conjecture and views.

SPECIALISTS AND SPOKESPEOPLE

Press releases provide many opportunities for an organisation to demonstrate expertise within the business.

You will learn that specialists within your organisation:
- can add a lot of value to your publicity.
- can help you to create better publicity campaigns.
- can give your business greater credibility.

Quotations can be an influential part of a press release.

Some quotes should come from the business leader, or perhaps a board member who has a specific remit (the head of marketing or sales, for instance).

There's nothing wrong with that, but if quotes *always* come from the top, then it is possible you could deal yourself out of many publicity opportunities. Influencers, journalists and other people know that it's a rare thing for a business leader to be a sharp-end practitioner. Quotes from the top are what's needed when a press release covers business performance, acquisitions, expansion and so on because the business leaders *specialise in running the business.*

A press release about a new product, innovation or service can gain greater credibility when underpinned by professional knowledge. It's time to consider raising the profiles of specialists from within the business.

WHY DEVELOP THE PROFILES OF SPECIALISTS?

Specialists provide insight from the coal face. They have a hands-on authenticity that business leaders lack. Because of this, they can give your company greater credibility – gaining recognition for its expertise.

Identifying and profiling key specialists can improve focus when promoting specific services; it also stops the media from becoming jaded by continually hearing the same views from the same voice.

It's not just about including specialists' views as prepared quotes within your press releases. News outlets like to talk to practitioners; they know they'll get the real low-down on a topic, rather than having to listen to someone posturing about the business. Connecting the media with specialists can be of great value, but – better still – once a relationship develops between them, the specialist's views may be sought out for news stories other than your own.

Specialists are also likely to be more available to chat to the media than a business leader. Work with outlets to give them what they want. Provide access to business leaders when that's their preference, but encourage them to talk to others where it delivers value. Build up the profile of specialists so that the media *wants* to talk to them.

KEEP IT EFFECTIVE

Keep your team of specialists manageable. The more specialists you try to elevate with the media, the greater the work required.

Small- or medium-sized companies may require just one person; larger companies may benefit from a few.

It's also harder for your audience to identify with too many specialists: how many people could *you* recall from a large cast, or would you just remember the lead actors?

CHOOSE THE RIGHT PEOPLE

Not everyone is suited to fronting a company's publicity.

You need people who:

- can think on their feet, but aren't loose cannons.
- are articulate, but not pompous.
- know their subject in depth – they're not just fascinated by it, but also have a good commercial grasp of the topic.
- are well-liked by their peers.
- can operate and speak within a defined framework.

These specialists will represent your company to the wider world. You likely won't be able to curate their conversations. They should be people upon whom you can completely depend.

INVOLVE THEM

You don't want your specialists to feel they are merely your poster girls and boys, randomly nominated to adorn your announcements. This is another way your organisation can benefit from their expertise. Involve them in your publicity, seek their input before you write, and make them a part of the process.

It can be hard to get busy people to give up their time. Making them a real part of the publicity process will help gain their buy-in – and their enthusiasm and knowledge will almost certainly enrich your press releases. When you reach the point that you're working as a team, real publicity magic can happen.

TOUCH BASE OFTEN

Specialists are busy, too busy to be thinking about publicity all day long. Make it part of your schedule to touch base with your company's practitioners, chat about what's happening and listen to what's going on in their world. This pays back in two ways:

- you become a part of their routine, and they start to think about how they can include developments from their working life into yours.
- you'll discover far more about their specialisation and become more effective at marketing it.

All too often marketers call on specialists at the last minute, expecting an enthusiastic commitment to the latest campaign. Better to let them help shape the campaign from the start.

Specialists can also *supply* news opportunities – they talk to many people, are involved in many initiatives – some of which, when you've built a relationship, you can participate in, or time campaigns to run alongside.

COACH THEM

For the most part, news outlets aren't trying to catch out those they interview, so your specialists don't typically have to be wary of questions.

But it's worth coaching them to think about the context of their answers. When interviewed, they're not offering a personal view: they're your representatives. While you don't want them to be promotional automatons, they should deliver answers that support your business strategy and are relevant to your customers. In other words, encourage them to think a little before they speak.

They should remain who they are; don't groom the value out of them, but rather help them to remember that their role, at least when working with you, is one of publicity.

WORK WITHIN A CONTENT STRATEGY

There should be a purpose to each specialist's contribution. It's not just a free-fall expression of views, no matter how worthy. For each area of specialisation, you should have a content strategy: goals and key messages that are woven into marketing, sales and communications related to that specialisation, not just press releases. They should underpin your business goals.

IT'S NOT JUST ABOUT PRESS RELEASES

Remember: *the goal is publicity.* Press releases are but one tool. Specialists can offer more than just a few quotes in a press release or an interview with the media. They could do more – and perhaps want to do more. Perhaps they can also:

- speak at conferences and trade shows.
- write articles for industry outlets/websites.
- contribute guest blogs to specialist websites.
- give presentations or demos online.
- use social media to build a following (although your company will have a social media presence, individuals can reach a wider or more specialist audience).

Exchange ideas; brainstorm; find the stuff they love – and in what they want to be involved.

BEING POACHED

Some companies harbour a concern that raising the profile of key people makes them easier to be poached by competitors. It certainly increases their 'visible value', but these days it's not that hard to track down someone you might want to hire. Just as it raises their value, so it raises yours. You have a choice: raise your profile by raising theirs, or leave your profile where it is.

Publicity is about setting yourself apart from your competitors – and specialists are a vital part of your organisation's DNA. Better to push your communications agenda in the media, using your best resources, than have your competitors beat you to it.

> *Specialists' knowledge helps set organisations apart from others.*
> *Why wouldn't you make that a core part of your publicity?*

CITING RESEARCH

Research can give a press release additional credibility and interest,
encouraging outlets to carry it and readers to share it.

You will learn that:
- research can support your press release's key point.
- to be useful, research must be relevant.

While you write press releases in a neutral tone of voice, publicity is not an entirely objective means of expression. A press release gives your side of a story, putting your company in a favourable light. This is part and parcel of the medium, but you can add credibility to your message by citing research.

UNDERPINNING NEWS WITH RESEARCH AND STATISTICS

Independently investigated and verified facts can support a story enormously. Also, people like to learn; even just a takeaway fact or sound bite from a study can make a story more engaging and shareable.

Research helps to persuade readers; it also carries weight with editors and journalists, who need your story to be credible. Citing relevant research helps get a story published.

Research should be pertinent. It isn't fairy dust, to be sprinkled over every press release in a cynical attempt to chicane otherwise lame stories into the media. It's a useful tool, to be used where it supports a good story.

Any research cited should be relevant to the *central point* of your press release. It should substantiate what you say. What's *relevant* depends on your story, but if your story is about workers in Texas, then citing workforce research in China isn't credible. Research should be relevant to your sector, your services or product, your geography, and be reasonably recent.

Research should be independent. Ideally, it should not be sponsored by a party with a vested interest in the outcome, but this isn't always possible. Plenty of excellent research is sponsored by industry or government, with the aim of validating their strategy, products or services – but is still perfectly trustworthy. Editors and journalists *must* feel that the source is credible, otherwise they simply won't use it. They'll either strip it out or can the whole release – mistrust is contagious, it can spread from a single sentence to the whole story.

Unless you subscribe to commercial research services, you'll likely find what you need using search engines. Don't use the first research you stumble across. Look further – build a bigger picture and ascertain which works best for you. It's up to you to ensure the credibility and validity of the research: search for counter-research which might challenge or undermine citations from your chosen study. Most importantly, find anything which criticises it; a study undertaken four years ago may have been debunked in the last year.

Don't take a solid point from a study and then extrapolate it into something it isn't, or something which is a bit of a reach. If it benefits you to speculate on the research, or to provide an interpretation, do so as a quotation from a specialist.

Just as search engines make it easy for you to find and incorporate research into your press release, they make it just as easy for the media to verify it – checking whether you've quoted it accurately, used it in context and whether anything more recent or more credible derails it.

Cite research sources accurately. Give the name of the study, when it was undertaken, who conducted it (and who sponsored it, if relevant), with a description of the study and, where possible, a link to it. Without these, readers can't validate the research for themselves. However, the rapidly changing nature of the Web means that such links may soon change or expire – especially with content that might hang around a while. If you feel that providing links which ultimately won't work is more frustrating for your audience than not providing them, be sure at least to cite sources clearly. Generally, people can still find the research by searching online.

If you undertook the research yourself, or your company sponsored it, then you should say so. You can improve credibility by commissioning an independent company to manage your research.

Ensure that you have the right to cite any research. If you're citing elements of a study which have been published online, perhaps in multiple places, these may be covered by *Fair Use*, a legal principle which allows limited use of copyright material without the explicit permission of the copyright owner.

(A useful overview of Fair Use can be found on Wikipedia: https://en.wikipedia. org/wiki/Fair_use)

Getting authorisation to use research, or ascertaining its Fair Use status, is your responsibility. Extracts from commercial research (research for which payment or a subscription is required) should not be used without permission – and may require payment for use. An exception to this might be if the information you wish to use is in an *openly published extract* (which is to say, published by the researchers and not a third party) from commercial research.

Research works best when used sparingly. A press release does not need to cite a handful of studies: typically one is enough. The more you add, the more you cloud your key point. And, from a practical perspective, you're robbing the press release of word count which could be more profitably used.

While research can strengthen a story, it won't rescue one which is fundamentally weak. If you find yourself hunting for research to shore up a lacklustre story, then the story is likely at fault and you should consider dumping it.

Write a strong release and *then* decide whether research is needed. If research would work well, go for it. Use it where it helps to explain the story, shows the impact of what you are doing or gives it a real-world context.

WHEN RESEARCH DRIVES THE STORY

Sometimes a story is entirely about the results of research. Stories based on research, facts and interesting statistics tend to be well-read, liked and shared – so they can make for excellent publicity.

Where you've undertaken research yourself, have a clear timetable and agenda for the press releases which announce the results. Small polls may lead to a single press release, but if the research is significant, then it's usually better to write multiple press releases and distribute these over time. This allows each important key fact from the study to become a self-contained story, building a larger campaign. Otherwise, you may squander dozens of points which could have provided publicity for weeks. Another downside of combining all of the results within a single release is that you have to choose which of your findings is 'most important' for the headline, or you compromise by writing a less effective headline, where the release of the research itself becomes the story – which is almost certainly less newsworthy than the findings.

As when citing others' research, avoid stretching conclusions to serve a promotional agenda. Readers will spot this a mile away.

Some readers may well be sceptical about how unbiased your own research is. Consider hiring someone to do the research for you, citing them as the research company. However, you should still say that the study was commissioned by yourself, to ensure transparency. If you undertake the research yourself, say so. It's also best to publish detailed findings in a results document, in addition to main facts in a press release.

Original research can inspire powerful promotional materials, such as infographics and videos, enabling you to turn a single initiative into a far bigger campaign.

You can also take others' research and turn it into publicity for yourself. For example, you might publicly back or support an industry study – or allow a research company to cite your organisation in a study. Where possible, work in close collaboration with those who undertake the research, to coordinate promotion and avoid contradiction.

CHALLENGE OTHER RESEARCH

There may be recent studies with which you disagree, on which you have a strong opinion, or where your research (or experience) delivers a contradictory viewpoint. This can also provide firm foundations for a good press release.

Try not to lay into the original research, even if you take a contrary stance. You can counter research with alternative information in an intelligent way, without it becoming an attack on the research, researcher or research company. Publicity is a medium where you're working to be seen in a positive light. Add real value: don't rubbish things without explanation.

Also, have good reason for entering the discussion: don't simply piggyback on something for its own sake.

Research, facts and statistics can form the basis for great publicity. Citing solid, relevant research can help to get a press release published, read and shared. Validating any research you use is essential.

CALLS TO ACTION

Calls to action can improve both response rates and conversions, by directing people to a planned next step.

You will learn that:
- calls to action in press releases should not typically be sales-led.
- calls to action are part of the news story.
- like the rest of a press release, calls to action should be written in the third person.

Although many press releases are written to inform the market, or to keep a company's profile buoyant, most are intended to trigger a reaction from the reader.

A company might want customers to download an evaluation copy of a new software product, register to attend a seminar, watch a video or simply just read some more information – there are lots of possibilities.

Calls to action makes it easier for readers to respond. They can also direct people, efficiently, to additional information or resources.

In leaflets and advertisements, calls to action would typically suggest a sales touchpoint (*'call us* today for a free sample'), be in the first person ('click here to visit *our* website'), have a sense of urgency ('register soon') or make an offer (*'save* 40% if you book this week'). Such sales-led calls to action are not suitable within press releases.

News outlets won't include sales-led calls to action in a news story. They'll strip them out, as they call into question the objectivity of the piece or turn the news story into an advertisement, undermining their impartiality. In some cases, calls to action can compromise a story to the point where it's easier for busy media professionals to discard the story rather than run it.

Inappropriate calls to action include special offers, a direct request to call 'sales' for 'more information' and needy requests that people 'share this story'.

Think about how calls to action will read when on a website, or printed in a newspaper or magazine. It should use the vocabulary, style and structure of a press release and, ideally, be newsworthy itself. Write calls to action in a format that outlets can directly and immediately use, regardless of the final publishing platform/medium. Make it easy for them to do their job.

Good calls to action include asking people to obtain more detailed information, watch an overview video, download evaluation software, or join an event.

Remember that your press release can be published *anywhere*, so using language like 'click here' creates editing work for print media (where no one can 'click here'). It's better to say that 'more information is available from [URL]' – if the visible URL is also a clickable link, *both* online and print media can use it, without alteration.

Since the point of calls to action is to channel responses more efficiently, it's counterproductive to create multiple calls to action. These force people to stop and consider which one is best for them, and, while they hesitate, there is a real chance you will lose them. If you need readers to choose from multiple calls to action (or you provide a selection of resources) gather these together on a single landing page, so that your press release needs just one.

A landing page (a specific campaign page, with aggregated information and resources, to which you can direct visitors) is a highly effective way to channel interest. By offering a link to 'more information', you can let the landing page do the sales work. While offers and sales-led calls to action have no place in a press release, there's nothing wrong with placing them on a landing page – indeed, it works very well.

It's fair to say that a goal for many press releases is, ultimately, to get readers to buy. You may have stakeholders pressuring you to make this the readers' next action. This is understandable but flawed: in a typical sales process, buying is the *final* act, but, from a press release, seldom the *next* action. A press release is not an advertisement. By all means, lead people from the announcement to an advertisement. That's fine. In fact, it's more than fine. It's very effective.

A press release is most successful when part of a bigger process. Think about this end-to-end. What's the news? What's the outcome we want from people reading the news? What's the best process to achieve this? It's not 'announce – purchase', it's more likely to be something like 'announce – more information – engage – purchase'. For example, we could direct people towards signing up to a mailing list, from where sales-based marketing can take over in due course.

Finally, think about your two audiences: news outlets and the public.

Calls to action for the media sits outside the main body of a press release and should be labelled clearly. This enables outlets to grab additional information or resources relevant to them, without having to sift through sales materials. It's quite acceptable for the media to have multiple calls to action: ensure that these are clearly labelled. These might include: 'download high-resolution images' and 'watch our briefing video'.

Calls to action for the public sit within the body of a press release and work best when there is only one.

> ***Calls to action can channel people very efficiently towards your end goal. They work best when written in the accepted style of a press release, leaving other, more appropriate channels to 'do the sales job'.***

QUALITY CONTROL

You don't want to divert readers' attention from the story,
or for it to be undermined by mistakes or inaccuracies.
This means one thing: thorough quality control.

You will learn that quality control:
- isn't just a quick skim read at the point you've finished writing.
- can inspire new ideas as much as it can eliminate fatal flaws.

Since everyone makes mistakes, quality control processes are not optional. It's far better to squash flaws before you distribute a press release than be mocked afterwards on social media. We're not just talking about typos: quality control goes beyond checking only spelling and grammar.

Ideally, there should be several levels of quality control.

You should check:
- if the press release is newsworthy.
- the accuracy of information.
- how well the story is presented.
- if the press release is optimised for search engines.
- if the press release achieves its goals.
- if all approvals are in place.
- spelling and grammar.

Quality control is most effectively approached with a positive mindset: that it's not a process of 'fixing errors', rather an opportunity to make things better.

It pays to build quality control into the writing process, rather than apply it afterwards. That way, you can feed new ideas or changes into the press release, not just identify errors, saving time on basic remedial work. Involving stakeholders and managers along the way makes it less likely that they would bounce or drastically change your story when it's passed out for final review – since this won't be the first time they've seen it.

IS IT NEWS?

While you should validate the newsworthiness of a story before you begin work, sometimes a dud can slip through. Even after you've written a story, continue to challenge the brief. How good is the story? Could it be approached in a better way? Would an advertisement or mailer be a more suitable vehicle for the message? Even though it means writing off work, sometimes it's better to give up on a poor press release than be accountable for its inevitable failure.

HOW ACCURATE IS THE PRESS RELEASE?

Check your facts. While preparing the story, you may have garnered information from specialists, stakeholders, research documents, customers and so on. You can't take all of these at face value. You must check their accuracy. Being diligent during the research and writing process – noting the sources of information – will help a lot.

Quote sources within the press release, or facts will look like assertions or fabrications. If a specialist has stated something as fact, get her or him to provide a source. If they can't, it doesn't necessarily mean that the information can't be used – though it may need to be used differently, perhaps within a quotation from the specialist, where it can be positioned as opinion.

A press release will contain other facts. Product and service launch dates, prices, availability information, upgrade information, offer details and so on. Double-check these before distribution: it's possible some facts were correct when the press release was written but they've since changed.

You may well have drawn comparisons, for effect, within your press release. How accurate are these? Can they be substantiated or at least defended?

To be accepted as news, it's important that facts within a press release are accurate.

HOW WELL IS THE STORY WRITTEN?

This is a challenging self-audit. After all, it's about the quality of *your* work – how well the writing puts across the story. As a creative skill, the appreciation of writing is at least partly subjective – but you can objectively assess many facets of the story. Ask yourself if your press release:

- is on-brand, speaking the language of the organisation; delivering messages in an agreed way?
- delivers a clear message, getting quickly to the point without meandering around?
- is written around one key topic and isn't hitting the reader with a volley of information?
- is written around the right main topic, when something else would better resonate with readers?
- covers the *impact of the news*: what the *effect* of the news will be on customers, competitors and the sector?
- is clear about *why* your company is making this announcement – and why it's important now?

Don't be afraid of revising a press release several times. Multiple revisions don't mean that you're a poor writer, it means the opposite. Professional writers typically edit a text two, three, four or more times: no professional writer would submit the first draft. It's not unusual for revisions to be up to half of the 'writing' process. Encourage yourself to see writing as a series of cycles of improvement, rather than being confined to a single writing session.

Throw away text if it doesn't quite work or if there's a better way of writing it. This can be emotionally challenging, especially if you've laboured over what has become a well-honed paragraph – something to which you've grown attached. See what you can cut, expand, rearrange or rewrite. Experiment. Be open-minded. Don't be precious.

IS THE PRESS RELEASE OPTIMISED FOR SEARCH ENGINES?

It's important that the story can be found online. Ideally, you'll have identified the most relevant keywords before starting, and then woven them into the press release as you wrote. It's easier to do this than it is trying to pepper them in later.

At least one pass of your review workflow should be to assess the text from a search optimisation perspective, to check if:

- the most important keywords appear in the heading.
- some of the most important keywords appear in the synopsis.
- all keywords appear within the body of the press release, around two or three times.
- your company's name appears in the release.
- the press release links to your website at least once, and that the link has value for both people and search engines (i.e. itself contains keywords which describe what will be found on the page to which you're linking) but isn't over-optimised.
- you have over-optimised the press release: whether keywords appear too many times.
- inserting keywords has compromised the readability of the press release.

While optimisation is important, humans come first – always. Over-optimising a press release can hinder readability and obscure key points – and have a detrimental effect on search-engine performance.

DOES THE PRESS RELEASE ACHIEVE ITS GOALS?

It is important to understand what the press release is meant to accomplish.

Sometimes, goals are specific and measurable: an increase in enquiries or website traffic, for example, or a target for social shares. Sometimes, goals are less measurable or are part of a long-term objective: wanting to be seen as a thought-leader in a particular sector, or for a specific topic.

Whether your goals are objective or subjective, you should assess a press release for how well it supports those aims. No one will know for sure just how it performs until distributed, but it stands much more chance of success when aligned to predefined goals.

ARE APPROVALS IN PLACE?

Getting sign-offs is often tedious but always necessary. Despite the inevitable time pressures, you should avoid the temptation to skip any of these. Should something be wrong with a press release once distributed, it's far better there's collective blame than a personal one. More than that, it gives stakeholders one last chance to not just validate the press release but also improve it.

Creatively, it's your press release, but from a business or commercial perspective, it could well 'belong' to someone else, perhaps a subject-matter expert or business manager. Since the press release supports them, they must be happy with it. Keep in mind that people should approve what is relevant to them - not always the entire press release. If you think someone is wrong about a particular 'improvement', then make a case firmly, but be objective, not react emotionally to someone changing words over which you've sweated.

Task subject-matter experts with ensuring that the story's facts are valid.

If you've quoted someone within your press release, secure her or his approval. This is especially important for third parties: customers, specialists, analysts, suppliers, partners and so on. However, a word of warning: when escalated to a third-party's marketing team, timescales for approvals can slip out of your control. Not only that, the approved quote may either not be forthcoming or be watered down and have significantly less value. This isn't a hint to circumnavigate an approval process, but it's prudent to prepare alternative content should you need to ditch the original or can't wait any longer for sign-off.

If you mentioned another company's name, be sure that you can do so. Some companies won't approve the use of their name if it appears to be an endorsement. It typically pays to be factual when using another company's name. For example, 'XYZ Company, customer of Your Company' is likely to be fine (since it's simply a fact), whereas 'XYZ Company, which depends on the services of Your Company' is more likely to require sign-off. Be respectful of companies' brands.

If you're interviewed by a journalist, such etiquette almost never applies. The journalist will take an interview as its own permission to publish, and may even embellish what you've said. You're not a journalist: you're a publicist. The rules are different for you.

A press release is often created to support someone or something within a business. That person or business entity needs to have okayed the facts within the release, and have agreed on campaign logistics, such as distribution or circulation dates.Internal approvals can, if it's acceptable within your organisation's culture, be dealt with differently, simply to keep things moving. Rather than waiting for approval, you can circulate drafts and supporting information, with an intended publication date and a date by which people should respond if they wish to make changes.

The goal with approvals isn't to cover your back. It's to make the press release as good, and as accurate, as it can be.

The 'owner' of the press release (usually the head of marketing or head of publicity) should also sign off the release.

HAS THE PRESS RELEASE BEEN CHECKED FOR SPELLING AND GRAMMATICAL MISTAKES?

Just one typo can undermine all of your hard work (and the credibility of your company). While people approach proofreading in different ways, the only sure thing is that *not proofreading* isn't an option.

That the public would judge the spelling and grammar in your press releases assumes that your stories get published. Outlets to whom you send your press releases all write for a living. They can spot mistakes a mile off; the odd one, they *might* correct. If they do, it's likely they'll negatively judge your company on the quality of its output. Don't create work for them; of course, they proofread their own articles, but they'd rather not spend avoidable time on your press releases, if their choice is to publish as is. A great news story will get published even if it's not perfect but, in general, a company which delivers clean press releases builds up the trust of news outlets with news stories that are easier to process. You want outlets to welcome your news stories, not be wary of them.

A writer is often the worst person to proofread her or his own work. Writers have an appreciation of their own work which exceeds that of any reader; knowledge that can 'fill in the gaps' of incomplete text, rendering issues invisible that are obvious to a third party. Also, the brain tends to feel that the task is over when writing is complete. People become resistant to making changes. Revisions and proofreading can seem like 'more work' rather than 'completing the task'. Writing is, at the most, 50% of the work of creating a press release. The rest of the time comprises taking the brief, researching, planning, editing, revising, gaining approvals and proofreading.

While using an external proofreader costs money, it's almost always going to get the job done faster and to a higher standard. After all, proofreaders do it for a living. There can be a misplaced belief that 'if you're writing it, it's your responsibility to get it right'. Well, if that were the case, *professional writers* wouldn't use editors and proofreaders. They recognise that their skill is writing, and that, like everyone, they make mistakes. An outside eye is almost always better when it comes to reviewing text, and better still when someone does it for a living. A professional proofreader will have a far firmer grasp of what's right and wrong than 'someone in the office who is good at spelling'. They should also check for more than typos: key facts, the use and spelling of company names and so on. (Such mistakes can create lasting damage and lose you the support of a customer or partner. It's important to verify that it's 'Tesco' and not 'Tescos' – and 'HP' or 'Hewlett-Packard' and not 'Hewlett Packard'.)

It helps to use a professional proofreader because it's their job: not only will they be more knowledgeable, they'll also be more diligent, more passionate and yes, more pedantic. They're also being paid to do it; if you hand your text to someone in the office, it's typically someone who has to fit it in as a non-core task around their 'real work'.

If you've decided to proofread internally, then choose someone who can do the job well. A degree in English isn't a guarantee of being an excellent proofreader. For example, even graduates can use the phrase 'people were evacuated' without realising that *evacuating people* means to empty their bowels (even if it is a common enough saying): you evacuate people *from* a building or evacuate a building. This is important stuff; your text will be circulated on the Internet, right around the world. Getting it right counts.

It's hard to proofread your own text but, if that is the only option, then there are some simple things you can do to improve your success rate. The first is to *never* proofread on a screen; print out the story on paper, get yourself into a different room, shut yourself off and focus on the text as if you've never seen it. Try reading it aloud, speaking more slowly than you would usually. When reading, try punctuating it unusually, so that your mind isn't tempted to skip ahead without reading the actual words.

If you're reading in your head, try adopting a well-known voice. This forces you to 'read' with different inflexions and helps you to concentrate. Morgan Freeman's is a good voice to use, as is Maggie Smith's. And you know what? It also makes the process a little more fun.

Finally, there's always the option of using your computer's built-in text-to-speech function, to have the text read to you aloud. Yes, the voice is stilted, but for our purposes, this can be a good thing. This function is built into Windows, MacOS and many versions of Linux.

WRITING AIDS AND SOFTWARE

There are quite a few useful tools on the market which provide better functionality than built-in grammar and spelling tools. They can highlight more grammatical errors than most word-processing software.

They often offer helpful tips and advice, as you write – also helping you to improve your writing. You learn as you go; your mistakes reduce, and your vocabulary grows. They also check for things which word-processing tools typically don't, such as repetition, commonly misused words, words which others use too often and so on. They also help to spot words which are correct but used in the wrong context, such as lose/loose or there/their/they're.

They are not perfect and will sometimes suggest changes which are themselves incorrect, so you should always be the final arbiter of your work – and they are not a substitute for 'real' proofreading. Most tools either work online or integrate into word processors such as Word and are paid for by subscription.

Examples include Grammarly (grammarly.com), Ginger (gingersoftware.com) and ProWritingAid (prowritingaid.com).

PROOFREADING ISN'T A ONE-OFF EVENT

Ideally, there isn't a single proofreading cycle, if only because the person to perform the proofing should be the last one to handle the press release. Some form of proofreading should be done before the text goes for internal approval, so that stakeholders are not distracted by literal errors. Since stakeholders *will* make changes, the unavoidable reality is that there really *must* be at least more than one proofreading cycle.

BEWARE LAST-MINUTE CHANGES

Ensure the final proofreading is after any last corrections. Many errors are introduced during last-minute changes. These may be typos, but they may also be logical errors, where changing one thing demands that related items also need changing. Such errors are no less embarrassing or excusable because they arose out of a need for speed. Readers don't care why or when an error was introduced, just that one is there. And the end result is the same: credibility is undermined.

Quality control isn't just a single step at the end.
To be most effective, it should be a core part of the creative process.
It's not about fixing stuff, it's about improving it.

DELIVERING ADDITIONAL INFORMATION

It's impossible for a press release to contain every single piece of information about a news story without compromising that story's impact. Don't try to shoehorn everything in: provide it elsewhere.

You will learn that:
- a press release shouldn't contain every last scrap of detail.
- images, infographics and videos give your story greater prominence, increase visits to your website and encourage sharing on social media.
- additional resources can include promotional messages which wouldn't be acceptable in a press release.

Mark Twain said, "I didn't have time to write a short letter, so I wrote a long one instead." Anyone who has been challenged to write succinctly will recognise this as truth: concise writing takes far more time and effort than verbose writing. For those writing press releases, conveying everything deemed to be important, within a meagre few hundred words, is demanding.

This is especially true when that information has genuine value, for example when launching a new product which has dozens of new features. Why wouldn't everybody want to know everything?

It's not the role of a press release to convey everything. A press release is *an announcement*. The more detail you add, the more likely it is that you'll kill the impact of a story.

Consider very carefully whether something genuinely strengthens a press release, or whether it dilutes it. If it dilutes it, be bold – either omit it entirely or provide it separately. How do you decide what to keep and what to drop? If something *directly* supports the key point of a press release, try to include it; if something is secondary to that story, provide it separately. Anything else you can kill across the board. This keeps a press release sharp. Secondary information is still relevant, valuable or useful, so it's easier to incentivise interested readers to take the next step.

Focus on grabbing readers' attention and don't overload them – push additional information to places where they can get it if they want it. Where more detailed information adds value, provide it outside of the press release. Make it available via a link either within the press release, or at the foot. There are compelling benefits to providing additional information and resources.

- By far the greatest percentage of news stories are text-based, yet many outlets willingly accommodate other media, such as images or videos.
- Images and videos can deliver a big increase in 'click-through' rates to your news story.
- People are more inclined to share news stories if they include images or videos.
- Some people don't read an entire news story, but may watch a review video or scan an infographic, taking away more information than would have otherwise been the case.
- Resources which encourage comment or interaction tend to be shared more and generate more links back to your website.
- Products which the media can review (such as software, consumer electronics and so on) can lift your story to another level – so, make it easy for outlets to download evaluation software or obtain physical evaluation products.

Additional resources shouldn't be an afterthought, but rather part of a more rounded way of communicating news and of maximising stories. Rich media, such as videos and infographics, makes campaigns far more compelling and will typically achieve better results.

PHOTOGRAPHS

A good photograph can contribute significantly to the story; think about the story's core message and the image that would best support it. For example, this can be a shot of a product's packaging, the product itself, or a photograph taken at an important event.

You should provide some items as a matter of course, such as photographs of those who comment within the story.

You should *always* have on file professionally shot, high-resolution photographs of your top team, specialists and spokespeople. Photographs should be taken at the same time and be consistent in terms of lighting, camera angle, background and the way they're cropped. Don't supply stylised images (for example, colourised or black and white) as it's quick and easy for a website or publication to make that change, if that's what they want.

When launching a new product, a pack shot is a good idea. Ideally pack shots should be supplied with the box on a background *and* isolated against a white background. This gives the media flexibility when using the images. Pack shots shouldn't include other graphics, such as a company logo (other than where it exists on the pack). If you don't yet have a physical box, your marketing team can simulate one. When launching a new service, commission photographs of that service in use.

Can you shoot the images yourself? It depends on your skills and equipment. While it's true that even smartphones are technically capable, amateur pictures seldom match up to those taken by professionals. Photographs are part of your brand, part of how your company is perceived. You need to be confident that any photographs, however produced, meet whatever standards/brand guidelines you set.

Photographs should be RGB JPEG files at 300dpi (dots per inch). You shouldn't have to worry about the files being CMYK (the format used for litho colour printing), as outlets will make this conversion if they intend to use the file in print. (Your photographer or marketing team will understand this technical stuff.) Don't send high-resolution images as e-mail attachments. Make them available for download via links.

DON'T USE LIBRARY PHOTOGRAPHS

You could use library shots, but there are many drawbacks.

You *must* review the licensing terms for any images used. Most 'royalty-free' images are not licensed for news distribution, or for use within any vehicle that is itself resold. If your story gets picked up in several places, you could get hit with a huge bill from the image library's lawyers, who scour the Web, using reverse-image search software such as TinEye (tineye.com), looking for unlicensed images. Image libraries typically provide 'editorial-licence' images, for news usage, which cost more than royalty-free images – often, significantly so. However, an invoice for image misuse can be substantially higher than the purchase price of the image. Moreover, while library shots get the job done quickly, publicity is all about building an organisation's uniqueness, which is hardly best achieved by using resources which anyone can obtain. Images should be about you and your company.

Many library shots simply aren't suitable for news photographs: they're not *reportage* in style, they're too full of corporate gloss, aspirational and generic.

The biggest reason to avoid library images for news stories is that most media outlets won't use them anyway – for a combination of the reasons already stated. Glossy library images compromise the distinctive, news nature of the story, to the point where it can undermine the visual legitimacy of their outlet. It also exposes them to potentially large legal costs down the line.

INFOGRAPHICS

Infographics can be useful to demonstrate a process, statistics, a shift in behaviour, how a product or service solves a problem, and many other things. People love to share them. Ensure that an infographic educates – provides knowledge to the user – and doesn't simply push a sale, which puts the media off using it, as it will be essentially an advertisement. Think of the big picture when commissioning an infographic – what is the problem or issue that your product or service solves? What are the benefits to buyers? Quality is again important: unless you have the skills to do these in-house, to a professional standard, get a designer to create them for you.

The usual format for an infographic is as a 24-bit PNG file. It should be readable at a *relatively* small size, but provided to outlets at a larger size/higher resolution, so they can scale it to their required size for use online or in print.

As with photographs, don't send high-resolution images as attachments. Make them available for download via links.

VIDEOS

Videos can enable you to present an entirely different perspective on a news story. There's little point in providing a video which repeats what the press release already says. Videos can include interviews, sales pitches, presentations, demonstrations, customer endorsements and more. While *all of these* are inappropriate in a press release, they are usually completely acceptable in an accompanying video – an exception would be providing an advertisement, which would be unlikely to be used.

While you probably couldn't make a video for every press release, because of the cost and time, it's a worthwhile investment for key stories. Videos should be prepared professionally. This doesn't mean you have to spend vast amounts – and it's certainly something you can resource in-house, if you have the right skills and equipment. Using a cheap domestic video camera for corporate videos (even if it's HD or better) creates a poor impression. At the least, you *need* a good *prosumer* camera, off-camera audio equipment, lighting and good editing software. If you genuinely don't have the budget for this, don't cut corners and produce something cheap. It's not the case that 'something is better than nothing'.

Provide videos in full HD (1920×1080). Some websites use a lower resolution, such as 720HD (to save bandwidth), but let them make that call.

Don't send high-resolution videos as attachments. Provide links which make them available both for download *and* for embedding. Many newswires and media websites will embed the video from the source you provide; those which want to host the video themselves can download it from your links.

It's worth bearing in mind that the majority of people – up to 85% – watch videos on social media without sound (source: Facebook). Many people flick through Facebook, Twitter, LinkedIn and so on with the sound off, because they are at work, on the bus or train, or at home watching the television with their family or friends. This means that videos with subtitles can work better than those without. In general, videos specifically targeting social media should work with and without sound.

It's common to provide videos via a video hosting service. You could use YouTube (youtube.com), which is free, or a professional hosting website such as Vimeo (vimeo.com) which can provide an unbranded media player, or a player branded with your own logo. However, an outlet is unlikely to embed a video which uses a branded player. Vimeo and Wistia (wistia.com) enable you to do smart things such as embed a form to capture viewers' details *part way* through viewing the video – or perhaps allow them to download something in exchange for providing an e-mail address. Such services can also provide analytics on your video, such as which parts people skip or rewatch. However, most media websites will not embed a file which incorporates data capture. If you intend to do this, you should warn media sites that your video includes embedded forms and provide an alternative.

DEMONSTRATION PRODUCTS

New products can be made available for demonstration purposes for those outlets which would wish to create a hands-on review. It's better to proactively offer these than it is to have the media chase you: they can choose whether to use it or not. Provide links to software, downloads and an easy process to quickly obtain physical products.

TEXT

You can make a wealth of additional text available outside the press release, which outlets can then use as needed.

You should always have full bio pages of each of your key people, ready and available. You can include links in your press releases' boilerplate/footer text, and on a 'newsroom' page on your website. This enables journalists and editors to expand a person's profile, if needed, without contacting you.

The same goes for company information: while your 'boilerplate' information delivers the essential details, this may not be enough. Provide a company profile which is a non-sales document, structured around key facts, such as dates, turnover, company size, growth statistics and so on.

New products and services can benefit from detailed pages to describe them more fully, perhaps with technical specifications, if appropriate. Resist the temptation to send the media to your website's 'marketing pages' for this product – that *is not* what they need.

CATERING FOR THE PUBLIC AND NEWS OUTLETS

Your two audiences – the public and news outlets – each want different information. **The public** can follow signposts/links from your press release to additional information, downloads or media. These can expand on the story and perform tasks which a press release can't, such as selling harder, offering discounts and so on. **News outlets** don't want your sales materials. A brochure is far less useful than a specially prepared briefing document, written in non-sales language. Provide longer customer quotes than would work in a press release, or more detailed case studies. Provide access to evaluation products, a video presentation or briefing created just for them, and so on. Give them things which they can use within a news story – but don't send too much, as this can be overwhelming.

USE A LANDING PAGE FOR EACH NEWS STORY

For maximum impact, and to make life easier for readers, deliver all of the additional content on a landing page. That way, a single link on your press release can provide everything. While you could point readers to a page which already exists, such as a product page, a campaign landing page is far better.

Just as a press release should be kept focused and concise, so should additional content. Less is more: while you could provide dozens of resources, try to use only those which best fulfil a meaningful 'next step'. Everything should earn its keep and have both structure and purpose. Giving readers everything you can lay your hands on will more likely overwhelm than impress.

DECLUTTER THE PRESS RELEASE

Delivering additional information outside of the press release makes it easier for you to write a leaner story. It puts supplementary information in its place and keeps a press release focused.

KEEP THINGS LIVE

Be mindful that a press release may have a short 'news life', but it's likely to have a far longer life online, archived on many news websites. Links to additional information should be kept alive, updated as needed, or redirected somewhere else when they are no longer valid. It's very frustrating for people to follow a link, only to get an error message.

ENCOURAGE SOCIAL MEDIA UPDATES

Don't forget that outlets will likely want to promote a good news story via their social media channels. Help them do this, by providing highly condensed versions of the news story, written in a way that better suits social media. It's a good idea to give them a few options – shorter and longer versions. Don't just replicate parts of the press release – express the story in a more conversational way. Don't forget to include any URLs, hashtags and @names. As ever, make life easier for outlets. Save them time. You stand more chance of getting coverage if you also supply images, infographics or videos – at the correct size and in the correct format for social media.

Keep a press release focused and find other ways to deliver detailed or additional information. Use multimedia resources such as pictures, infographics and videos for your end audience and provide the media with easy access to supporting materials. Doing this can significantly boost the success of a story.

CAMPAIGN LANDING PAGES

Press releases benefit from calls to action, but to where do you send people?
While it's easy to link to website pages which already exist, creating a
campaign-specific landing page has many benefits.

You will learn that a campaign-specific landing page can:
- make life easier for customers by putting additional information in one place.
- enable you to more accurately measure results.
- improve responses and conversions.

When you issue a press release, it's generally to solicit a reaction of some kind, usually via calls to action that direct readers towards next, best steps. Many press releases direct the reader to something which already exists, such as a product information page. This might be okay in some cases – and it's certainly easy to do – but is it the best way to handle this all-important next step?

When you want to direct people to more information, or encourage interaction, consider using a campaign landing page on your website. Although this does mean a little extra work, it can significantly improve responses and conversions. A landing page allows you to aggregate everything that's relevant to the press release *in one place*. It's focused.

For quick 'needed now' press releases, it's usually not possible, nor practical, to create a campaign landing page. That's fine – it's not something you need to do for every news story – and some stories are self-contained, so there isn't any 'more information'.

But where you want to maximise response, generate better – or specific – results, a landing page is a powerful way to funnel customer interest.

A landing page can contain many things: a more sales-orientated version of your story, special offers, downloads, links to social media channels, sign-up forms, multiple contacts, more detailed information, and so on. Many of these wouldn't sit comfortably within a press release, nor would there be room for them all. A landing page can handle this information overflow with aplomb.

As an example, if your company decided to give a percentage of a product's sales to charity, a press release can convey the most important messages. But it couldn't tell the whole story. A landing page could talk about this in depth, showing what you are doing and what the impact is. It can also encourage others to donate, or get involved, using language that might jar in a press release.

ENTICE PEOPLE TO THE LANDING PAGE

Think about how you set expectations within a press release, and how the landing page can most effectively meet those expectations. For example, by following a link, people will certainly 'find out more' but do those words promise enough to get people to click on the link? What will they discover that isn't within the press release? What else can they gain access to: for example, is there a time-limited offer, or some freebies?

Build a landing page that delivers content that readers will want – and direct them to that. Think about *their needs* before your sales requirements – though of course include options to buy, or enquire, on the landing page. A new product? Suggest a demo video. New software? Offer a 30-day trial. A different way of doing things? Provide a free seminar or webinar. A pre-launch announcement? Let them snag a discount if they register early-bird interest. Offer people something they need or want, something *specific*, not just 'more information'.

A PLATFORM FOR MEASUREMENT

Another advantage of creating landing pages is that you can gather campaign analytics. Directing traffic to a single page means that you can more accurately measure response to the campaign, enquiries and conversions.

For the publicity-writer, campaign analytics deliver valuable insights. Learning which press releases get the best and worst responses helps you to fine-tune publicity with greater confidence.

Direct people to landing pages using calls to action *within* the body of the press release, typically towards the end. Since they are part of the release, they should be factual and direct. Avoid sales and marketing language. Just as the rest of the press release is in the third person, so should be the calls to action.

LANDING PAGES FOR NEWS OUTLETS

Should you create a landing page for news outlets? For your most important campaigns, such as new product launches, this can be a great idea. For such landing pages, there's no need for a commercial goal; you simply provide all of the campaign's resources in a structured, unfussy way. You may also want to provide contact details for specialists related to the campaign – or even provide the facility for journalists and editors to schedule an interview, using an online diary. For most press releases, news outlets will usually be happy to download extra information and resources from direct links within a press release or e-mail. Calls to action for the media should sit outside the body of the press release and be labelled as such – for example, under a 'notes to editors' heading.

Creating campaign-specific landing pages does take a little more planning and execution. But for the right press releases, the benefits justify the additional effort.

FAKING IT

Not all changes in the news landscape are positive. Two particular concerns are the rise of fake news and clickbait.

You will learn that:
- biased news isn't new, but it is on the rise.
- clickbait articles are seldom newsworthy or stories of substance.
- publicists should recognise public mistrust of the media.

People know that not all news can be trusted. They understand that even good news stories can be written from different perspectives, presenting opposing accounts of the same events. They're surrounded by faux news articles, clickbait and trivia written to look like news – all created to get advertising revenue from your clicks.

MEDIA MISTRUST

Bias, fake news and clickbait stories all contribute to a growing distrust in the media.

Research firm Edelman publishes an annual report, The Edelman Trust Barometer. The 2017 report found that "trust in all four key institutions – business, government, NGOs (non-governmental organisations) and media – has declined broadly". In 2018, Edelman said that "trust in business, government, NGOs and media remained largely unchanged from 2017" and that it "reveals a world of seemingly stagnant distrust" and that trust within the USA has dropped to record levels (source: Edelman).

Statistics from global community YouGov found that trust in advertisements had risen to 61% in 2017 (source: YouGov), yet a 2016 report by Gallup found that Americans' trust in mass media was down to 32%, from 53% in 1997 (source: Gallup). So, not only is mistrust in the news at an all-time high, many people are more likely to believe an advertisement than a news story.

DECIDE WHERE YOU STAND

While, philosophically speaking, *all* news is to some degree fake (it's hard to report on anything *without* adding emotion or bias), this does present a problem for the publicist. To influence others, our stories must be believed. They have to rise above fake news and clickbait, not get lost in it.

Some news websites and writers have adopted clickbait-style techniques and over-sensationalised their stories, perhaps to compete for revenue with clickbait websites. This is a trap. You are trying to build trust. You don't want to mimic, or be part of, something where trust is crumbling.

- Recognise that you're putting out stories into an environment of some mistrust and be on your guard when writing.
- Tell good, factual stories.
- Write stories in an authentic way and keep exaggeration at bay.
- Avoid clickbait-style techniques. These frustrate readers, who hate it when a sensationalist headline leads to lacklustre content.
- Check any facts you publish – citing sources and not exaggerating conclusions. Journalists and influencers are now more diligent about the facts cited in press releases than ever before.
- Third-party research and endorsements build credibility in news stories. It's essential to include these when possible.

Be on the lookout for fake news, to ensure you don't use any of the same techniques.

- Avoid shocking or unbelievable headlines.
- Don't write headlines in capital letters.
- Don't use exclamation marks.
- Don't draw dramatic conclusions or make tenuous links which imply doubtful cause and effect.
- Don't use manipulated images or images out of context.

Painting your company in a positive light is not the same as faking it. If you're going to build trust, be authentic and avoid the tools of mistrust.

Those interested in protecting themselves from fake news can take advantage of websites such as Full Fact (the UK's independent fact-checking charity) at fullfact.org. However, be aware that – perhaps inevitably – some question the impartiality of fact-checking websites.

HANDLING COMMON NEWS TOPICS

There are many potential news topics,
but how do you write the most effective press release for each?

We've examined, in depth, how to write press releases. Hopefully you're armed and ready to go – but first, here are some pointers to help you to write the most common types of news story.

AWARDS: GIVING

Using the fact that you're giving an award as the main point of a press release makes publicity look like your primary motivator for doing so. Better for your organisation to step back and let the winners, participants and nominees take the limelight. Focus on the award, not you. What are the benefits to the recipient? What will be the benefits to the recipient's sector, employees or customers? Why this particular award? Why is this important to your company? Also, what are the facts? How long have you been giving this award? Who has won previously? What were the tangible benefits?

AWARDS: SPONSORED

That you are sponsoring an award is interesting, but typically not enough to carry the story. Why are you sponsoring that particular award and how does this connect to your business and its values? How does your company align with the award? (Think human: perhaps your founder was inspired by that field to establish your business.) What does the award recognise, and why is this important? Who are previous winners? Who is contending for the award?

AWARDS: WON

While winning an award can have news value in itself, it is *why* you won the award, what that means to others, that should drive the story. Did you win the award for breaking new ground? For saving customers time or money? For opening up new possibilities? For philanthropic work that changed lives or created opportunities? Try to write personal stories, focus on what individuals achieved rather than talking about your company as an anonymous entity.

BUSINESS REBRANDING

Customers seldom understand the reasons for rebranding and can perceive it to be an expensive exercise that prioritises you ahead of them. Make the rationale for rebranding, and its benefits, as real as possible. Avoid marketing-speak and intangible goals. Focus on the needs of the customer, your partners and your markets.

BUSINESS WINS (SIGNIFICANT NEW CONTRACT/CUSTOMER)

Business wins are exciting within an organisation but can fail to engage others. Underpin the announcement with facts relevant to outsiders. In other words, it's not 'all about you'. How are others affected? What will you achieve for the customer? What will you be doing that is new? Why did the customer select you? How will your services benefit the customer?

CASE STUDIES

In a world where many press releases are indulgent and introspective, case studies can provide a refreshing insight into something that's happened. It might be a project that was delivered well, a product that has changed profitability, productivity, fortunes or lives. Focus on the facts and let the story speak for itself. Avoid quotations from your organisation which say how "delighted" you are. Add substance. Get quotes from the customer or from people whom the story affected. Support the story with facts. Demonstrate change.

CELEBRITY/PUBLIC FIGURE APPEARANCES

If the celebrity is well-known enough, this can be news in itself. However, not everyone can afford to pay a Hollywood star or footballer to open a new office, so this is more likely to be an industry figure or local politician. This kind of appearance supports the event, but it may not be a story in itself. What is the event? Why is this happening? What will be the impact? Why did you choose this person to support the event? What is their connection to the event or your organisation? Is there some personal relevance?

COMMENTING ON EVENTS

Your comments on something that affects your industry can be newsworthy. The event should be significant and your comments of value. Such news stories gain more traction when comments are contentious.

Perhaps disagreement with new government policy; a view that's counter to established or mainstream thinking; a flaw in a product or process. Views expressed should be either based on fact or supported by facts. If you're highlighting a problem then provide the solution: but don't go off on a sales pitch. Commenting on outside events is not something you should do often: people like controversy but they don't like pessimists, back-seat drivers, cynics or habitual complainers. People can spot someone who's jumping on a story for a bit of exposure. Add value. Don't be mean. If you're endorsing or praising, ensure that it's not empty support. Do something to add real-world value.

COMPANY ANNIVERSARIES AND MILESTONES

Anniversaries and milestones are important – but they are most important to those involved. The fact that you've been trading for ten years (or have just welcomed a millionth customer) may be a source of celebration within the business, but resonates little with outsiders.

Think about how your company started; early successes which were the foundation for growth. Obstacles the company has overcome. Customers who have helped you to succeed – tell their stories. Talk about how you've changed the market. Your plans for the future. Think mostly about things which are meaningful to those outside your company.

COMPANY REORGANISATIONS

Company reorganisations are a major event for those involved but are not necessarily of interest to customers or the market. For these to resonate as news, the restructuring needs to impact materially on customers, not just "we're doing it to be more customer-facing". It must benefit them; solve their problems; make life easier for them: this is the heart of the story. It can be supported by endorsements for the change by well-known brands, but not in a glib way. Reorganisations can also provide an excellent (and rare) chance to admit you were wrong – in a positive way – because it's in the context of enacting change to improve.

CROWDFUNDING CAMPAIGNS

Crowdfunding campaigns can generate excellent publicity. The news here isn't that you're raising money, or the unique packages available for crowdfunders (though these are worth a mention), it's the problem you aim to solve. For what are you raising money? How will it help others? What gap in the market will it fill? How are established products and approaches failing customers? And the facts: when will this be available? How long have you been working on it? What inspired you to create it? Then, perhaps as an incidental paragraph, why you are crowdfunding rather than soliciting investment via more traditional means.

CUSTOMER ADVISORY GROUP UPDATES

Customers like organisations which listen. Customer advisory groups demonstrate a commitment to input. Setting one up is news, as are changes in policy, products, services and strategic direction resulting from a group's input. As with all press releases, the news is not that this has happened, it's the impact of it happening. What did the group decide? What was the catalyst for this thinking? How does this differ from what competitors or the market are doing? What unique insights did (or will) the group provide? How much influence does the group have within your organisation? Can you get the group's decisions or recommendations to be endorsed by third parties?

CUSTOMER GIVEAWAYS/FREE OFFERS AND CONSULTATIONS

Despite being 'of interest' to the market (because there's 'free stuff'), customer giveaways/offers can turn a press release into an advertisement, rendering it ineffective. Make your sales pitch in a mailer or advertisement. In a press release, focus on news, not the offer. What's new with the product/service in the giveaway? What can customers achieve with it? How does it impact on the market? Has it been trialled in private and what were the results? Why would customers use this and not something else? Why would they change from what they use daily?

The offer itself should not be in the headline, synopsis or even be the main thrust of a press release – but tagged to the end. Use calls to action to channel people towards more sales–orientated website pages.

CUSTOMER INTERVIEWS

It's great when clients are enthusiastic about what you do, are going to do, or have done. It's lightning in a bottle. However, if you're using this within a press release, you do need to identify what's new – what makes it newsworthy. Establish how you changed things for the customer – setting this in the context of the wider market so other companies can see the potential for them. What did you do that was unique, that others wouldn't have done in the same way? Underpin it with facts and statistics. Keep customer quotes factual rather than sycophantic. Avoid trotting out the usual sentiments such as, "We're proud to do business together."

DAMAGE LIMITATION

When something goes wrong, companies turn to publicity to put their side of the story. Do this with care. If your organisation is headlining in the media for the wrong reasons, a simple press release can make things worse, not better. Whether you are right or wrong, it's important to accept that the world may think you are wrong – and to act with that in mind. This means fixing something in the real world before using publicity to communicate the resolution. Stick to the facts. Be contrite. Put yourself in others' shoes: what do they expect?

Can you go further than that, can you exceed expectations? Apologies must be authentic.

ECOLOGICAL IMPROVEMENTS

How your company behaves ethically is of increasing interest to customers. They care about how principled you are. They want to make informed buying decisions: this is the starting point for your story. Hard though it may be, try to avoid crowing about accomplishments too loudly. Keep it factual and stick to real achievements, not statements of intent. Ecological improvements are another example of where you could previously have got things wrong and now be putting them right. Look at where you are, where you are going and why. Try to identify meaningful benefits for customers. Use facts and statistics. Bring personal stories into your news – how are you helping those in your supply chain to live better lives?

EMPLOYMENT CREATION

These stories are often about new offices, new manufacturing facilities, new products and so on – but the real news is how this affects others. Employment is about people; personal stories and local improvements. More capacity can benefit customers by providing cheaper products, an assurance of local parts and labour, a boost to the region's economy. Look, as always, at how this helps others, rather than how this makes things better for you. Provide statistics: how does this map to your year-on-year growth? What kind of people are you hiring? Perhaps you're giving young people a chance, retraining others, helping the long-term unemployed back to work, investing in skills, creating new high-skilled roles, creating new jobs or recruiting graduates. Perhaps you're responding to technological advances, new legislation or expanding your sector's skills in new ways. Simply saying you've hired five hundred people provides no context: the only benefit is to you.

ENDORSEMENTS FROM INDUSTRY SPECIALISTS OR BODIES

Third-party endorsements always give marketing a lift, but when they are from industry specialists or professional bodies, then they can be especially newsworthy. Look at 'why' this has happened rather than the fact that it has. Why have they cited you? Is it an award, recommendation or part of some research? What is the history of this? Why did you stand out from others? What changed in your business for you to be noticed and cited? What is the landscape around this – are other companies mentioned? What kudos does this endorsement carry? Who was cited previously?

EVENT SPONSORSHIP AND SUPPORT

You've perhaps read press releases which do the bare minimum: "We're delighted to sponsor ..." For the company sponsoring an event, this act alone seems newsworthy, but it lacks resonance with outsiders. The news here is about the event, not you. Is it a charity event? If so, what or who does it support? What are the goals? What has the charity achieved? Don't make it all about you: who else sponsors this, or takes part? What is the history of the event? Why has your organisation chosen this? Is there a personal story you can bring front and centre?

EXPERT OPINION

What your company has to say, and what it believes, can be newsworthy. Don't say things for their own sake. Add value. Create debate. Provide answers, don't just hit out at others. Expert opinion works best when it comes from specialists, not necessarily business leaders. Let your teams, your practitioners, be the ones to speak. The media will prefer to engage with them as they know they'll get in-depth answers which, while not without bias, will be less controlled than the corporate line. Opinions expressed should be timely, about something which has just been in the news – and are in themselves newsworthy.

FINANCIAL OR STOCK UPDATES

Financial press releases tend to be the most factual of all – indeed, there may be a regulatory requirement to present numbers without embellishment. Sticking to the facts is vital for financial updates – by their nature, information is aimed primarily at shareholders and traders. However, that's not to say there isn't the opportunity to make it relevant and exciting to others. Avoid adding a business leader's "delighted" sentiments. Try to find something that's new, something that's changed. Point to how customers have contributed – but in a material, meaningful way. If the financial results aren't great, say why – and what you're doing about it.

FREE CONTENT: E-BOOKS, TUTORIALS, TRAINING COURSES AND VIDEOS

Leading with 'we have free content' turns a press release into an advertisement. Keep the sales aspect of the message firmly in its place. In a press release, focus on what people can achieve with the free content: what are you helping people to do? What is the market value of that content? Can you humanise a press release by adding personal stories from those who have used the content on offer?

HELPFUL TIPS

People like tips: they generate website traffic and get shared. To include them in a press release, tie them to something new; something newsworthy. Interesting and valuable though 'top ten ways to cut fuel costs' is, it's not news. In this example, a change in government energy policy could provide the news needed as the platform for your tips, as could an overall (publicised and controversial) rise in energy prices. Don't think about the tips as being news, reflect on how they can help – can they save money or time? Can this be quantified by solid figures? Can you create personal examples, such as a one-parent family's costs, or those of an average family?

INSPIRATIONAL STORIES

These can make great press releases. Personal stories – how customers have overcome challenges – resonate well with readers. They have relevance. Avoid the pitfall of crowing too hard about your involvement: keep it about the person, what they achieved, what they started out from, how it has changed them. Let your company's brand gain reflected benefits from this, but don't make it about you.

INTERNSHIPS, APPRENTICESHIPS OR SCHOLARSHIPS

It's not unusual for organisations to offer internships, apprenticeships or scholarships. Press releases which carry this as the heart of the story can fail to gain traction because it's reporting 'business as usual' as if it were news. Also, bear in mind that internships have received some negative press, so publicising yours in vague terms can tar you with the same brush, even if only by omission. Think about what's new; what's different. What are you trying to achieve? How has this changed or is changing? What opportunities does this open up? Can you write personal stories of interns who have gone on to higher positions and have become significant contributors to your organisation? Focus on the benefits to those entering the programmes. Avoid general statements about 'corporate social responsibility'.

INVESTMENTS, MERGERS AND ACQUISITIONS

Investments, mergers and acquisitions typically mean growth or change: this is almost always news. Try to avoid the investment itself being the focus of the story, so, rather than, 'XYZ Company invests $400,000 in ...' it's better to say, 'European growth drives $400,000 battery research investment' or, 'New mobile phone technologies underpin $400,000 investment'.

It's not about buying a company, but what this will achieve. The story is *why*. Add facts: include research to demonstrate the logic of the move. What will change as a result of it? More employees, more sales and so on? Be specific: cite numbers to build credibility.

LOCAL BUSINESS SUPPORT

This is another great example of 'people stories', even though it's about business. Make the story personal, keep it about support for other businesses – and the people within those companies. State the tangible benefits. Keep your organisation away from the centre of these stories; otherwise, it looks as if your actions were for publicity alone.

MARKET EXPANSION, NEW TEAMS OR DIVISIONS

Growing your business by sector or geography, or entering new markets, can make great news. There will be reasons behind this, outside of 'making more money'. It's these reasons which should be the heart of the story, rather than the act itself. What opportunities are you pursuing? How did this journey begin? What will be the impact on that sector or geography? Will there be a shift in how people do something? Will it lead to greater employment? Is it part of a bigger plan? Remember the facts: what is the investment? What are the expected returns? Most of all, think about it from the customers' perspective. How will they benefit, in material terms?

NEW HIRES: FOR SENIOR OR CRITICAL ROLES

People moves are typically more interesting to those within an industry rather than those outside of it – and it's only the senior or significant roles which are usually newsworthy. An appointment itself may be the reason for writing the press release, but the story is the 'why' behind it. It may be a personal story, or stories (of the person stepping down *and* the one stepping up). It may be to take the company in an entirely different direction. It may be to provide a top-to-bottom shake-up. It's these things which most interest people.

NEW USES FOR PRODUCTS

There are plenty of blogs and videos about 'life hacks' – using an everyday item differently. While these don't usually qualify as news, there can be instances which are newsworthy. These can be unexpected, personal, useful and in some cases life-changing. Think about these kinds of stories as a film unfolding, rather than a product to be promoted. What problem was solved? How did the person (or people) stumble across this? What will be the impact? These stories need to be newsworthy: adding an unusual cheese to a lasagne won't make headlines.

PARTNERSHIPS

Partnerships often come about because each side is lacking something the other has – together, the two parties can offer more, or respond faster, than when they work on their own. This is the heart of the story: what the partnership will offer, what it will result in – not the act of partnership itself. It's also an opportunity to show humility and the recognition of others' expertise. Each partner should write press releases that are more about the other partner than about themselves. Focus on what's changed or will change. Explain why going it alone would have been less good for customers. Also, provide some assurance: people can worry that a favourite brand might be subsumed into a competitor they dislike.

PATENT AWARDS

While press releases announcing patents should have lots of factual information to ground the story, they can be little more than puff pieces. This isn't about how great you are; it's about the problem the patent solves. What does it do which eluded so many others? What was the thought process leading to the patent? How do you plan to capitalise on it? How does it affect your products/services, or those of other companies? Don't forget the facts: the patent number (to save everyone from hunting for it), the scope of the patent and how it aligns with your other patents.

POLITICAL SUPPORT AND AFFILIATION

Tread cautiously here: organisations often avoid overt political connections because, by definition, it can alienate a (sometimes large) percentage of customers. Keep this about the *aims* of the party you're supporting. This could be a stance on energy policy or education policy, for instance, which makes this party the only one to align with your views. The story here is about what your company believes and supports – its ethics.

PREDICTIONS

Looking ahead to new products, services, markets or even the coming year can make for an interesting story. Ground your story in something that's happening now; something that's already in the news. Or, use an announcement of a new product or service as a vehicle for prediction or speculation about change. Concentrate on the impact of change, not change itself. How will it improve customers' lives? How will their businesses benefit? How different is your approach to that of the market? What will be the hits and misses?

PREMISES CHANGES/OFFICE MOVES

Change makes solid news, but not when it's business as usual or change for change's sake. The business driver to move location is more important – in publicity terms – than the move itself. Needing more space is hardly newsworthy. However, a planned expansion, move into new markets, significant recruiting drive or an important product diversification can make the basis for a great story. Avoid praising yourself. Look at what this means in terms of employment, increased business, new opportunities and so on.

PUBLIC SPEAKING/EVENT SPEAKING

It's not unusual for business leaders or specialists to be asked to speak at events or in public. However, the news is not that this is happening, it's what will be said. It's about the topics on the agenda, perhaps presented in a contentious light. How will people benefit from attending? What will they learn here that they can't elsewhere? How can they participate? What's the basis for the speaker's expertise; what are her or his credentials? What facts will be presented?

REQUESTING REVIEWERS

Product and service reviews can be massively beneficial. Reaching out to news outlets isn't always easy, and a press release can seem like a quick way to do this. However, if it's not news, then it makes for a weak story ('we're looking for people to pat us on the back'). This can become newsworthy by citing the reasons for their input – and having a real process to act upon feedback – so, not only is reaching out newsworthy, there can be follow-up stories after, too. Why is this input important? What do you hope to learn? Why could you not learn this without them? It's okay not to have all of the answers, all of the time, when you have a process for finding them. Show that you listen.

RESPONSE TO AN EVENT

When events make the news, this can provide an opportunity to present your views. Add value to the debate – it's easy to give the impression you're exploiting the news, especially if it's someone else's misfortune. Perhaps another business hit the news for losing data; while it can be useful to say how something could have been avoided, it can be a genius move to provide the solution directly to that company – and then release a story about that. Try to be a positive voice. Deliver answers, don't just flag problems. Avoid 'I told you so' finger-wagging.

REVEALING SCAMS

It can be frustrating to see customers flock to a flawed product or service (especially when you offer one that's better). Publicity can help you educate a market or shift what you perceive to be incorrect perceptions. However, there are some caveats. You need to be sure of your facts; you could enter a fray should things backfire. You should also understand why customers embrace a product which you see as a scam – they may not entirely like how it works, but are happier with this product than yours because it's a quarter of the price. Better to cite the scam product as meeting a certain need, so that people don't feel you're saying they're foolish. Then explain why alternatives are better. Talk about real, meaningful gains: don't be vague. Give examples: personal stories where possible.

SEMINARS AND WEBINARS

Seminars and webinars are a popular way of introducing customers to new products, services, concepts and methodologies. Concentrate most on the solutions that these provide: how will customers benefit? So, rather than 'XYZ Company talks about project management', topics such as 'How project management can cut costs in half' creates more interest. A seminar is about learning something – not being sold something (even if that is your primary goal). Talk about what people will learn and how it will benefit them.

SERVICE DELIVERY CHANGES

When you change the way you do business, most people aren't that interested – or they can react negatively if they're comfortable with the way you've traditionally done things. Publicity is best when approached from the customers' perspective: what will they gain? Why and how will things be better? What drove you to make the changes? Will they save time or money? Be realistic about customers' reactions and handle these in advance. Don't write off potential concerns as being 'a worthwhile trade-off'. If you can get some customers to trial the changes, and include that, it can help. Include personal stories of customers' frustrations with the old way of working.

SOCIAL INTERACTION

People love informal, responsive corporate interaction on social media – and such exchanges can make great news stories. You can write about some of your successes by keeping the focus external: it's about those with whom you interact more than it is about you. What problems did you solve? What problems did those contacting you have and how did you respond? What was the outcome? Did others join in the conversation? Did they contribute to the solution?

If the exchange was fun, all the better. Social media works best when it's giving, and is big-hearted, so keep stories of social media interactions in the same vein.

SOCIAL RESPONSIBILITY

Charity support can be an excellent source of publicity, but it would be wrong to put you at the heart of it. Rather, use publicity to further the cause(s) of those you support. Your company's involvement should be little more than a paragraph; fewer words deliver greater benefits, and avoid risking the perception that you're only in it for the publicity. Talk about what your charitable cause does, what it achieves, the challenges it faces, how others support it. Be humble – you're likely to be playing a small part in their work, even though they will be grateful for your involvement. Make them the heroes.

SURVEYS, POLLS AND TREND ANALYSIS

Statistics make for good publicity. To have the most impact, they should surprise rather than confirm – and press releases can score well when they deliver unexpected or contentious information.

The facts themselves can be the story: 'Three quarters of people hate their smartphone' needs little interpretation, for example. Facts are vital to such stories: make sure they are accurate and that you don't exaggerate the reasons driving the statistics. An expert opinion can provide some background: this comes better from specialists within your business – or from third parties – than it does from business leaders. Running surveys is an excellent way to gather and publish data – but make sure that you remain objective and that your survey methods are open-book.

TAKE A STAND

When businesses take a stand on an issue in which they believe, it can create great publicity. However, be aware that sensationalist press releases can be incredibly off-putting; some people may cynically question your motives – especially if your stance benefits you commercially. It helps to put your support into context: perhaps your founder's mother had a rare illness that you'd like to eradicate; maybe cutting your organisation's energy bills can also reduce your carbon emissions. Think about how this benefits outsiders and make it their story: you're supporters of a cause, not evangelists. Help the cause and be happy to take small credit, rather than dominating the message.

TRAINING AND CERTIFICATION

The knowledge within your business is important, so increasing it (and demonstrating that via accreditation) is good publicity. However, be wary that many customers may already expect you to have that level of knowledge, and renewing a mandatory certification is merely business as usual. Focus on going the extra mile and what this means for customers: concentrate on tangible benefits to them. Certification can open up the delivery of new services, or make new products available, for example. It can also demonstrate that you're an enlightened employer.

WHAT SELLS BEST, AND WHY

Whether you supply products or services, you will likely have a market insight into what customers do and don't like – even what works and what doesn't. This is often interesting to others but, in a press release, should be tied firmly to something that's new or newsworthy. As with most topics, think about this from the outside perspective: it's not about what you sell, create, build or deliver – it's more about what customers like, why they like it and how it benefits them. It's about their dislikes of less successful products or services. It's about how those preferences drive change in the market and what's surprising or counterintuitive about these things.

WHEN A GLOBAL PANDEMIC HITS, SHIFT HAPPENS

So, there we were, just putting the finishing touches to this book when a once-in-a-lifetime event struck. SARS-CoV-2 (COVID-19 or just 'the coronavirus') swept the globe. Whole countries locked down. Business halted. Economies stalled. This puts everything in our lives, not just publicity, into a different context entirely. It's fair to say that we hadn't considered writing a 'how to create press releases in a global pandemic' chapter. It's also fair to say that, with the exception of some broad advice, it's not that helpful to do so. One way or another, life will resume – broadly speaking.

And yet, the pandemic did make some welcome and sweeping changes to the way in which many companies communicate.

Where the whole world is focused on survival, everyone is selling, and no one is buying. The coveted sales traits of tenacity and perseverance count for nothing, indeed, in this world they are worse than useless – they are an annoying distraction. Even the smartest marketing campaign is unlikely to draw much in the way of results, unless you're selling something in short supply. The lesson here is that it's OK to hit the pause button when you need to. Don't listen to sales 'experts' who tell you that you simply just have to be more determined, and pushier, to get results. Be human; a good human – and not a bothersome human. Prepare for when things ease up: so that your publicity is ready to roll and well prepared.

'Be human' is the great compass to guide you. Yes, your business is hurting, but so are the businesses of those you're trying to sell to. Recognise this.

- Don't use messaging or offers which exploit the situation. If you're providing some kind of temporary solution, avoid leveraging events.
- Avoid talking too hard and loud about how well you are doing, what a good job you've made of adjusting to the situation and so on. Focus on the well-being of others. It's OK to talk about your positives but keep them in the context of how they benefit others. (This is actually sound marketing and publicity advice at any time.)
- There's enough negativity, so be a positive force: but don't be too upbeat, as it may come across as being tone-deaf. Be a positive voice. Be a positive role model. Be a leader. There's understandably enough negativity around.
- Retain your normal brand tone. Be who you always were.
- Don't put unknown personalities in front of customers – wheeling out a business leader who isn't normally in front of customers isn't as effective as using those with a connection, a relationship which already exists.
- Create messages with empathy. Understand.
- Face the truth and be as transparent as you can, especially within your own teams. No one is going to judge any company for not being able to fly high right now.
- Put a practical perspective on things – for example, adding realistic timescales to product announcements.
- Do the right thing; your instinct tells you what this is. Be a helper.
- Most importantly, be different. When everyone is selling, there's a lot of noise. You can't cut through that by doing what everyone else is doing.

It's interesting that at a point in history when most of us have been focused into the same situation, there's been a rapid shift in communications tone – towards being more human; more authentic without trying. This is a good thing – and it would be great to have 'being human' sitting at the heart of all communications, not just publicity.

REINVENT THE PRESS RELEASE; REIMAGINE YOUR PUBLICITY

Don't accept that a press release or announcement must be confined to a single-page story, when so much more is possible.

You will learn that:
- you can take the same story to a wider audience by rethinking how you announce news.
- press releases can be at the heart of a reimagined publicity strategy.

One of the great attractions of a press release is its efficiency: your story is told once, in a single page, which is then sent to everyone. This strength can also be a limiter, holding back your announcement when other media could help to tell your story in even better ways.

Although there's an accepted framework for a press release, any other ways you can build upon your announcements absolutely aren't set in stone. There are no publicity police, constantly patrolling the Internet, looking for indiscretions. What matters is that you find ways in which to better tell your stories – to get better coverage.

So go on. We dare you. Don't accept that 'one story, told once' is the only way. Take your stories further – reinvent the press release. Let's look at ways in which we can overcome what are the perceived limitations of traditional press releases. We talk about many of these throughout this book – and combined, these can transform your publicity.

One story goes everywhere. This means that everything from language to benefits has to be generalised.

Write the story in different ways for different audiences. This allows you to talk directly and with greater resonance to specific groups of people: such as shareholders, employees, customers of a certain product – and so on. It's true, this is more work – but it's also far more successful than using just one story for everyone.

The story is written 'to brief the media', almost as a list of facts. This means that the story can come across as dry and not resonate well with those outside of the media.

Write your story as if it is to be the final, published piece. Unless you overdo it with superlatives, this is unlikely to put off anyone within the media and it will connect better with others. Building on the notion that the story is written in different ways, for different audiences, you can keep the heart of the press release the same but take different directions with writing style, benefits, supporting media and more.

The formal media is reducing in size

While it is undeniably true that traditional media is contracting, that doesn't always mean that its influence is less – don't be cheated into thinking that the media has diminished value. You still want to engage with the media – but also work hard to engage directly, through social media channels, via your own distribution channels and via newswires. Your story can find many audiences, via different means. Again, this works best when stories are told in different ways – talking directly to, and making the most of, each communication channel.

People get news via social media

Well, this is partly true, but much of it still comes into social media via formal media outlets, not just informal ones. Things don't typically magically appear on a social media outlet unless it has traction elsewhere (or is paid for). Your own social media channel isn't likely to have the reach of recognised, independent, respected news channels – or the channels of other influencers. Create social media updates for your stories to engage with those people via other channels, not just your own. It's unlikely that you can 'tell the whole story' via a tweet or update, so linking back to the more complete story is essential.

TL;DR: people want snappy stuff

The received wisdom is that people don't read long stuff any more and want short sound bites via video or infographics. As with all received wisdom, there's some truth in this, but it's far from being an absolute truth. Not everyone wants detail, but some people definitely do. The media for example, or enthusiasts, specialists, or even just those who are seeking to buy and want to perform more of a comparison on products or services. Or someone who just thinks the story is interesting and wants to find out more.

Tell short stories, use video, infographics, photographs and other supporting media – but also tell the full story. Plenty of people want it. If your video is engaging, they'll want to find out more.

Telling your stories in different ways, via different channels, not only lets you reach more people, it enables you tell more complete stories and helps ensure that people are exposed to your stories more than once.

'I can't measure it'

Who says you can't? There are lots of ways to measure the performance of your stories, some free, some premium and lots in-between. Use landing pages to measure response and track conversions. Deploy measurement tools to track the metrics most of interest to you. Use mailing software to distribute your press releases, so you can track opens, forwards, bounces and so on. Or use built-for-the-job publicity measurement tools. If you want to measure it, it's likely you can – but you may have to adapt your processes to do it.

CREATE PARALLEL SOCIAL MEDIA RELEASES

Social media channels – yours, and those of media outlets and influencers – are essential places to publish your news.

Don't be tempted to simply repurpose parts of your press release. It's written in a specific way, to do a specific job. The language of social media is entirely different. There's a lot of scope to put different slants on the story, express emotion or add a little fun.

Write text for social media posts at the same time as writing the press release.

Social media channels provide significantly less space for a story than a press release (sometimes as little as 90 characters). The important key point of your story must be conveyed instantly, in the most compelling – and possibly creative – way possible. You can preface your press release with 'news' or 'breaking news' and hashtag it as #news and #pressrelease – helping to separate it from your other updates. Video and images are essential parts of a social media release. They help your announcement to both stand out and encourage shares and retweets.

Don't be shy about boosting or promoting updates to reach a larger audience – this is what publicity is all about, reaching beyond your connected network. It's a good investment.

Remember to provide a link back to your news story. Keep the link as short as possible or use a link shortening service.

Above all else, social media is about engagement. Obviously, be prepared to respond to all comments on your post, but it's also important to write in a way that encourages conversation.

Prepare updates for your own social media channels as well as priming outlets with updates you suggest for them. For outlets, create a few versions, simply to give them some choice. For yourself, it's still worth creating a few updates per story – partly because people may not see each one, but also because it allows you to make different points in the strongest possible way.

Just as your press release benefits from supporting media, so do your social media updates. Prepare images, infographics and videos – for your own use and for social media channels. On your own channel, don't feel as if you need to stick entirely to campaign images, if something off-beat will get more attention – but always keep on-brand.

Make it easy for channels to get your news out. Squeeze every ounce of value from each story, over a series of updates.

Ensure that you include relevant hashtags to help people find your update, along with @names for anyone or any business you're mentioning. Use these prudently, don't @ big brands for the sake of it, there needs to be a valid reason.

Social media updates are a retelling of the story in the press release, but they are also mini campaigns. Too many organisations simply tweet out a press release heading with a link back to the original. Think bigger than this. Get the story rolling in a different direction.

The difference between an organisation which undertakes this more comprehensive, richer view of publicity, and one which cranks the handle on one-page releases, distributed to just a media list, is huge. Reinventing the press release in this way can take your publicity not just 'to the next level' but to a level of performance that would be otherwise unattainable.

So, are you serious about publicity? Get reinventing.

While press releases are good, reinvented press releases can be even more powerful. Don't limit your publicity.

DISTRIBUTING

DISTRIBUTION CHANNELS

Many organisations could be more inventive when distributing press releases. If you're sending press releases only to news outlets, you're missing out – and could multiply your distribution manyfold.

You will learn that press release distribution:
- shouldn't be limited to just news outlets.
- isn't the same for every press release.
- needs to be targeted.
- can, with some thought, be significantly expanded.

A news story is only as good as its distribution channels. Getting your distribution right is critical if your publicity is to be successful. So, to whom do you send press releases? The obvious answer is 'news outlets' but this begs two questions:
- What exactly is meant by 'news outlets'?
- Does targeting news outlets alone mean that you could be missing a trick or two?

NEWS OUTLETS AND INFLUENCERS

News outlets are an important target for press releases, but not the only one – nor are they always the most important. Think about 'news outlets' in a broader and less formal sense.

What separates other influencers – such as specialist commentators – from a news outlet, for example? Authority? Some influencers' voices carry authority that's comparable to (or perhaps greater than) news outlets in their sector. Even if a news outlet has greater *perceived* credibility or status, an influencer's view may be more trusted. And what separates someone like a blogger, specialist commentator or other influencer from an industry analyst, in real terms? Their specialist knowledge, influence and following may be roughly the same.

Don't judge the validity of a distribution channel on its standing within the mainstream media. It doesn't pay to submit a press release based on the perceived kudos of being covered by a specific outlet. While it's exciting to get a story placed in a mainstream news outlet, other influencers such as specialists and commentators can enable you to reach a more *relevant* audience. The size of your distribution list may well be important, but targeting *relevant* recipients is vital.

WHO ELSE SHOULD BE ON YOUR DISTRIBUTION LIST?

Forget for a moment that it's called a *press release*; concentrate instead on it being an announcement.

Why not send press releases to employees? To business partners, suppliers and sales channels? What about professional bodies? And let's not forget customers. These are all great examples of people to whom you should directly send your press releases. Why wait for the story to be picked up by the media?

With a little thinking, you can multiply your distribution manyfold, to include:

- analysts.
- bloggers and vloggers.
- business media.
- business organisations.
- commentators.
- conference and exhibition organisers.
- customers.
- employees.
- freelance journalists.
- local and community press.
- magazines.
- newspapers.
- news websites.
- newswires.
- partners.
- political or council representatives.
- professional bodies.
- radio stations.
- social influencers.
- social media.
- television.

Before we look at each of these, it's worth understanding that such communities often operate in tiers. Outlets can be mainstream, topic-interest media and niche. An example of this is the IT sector; the sector itself is massive – one of the biggest in the world. The mainstream media covers a broad range of IT topics but typically only reports on those stories which are significant. Then, some outlets focus on a single topic from the IT sector, perhaps something like customer-relationship management. What's news to *this* community may well not be that newsworthy to others. Then, other outlets will focus on just one niche customer-relationship management product or methodology. What's exciting news here may well not be of much interest outside of *this* community.

While it's tempting to aim only at the bigger outlets, these are not always the most effective. Target publicity where it is most relevant.

ANALYSTS

Every industry has its analysts. They're the people who keep their finger on the pulse of that sector, watching for new products, services and other changes. Others seek their views: business leaders, strategists, journalists and editors. They are highly influential (and sometimes controversial). They're perceived as independent thought-leaders.

Sometimes, they are practitioners, which means they might also work for a competitor. Some people worry about marketing to their competitors, but it's usually an unfounded concern: your competitors know what you're up to soon enough. And if competitor-practitioners get your message directly, and participate in its distribution, they'll find it harder to undermine you in front of customers.

If the analyst is also a practitioner, she or he will already know that putting self-interest first will blow all industry credibility, so, again, don't worry too much.

Analysts should typically receive only your most strategic press releases, and you should try to engage in a one-to-one dialogue with them where possible. They're people with whom you want a relationship, and as there usually aren't that many influential analysts in a sector, it's an achievable goal.

BLOGGERS AND VLOGGERS

Bloggers and vloggers may sometimes be 'informal fans', but they can also be incredibly influential and have a significant following. They can, in many ways, be as authoritative and influential as an analyst – or even a mainstream news outlet. Most often they will be self-employed or employed within the sector: so again there may be a business conflict conundrum to deal with, but, as with the analyst, it's best to set this aside and concentrate on the publicity aspect of your relationship.

Get into contact with the most influential. They often welcome an early warning of something new, so they can jump on it when the press release comes out. Don't judge a blogger by the design of her or his website or social media channel. To the corporate eye, it may lack credibility and visual polish – yet can boast a following that industry leaders envy.

Text-based blogs can have a substantial readership, and video bloggers can have a bigger following still – perhaps in the tens of thousands or higher. YouTube is one of the most visited websites, and video bloggers can have a substantial following. This means that product reviews by video bloggers can be massively beneficial to sales.

BUSINESS MEDIA

Almost all industry sectors have a series of trade journals, online magazines and online news websites.

The number of these vary per industry; there are typically fewer for niche sectors and more for larger ones.

Don't be drawn to just the larger outlets: smaller, focused niche players can deliver great benefits, and may more readily place your stories. Also, they often have highly engaged followers and loyal readers.

Business outlets are most interested in stories which have an impact on the sector and direct relevance to their customers.

Again, there's a lot of value to building relationships with the journalists, editors, and website owners.

BUSINESS ORGANISATIONS

There are many organisations – typically membership-driven – established to help businesses in general, rather than to support those in a particular sector.

In the UK, this includes the Institute of Directors, Business Link, British Chamber of Commerce, Confederation of British Industry, Federation of Small Businesses, Small Business Bureau and the Forum of Private Business. In the USA, this includes the Entrepreneurs' Organization, the National Federation of Independent Business, the National Business Association, the National Small Business Association, United States Chamber of Commerce – and many more.

For some campaigns, it can be worthwhile including these on your publicity list. Who you choose from these organisations depends on your news or campaign, but most usually it would be a marketing or publicity contact. They are most interested in news which directly benefits their membership, so don't inundate them with everything.

COMMENTATORS

Sector commentators are highly influential people who write, blog or video blog, present, judge, review, podcast, provide thought-leadership and, as a result, may well have a significant social media footprint.

What these people say is of interest to those who work within an industry, as well as to its customers and suppliers. They may have built a reputation around specific disciplines or types of product.

They may even be vocal peers who work for a competitor or supplier. Their output tends to be frank and sometimes challenging, but they enjoy a unique position because of this, not in spite of it. Their assertiveness can seem like a publicity risk, but it is generally way better for you to brief them directly than let them be informed by your marketing – or your competitors.

CONFERENCE AND EXHIBITION ORGANISERS

Most sectors have several industry conferences and exhibitions.

The organisers of these events have relationships with most people within your sector, including suppliers and buyers.

They will, of course, try to sell their services to you. Fair play, some services may be of value, so be open-minded. Event organisers in your sector should know that you exist and what you're up to. You should develop a relationship with them. Conference organisers are often looking for people to contribute articles to periodicals or give a presentation at events.

CUSTOMERS

Companies often omit customers from publicity distribution lists, yet they're the people who might most benefit from your news.

It's worth pausing for breath before you hit that send button though. Your press release should usually be reworked for a customer audience. You might shorten it, make it less formal, paste it into an e-mailer rather than send it as an attachment. These changes usually take a little effort, but will make your message far more relevant.

It's good that customers hear the news directly from you, rather than via another source. The usual caveat applies: it's better to segment your customer list and send only those releases which are relevant.

Pressing 'send to all' may be easy, but it can result in more people opting out of your mailing list – or, worse, becoming resentful of your company and its communications, because they're not of interest.

EMPLOYEES

Employees should always know what their company is up to.

Sending a press release as it stands is usually fine, though many benefit from additional insider rationale: a perspective on the story that the outside world may not need.

If the story is part of a bigger campaign, then also send other supporting materials – to help employees answer questions from customers. Although many of your staff won't be proactively customer-facing, they are still representatives of your company. As Francis G 'Buck' Rodgers, IBM's head of global sales and marketing from 1970 to 1984, said: "Everybody sells" – a successful company knows that each employee should treat *everyone* as if that person was a potential customer. Because you never know: they could be.

Simply circulating a press release isn't the best way to get your company behind a campaign. It's fine for those employees who aren't involved in marketing and sales, but customer-facing employees will benefit enormously from a fuller briefing in advance, and need arming with additional materials.

At the least, circulating press releases helps employees see what's said to the outside world. Employees resent being the last to find out what's going on – it can make them feel unimportant, or put them in an awkward position when an outsider references news they haven't yet heard.

Use press releases to help keep your employees informed.

FREELANCE JOURNALISTS

Many journalists aren't employed directly by a single publication. They write freelance, sometimes commissioned and sometimes speculatively. Published news stories and articles typically have a byline (who wrote the article). If you see a great article in your sector, then search online for the journalist. Check out her or his other articles. If they write for your industry and look like they might be interested in your company's news, get in touch: it's rare that you can't find their e-mail address, but if not reach out on social media. They're usually available people. Bear in mind that they are busy: respect their time and focus conversations on what's best for them.

Don't assume that news stories will be a gift to them. If they're not interested in your current stories, find out why. Be open-minded and take a steer from them as to what's newsworthy.

LOCAL AND COMMUNITY PRESS

Unless you're a small business, you may not think so much about the local press: the media within your sector will be of far greater benefit to you. But it pays to keep them in mind. Even national businesses have local offices, and all customers have to be local to somewhere.

Publicity goals may well be different at a local level, but they are still good goals to have.

Ensure that stories you send are relevant to that publication. Provide them with a local contact for the story, if you can.

Bigger companies can fall into the trap of believing that all publicity should be strategic, national or international. Good local stories can add a human spin on the bigger picture and create footfall, and drive interaction, where a company does business.

MAGAZINES

Sector-specific magazines can deliver a different kind of publicity opportunity. While they'll still be interested in your news, those with print production cycles mean that news can be less relevant to their readers by the time it's published: readers may have already seen it somewhere else.

In general, both online and printed magazines have been lowering the percentage of news they carry while increasing articles and features. In publicity terms, this means your news story is less likely to get placed unless it's got real value. But it also means you might be asked to contribute (or contribute to) an article that's based on the events in your story. Submitting news stories still has value and can create such opportunities. It also keeps you at the front of the editors' and journalists' thinking.

To get the most from sector magazines, you should form relationships with key people, be able to write well, or employ someone to write on your behalf (should they ask you to submit an article). It's also useful to obtain their advance schedule of articles, and then talk directly to the editor, journalists or writers about your views on the topics within upcoming articles.

NEWSPAPERS

While newspapers may be one of the first things to spring to mind when you think of 'the media' they can be the least relevant when it comes to business publicity, and (along with television) the hardest in which to get stories placed.

Only send significant news stories, those with real impact, to national or regional newspapers. They have lots of news and quickly sift out the promotional stuff: to win some coverage, it has to be *real* news. Something that genuinely matters to the readership. That said, many mainstream outlets have distinct sections which may be interested in your stories. For example, in the UK, the technology or business sections of the Guardian; in the USA, the technology or travel sections of USA Today.

For bigger newspapers and news websites, submitting press releases directly is an almost total waste of time. They simply don't look at them: they get their press releases primarily (sometimes exclusively) via high-level publicity channels such as Associated Press and Reuters – and these take only press releases from a limited number of trusted newswires. If you have a big story and want to get it placed, those newswires are the way to go.

NEWSWIRES

Newswires syndicate press releases to the outside world, usually without alteration.

The best newswires provide a paid-for service. You may not use them for every press release, but you should use them for important ones, especially ones where you want to reach the mainstream outlets. The only way to get press releases to large outlets is through organisations such as Associated Press and Reuters, and the *only* way into those companies is by using paid high-quality newswires.

Market-leading newswires include:

- Business Wire (businesswire.com)
- GlobeNewswire (globenewswire.com)
- Newswire (newswire.com)
- PR Newswire (prnewswire.com)
- PRWeb (prweb.com)
- Realwire (realwire.com)

There are also newswires for specific market sectors. These don't concentrate on the size of circulation, but rather the *quality* of it, whether that's via visitors or syndication.

These can play a major role in publicity because their primary audience consists of people who either reach your target market or are part of the target market itself. Stories placed on vertical newswires may not always make it to the mainstream media, but that's not their role: they're there to inform the sector, its suppliers, customers and commentators. They typically also reach that sector's specialists: market analysts, bloggers, professional bodies and so on.

If there's a risk with newswires, it's that many people perceive them to be a quick fix: that it's the only thing they need to do. It isn't. Don't ignore other means of distribution; your quiver should contain more than a single arrow.

Newswires extend your reach: they go beyond what you could otherwise achieve via networking and list-building. This works best where the newswire is good, and relevant to your needs. Quality counts as much, if not more, than volume.

There are free newswires (and plenty of them), but they offer limited benefits and have quite a few drawbacks, such as:

- lack of media credibility.
- uncontrolled advertising (a competitor's product could appear on the same page as your news story).
- a less than useful circulation (ask yourself if many of *your customers* go to these sites, for example).
- poor media traction – journalists typically don't get news from there.
- little or no sector targeting.
- poor news quality – they're generally the home of mediocre press releases and lame news stories.

So why do people use them? Well, they're free. If it's easy to do, and free, then why not add them to your mix? If the press releases they carry don't actually reach relevant influencers – and competitor advertising compromises them – what's the point? Many *were* once used, primarily, for easy search optimisation. 'Backlinks' in the press releases (links back to the company's website) *in theory* helped to boost the receiving website's popularity score, raising it in the search results. *In reality*, this is no longer the case and, when press releases are distributed on some free low-value newswires, it can have an opposite, *negative* effect on search optimisation. It can even lead to a blacklisting of your website on Google. (If you didn't read the chapter on search optimisation, check it out – we explain this in detail.)

NEWS WEBSITES

'News websites' is rather a broad category; some of the most visited websites are the big news sites – yet many useful websites focus on one market, or a single product.

The same principles apply as previously outlined: only the stories with big, broad impact should go to the major players. As with newspapers, the main route into the big websites is through companies such as Associated Press and

Reuters, which means using a major newswire. While news websites are savvy about receiving news via social media, this is usually news 'as it happens' – the rising numbers of multiple tweets about a big event, from people on the spot, rather than as a result of a company's publicity process.

Each sector has specialist news sites serving it. Research these carefully to understand which might work best for you, before adding them to your mailing list. Why? Some news sites specialise in delivering the news with a more cynical (even caustic) edge: you might feel that your publicity isn't best served by being picked at by the blunter members of the media.

Some sector-specific news sites will take and publish your story as is (a process sometimes referred to as churnalism) while others may want to take your story as a reference and rewrite it in their own style.

Keep your eye on journalists' names. They're as important as the website, since they may well be freelance, and in any event, they're key people with whom you should build a relationship.

PAID MEDIA

While the goal with a press release is to achieve media coverage, today's news stories can equally be directly targeted at customers, influencers, partners and more. With this in mind, it makes solid sense to exploit various forms of paid media to help boost the profile of your story. The most obvious paid media choice is a newswire, but you can also use targeted advertising on search engines and social media, banner advertisements on relevant websites or indeed advertising in other forms, such as on YouTube. Clearly, for this to be successful it's vital to have created other forms of media than just the press release – ideally all part of a larger campaign telling the story in different ways. You're more likely to direct people from your advertising to a landing page than to the press release itself, but you could also choose to retell the story in a more customer-focused way. For some reason, many people draw an unnecessary dividing line between 'reaching the media' and 'reaching an audience'. Be open-minded about using every tool at your disposal and explore how your story can be best expressed via that medium.

PARTNERS

It's worthwhile adding business partners to your mailing list: suppliers, subcontractors and so on. It pays to have their key people up-to-date with what your company is doing, and on board with your message.

In some cases, your partners will be your competitors' partners too. You might have concerns about them receiving your marketing information quickly and directly. Since the information will already (or soon) be in the public domain, there's really no additional risk - and communicating well with them is only likely to increase their perception of your value.

Partners may likely deal with someone within your organisation other than the marketing department: perhaps they deal with the sales teams. It's therefore important that these teams also receive press releases and, preferably, additional campaign briefings and materials.

It's better to keep partners up-to-date, with information that's structured in a way that works for you, than have them get your news via others. A press release is a great way to do this.

POLITICAL OR COUNCIL REPRESENTATIVES

There are occasions when news stories are relevant to political representatives. Representatives may be national or local, but they are most usually the latter. The former have bigger things to get on with, such as running the country.

Send press releases to this community sparingly and only if it has real relevance to the person's post.

It's also a good idea to e-mail them only if there is some way in which you want them to be involved, again, in line with their remit.

PROFESSIONAL BODIES

At the heart of your industry will be a small collection of professional bodies: membership organisations responsible for standards, raising the sector's profile, campaigning with politicians and so on.

How could you *not* send your press release to these people?

They'll probably hound you for membership, but these are *professional* bodies. They won't typically *demand* a quid pro quo. Having said that, it can be worth you being a member: partly for the benefits, but mainly to help forge relationships. When such relationships exist, publicity will be more readily received, and is more likely to be included in their outbound communications.

RADIO STATIONS

As with newspapers, there are national and local radio stations; so the same advice applies. National radio stations are only interested in bigger news, whereas local radio stations want something that's of value to local listeners.

Often overlooked, this medium may not be a cornerstone of your publicity activities, but there are times, as with local press, when it can be of great value.

Identify not just the voices on the air (newsreaders, for example) but also the routes into the radio station, such as the research team.

SOCIAL INFLUENCERS

Although your brand (or perhaps the people within your organisation) may have a sizeable social media following, it's unlikely to match that of some of the most connected people on Facebook, Instagram, Twitter, YouTube and so on.

These people can have followers in the thousands, tens of thousands and even millions. Their reach and influence can exceed that of celebrities. More importantly, these people are typically seen to hold independent viewpoints – which makes them highly influential. A mention or two from the most influential people can generate massive interest in your product or services.

There's a problem, though: press releases aren't always the best way to get the most from these influencers. More than anything, they engage socially, and that's often the best way to reach them.

At best, a traditional press release might keep them in the loop with developments at your organisation – and it's important to keep this in mind. If you want to reach specific types of influencers (for example, technology reviewers on YouTube), then a less formal version of your press release is a great help. This is an excellent example of when a reworked press release, or story in a different format, can work well.

SOCIAL MEDIA

Social media is a critical amplifier for your news, but it's not a channel that reacts well to hype or gloss.

While social media *can* reach journalists and editors, it's typically more useful when engaging directly with the public – and the less formal parts of the media, such as your sector's commentators and influencers.

For this reason, if no other, it's clear that just sharing your press release's headline, with a link to the story, isn't going to get the best response. Indeed, it's likely to get little or no response.

Social media requires an approach of its own: usually not just one update, but several. Updates should use images and videos as well as text. Social media requires interaction, for which you should prepare.

Updates should be conversational and free from hype; perhaps fun, even where the underlying news story is relatively dry. Pull out different aspects of your news story and present them in more interesting, human and conversational ways.

Social media can be a major force when there's news of substance. It can do you a lot of good: the story can be amplified enormously. But, if your story isn't well-thought-out, social media will call you out on it; it can be an embarrassing own goal.

Social media does provide a fantastic mechanism to build up a direct audience. With high-profile figures attracting followers by the millions, it seems like a great thing to do. And it is – but, without celebrity status, it takes a lot of time. It also takes a lot of content – whether those are tweets/updates which are interesting in themselves, or more in-depth content such as e-books and videos (or a mixture). You should definitely build your social media channels, but don't expect them to work hard for you from day one, or for them to obviate the need for (and usefulness of) other media.

TELEVISION

For many businesses, getting television airtime via publicity isn't a realistic proposition. Let's face it, you'd need to invade another country to hit the top slot.

There's potentially a place for news stories with a local focus. If you're increasing employment in an area, exporting to a new country, driving innovation and so on, then television news is a real option.

A press release is still of value, but you're going to need to get it into the right hands (the news research team) which means you can't send it blind. You'll also need to follow it up personally.

For a stronger chance of success, work through a publicity agent who has established contacts in television.

DIFFERENT AUDIENCE, DIFFERENT MESSAGE

Those are the main communities where you might target press releases. Don't hit them all with every story, and the right mix for your business is something to refine over time. Remember to tailor your message for each different audience.

KEEP DISTRIBUTION RELEVANT

A distribution list doesn't get awards for its size. Relevance is everything: relevance both to your business and to the story.

As an example, a story with a human interest angle – say a sponsored fundraising hike – would be relevant to local newspapers and radio stations, but annoying to a trade publication. A scheme to recruit dozens of apprentices would interest your local political representatives but be irrelevant to an industry analyst.

Segment your mailing list, so that you send press releases only to those who would find them relevant. Some news stories can go to everyone, but take each one on a case-by-case basis.

If people get too many irrelevant press releases, they will just opt out of your mailing list – or add you to their spam list.

To make mailings more relevant, enable people to sign up for, and opt out of, specific topics. After all, they may have a real interest in one thing your company does, but not everything.

IDENTIFY THE RIGHT PEOPLE

You should send news stories to a *named contact*. However, some outlets (especially larger ones) prefer you to use a generic e-mail address, such as editor@ – as this is monitored by several people, around the clock, all year round. The key here is research: build a list with information you know is accurate, using the contact method preferred by the outlet. This means that you must put in some legwork to create and maintain mailing lists, but this is no bad thing. Why? Because editors, journalists and influencers aren't mailing dumpsters. They're *actual people*. You should forge relationships with as many of them as possible, not barrage them with an endless one-way broadcast.

Where you use a generic e-mail address, don't fret: once outlets start picking up your news, you will have the opportunity to make contact with their editors and journalists.

MAILING LISTS

If you want to reach a large number of outlets, consider using a mailing list.

There are caveats. Publicity should be more about relevance, than volume – reaching 1,000 outlets relevant to your story can easily be better than hitting a general list 10 times that size. Even if you use a commercial list, you still need to build your own list, to generate relationships with the most relevant outlets. Commercial lists are useful, powerful and sometimes essential, but at the end of the day, you're usually mailing blind when you use them.

That said, there are some good list services available. Research these and make a choice based on relevance to your business, geography and available budget. Search online for 'PR database' or 'journalist database'.

Public relations databases include:

- Agility (agilitypr.com/our-solutions/media-database/)
- Cision (cision.co.uk/products)
- Cision Gorkana (gorkana.com/pr-products/media-database)
- MuckRack (muckrack.com)
- PRmax (prmax.co.uk)
- ResponseSource (responsesource.com/pr/mediadatabase)
- Vuelio (vuelio.com/uk)

Of these, MuckRack is unusual in that it reaches outlets via social media.

Some of these companies don't provide a list per se, but rather a service by which news stories can reach their outlets. Their software often includes lots of other features – and can be a complete publicity dashboard.

These lists typically focus on news outlets: editors and journalists. This is great, but remember that you also need to connect with many other influencers too.

ASK PEOPLE TO OPT IN

Don't assume that just because someone is a journalist, editor, commentator, blogger/vlogger or whatever that they'll welcome every one of your press releases with open arms. However many unsolicited e-mails you get, news outlets get at least ten times that, or a hundred – or more. Journalists and influencers simply can't read everything. Sending unsolicited press releases can lower your odds of getting published – an unsolicited press release is still spam to a busy journalist. Not only is receiving unsolicited e-mails annoying, in many countries sending it is illegal – for example, in Europe, under GDPR (the General Data Protection Regulation), there are potentially large fines. On a practical level, if the recipient

DISTRIBUTION CHANNELS 177

has no idea who you are, your e-mail might not even get through her or his spam filters.

Asking permission is a simple process. A friendly e-mail is often enough, but a phone call can be better where there's value in building a relationship. Your e-mail should be polite, friendly and personable. Ideally, it should reference their outlet and say why your news is of value to them. It should be concise. It should ask them to opt in and let them know they can leave at any time. Let them know you only send out a dozen or so releases a year (be honest about the number, they may remember this).

Some people will say no. Live with it. The fear of people saying no is one of the things which drives companies to add *anyone* to their mailing list, because 'I'm sure she/he will be interested in our news'. Let's be clear: if they are not interested, they *will* say no, they *will* put your stuff in the bin or they *will* add you to their spam list. The result is the same, so it's pointless sending it. Better to ask.

As with most rules, there are exceptions. You probably won't ask employees or business partners. Your customers may already be covered by any opt-in agreement you have in place with them. Also, you may have a particular news story which you are confident will be of great interest to a segment of your mailing list: perhaps some research that analysts will value, or a new product launch in which influencers will be especially interested. When this is the case, consider sending a specially written covering note, explaining why they're receiving this one-time-only unsolicited e-mail (and asking them to opt in to your list if this kind of thing might interest them).

While we're on the subject of opting in, remember to provide a mechanism which enables people to opt out of mailings easily. It's the law and it's good practice. It's also a practical way of keeping your mailing list clean. Speaking of which, you should monitor 'bounces' from press release mailings (using the analytics part of your distribution software) to enable you to remove e-mail addresses which are no longer valid. Why? Because sending stuff to dead e-mail addresses can flag you as a spammer. (Many businesses, Internet service providers and e-mail companies use what are known as 'blacklist servers' to help control spam. If your business is added to a blacklist server – which happens when lots of people flag e-mails as spam – even legitimate e-mails may cease to arrive, as they will be blocked automatically.)

It's worth having a polite reply ready, which you can personally send when someone important opts out. You can let a system send this automatically (and you *will* do this if your list is large), but if you do it personally, you create a chance of reversing their decision.

There's great value in people opting out – it enables you to learn which type of people want your releases, so you can improve your list. Ultimately, if you end up with a more relevant mailing list, sending press releases to only those who want them, this is no bad thing. It's an effective way to keep your list clean.

DATA PRIVACY LAWS

Under many data protection laws, you can't store personally identifiable information about people without their permission. This makes it a legal requirement to gain opt-in permissions. Regulations such as the EU's GDPR (General Data Protection Regulation) do include provision to send information that is of 'legitimate interest' – a stance you could argue works when sending press releases to journalists. However, all circumstances and content are different, so ensure that you build distribution lists in a way that is both legal and of value to the recipient. (Sending press releases via good newswires, or using social media, means that opt-in permissions are shifted from you to the publishing platform.)

SEND NEWS, NOT PROMOTIONS

A press release distribution list is valuable. It should comprise of people who want your news and want to be on the list. Nothing drives unsubscriptions faster than abusing this by sending out promotions instead of the promised news.

THINK RELATIONSHIPS

To get the most from the media, they have to know you. You should also know them, to understand what they want from your publicity, so you can deliver what they want for their audience.

It's a challenge. With how many people can you maintain a relationship? It's not thousands, or even hundreds – far fewer people than you'll want on a mailing list. It's important to find out those people on your list you can more closely work with. This may be a dozen or so people: people to whom you can pick up the phone and chat, or perhaps meet for lunch.

Not all relationships are the same, and there doesn't have to be a firm dividing line between those to whom you just send press releases and those you court a little more intensively. With e-mail and social media at your disposal, you can have a wider second tier of people with whom you also work, though perhaps not so closely.

When you have a really strong story, hold fire on that press release and consider getting in touch with your best contacts, in advance, to discuss it. At the least, they'll offer some pointers as to the best way to write it, but they may pick up the story and run with it without the need for a press release (or ahead of the story's main distribution).

WORKING WITH PUBLICITY PROFESSIONALS

Publicity professionals can be of great help to an organisation, not only by creating or writing stories, but also with distribution and story placement.

They have established relationships of trust with the media and are part of a professional network that could take you years to replicate. In short, they can place stories that you can't, often in places you can't reach.

They can also help you take publicity to a different level. They don't just have more contacts – they have more experience and ideas. They can approach publicity in completely different ways than you would yourself.

They can also add bandwidth to your publicity efforts, freeing up your marketing team to get on with other things. Even within large organisations, publicity is typically handled by a small team – a publicity company can draw on larger resources, including people who are specialists in particular fields, such as research, fundraising, community relations, government relations and so on.

ANNOUNCEMENT CAMPAIGNS, NOT JUST PRESS RELEASES

Throughout this book, especially in the chapter *Planning beyond the press release* (which discusses the PESO publicity model), we stress the value of taking announcements beyond the cookie-cutter approach of a single press release.

We talk, for example, of the need to tailor the message to suit different audiences, delivering more detailed additional information via links to your website, using other media to support the story – and deploying landing pages to both focus calls-to-action and better measure results. And, at the start of this book, in the chapter *Are press releases still relevant?* we address the criticism that 'press releases don't work any more'.

It's true to say that an announcement, told using a single press release, has a place; it's an efficient way to tell a story. But it's also true to say that many organisations really do need to seriously rethink not only how they write press releases, but also how they disseminate them. In today's multimedia world, a press release may well not be enough, on its own, to tell your story well.

It's not so much thinking about *how you distribute a press release* as it is thinking about *how you distribute your story*. In other words, distribution should be *story centric* not *press release centric*.

To get the best from any good story, a press release absolutely needs to be part of a bigger campaign.

This changes how you think about the story. There is an inherent difference in thinking between (for example) 'press release plus video and infographic' and a 'campaign to tell the story'.

Even those using unsupported press releases must surely concede that today's world needs stories which are told via multiple channels, using multiple media and even written in multiple ways. That makes for better publicity.

The best way to achieve this isn't to append your thinking to a press release, it is – as with all forms of marketing – to plan a campaign which does the announcement justice.

If you start to plan a campaign and your ideas for telling the story in different ways are exciting, then it's a good indication that you have a strong story – *it's news*. A strong story inspires a more powerful retelling, which encourages sponsorship of the story. If you find that such ideas seem either overblown for the story in hand, or difficult to conceive, then you know the story isn't that strong – *its news value could be questionable.*

The starting point for any announcement should really be to think of its potential as a campaign. If it's a good, strong story, that's the best way to get the news out and for the story to reach its full potential.

The view that you 'e-mail a database and the job's done' won't deliver the best results. There's little rocket science to press release distribution: just care, management and some thought. With effort, you can expand your circulation massively and make great contacts in the media. After having a great news story, distributing it well is the next priority.

INFLUENCING THROUGH INFLUENCERS

Influencer marketing aims to reach your audience, via trusted intermediaries, with a more authentic message.

You will learn that:
- influencer marketing can be an important part of your campaigns.
- influencers can provide access to communities both large and small – those who trust the influencer and act on what she or he says.

In the previous chapter, *distribution channels*, we listed possible recipients for press releases. While this list is diverse, many of them are, in one way or another, influencers. You're connecting to them, to reach the people they influence.

We flagged that with one community, social media influencers, press releases aren't the best way to engage (it's also true of some of the others on our list, though to a lesser extent).

A press release can't be expected to do everything; to work everywhere. To build a relationship, you should make personal contact. You can't do that with *any* one-to-many tool.

HOW INFLUENTIAL?

There are many social media influencers, on many platforms. They provide how-to guides. They review products. They entertain people. Although they're not always slick, they can have a huge following.

Social media influencers often make a decent income from their channels (usually via advertising and sponsorship), but they can seldom be bought. They're usually independent and therefore hugely trusted. According to Twitter, around 40% of Twitter users say they've "made a purchase as a direct result of a tweet from an influencer". In the same research, 49% of Twitter users said they rely on recommendations from Twitter influencers, versus 56% on recommendations from friends (source: Twitter).

Although young audiences trust social media influencers over television stars (Defy Media's Acumen Report found that 62% would try brands recommended by a YouTube influencer, compared to 49% from a movie star's recommendation, source: Defy Media) it's not just 'kids selling to kids'. Name a topic; you'll find an influencer – in fact, you'll find quite a few. People turn to social media when they're buying new shoes, a computer or need a recipe. They look for make-up recommendations and want to know which customer-relationship management system will best suit them.

According to a study by Tomoson, influencer marketing is one of the fastest growing customer-acquisition channels, ahead of organic search and e-mail marketing – and that businesses can make up to $6.50 for every $1 spent (source: Tomoson).

Research by the social media influence marketing platform Suzy, previously known as Crowdtap, found that those aged 12–32 spend 30% of their 'media time' consuming 'peer-to-peer' 'user-generated' content, versus 13% of their media time watching live television and 10% watching recorded shows (source: Suzy). The firm found that user-generated content was 35% more memorable than other media and 50% more trusted.

IT'S NOT ALWAYS ABOUT SIZE

While huge numbers of followers are impressive, it's far more important to connect with those influencers who are most relevant to your company and its products or services. Working with someone who has thousands of highly engaged followers can deliver stronger results than wasting time courting someone whose million followers have no interest in what you do.

IT CAN TAKE MORE THAN A PRESS RELEASE

The nature of influencer marketing is such that it almost always demands a one-to-one approach, usually over a fair amount of time. You need to build a relationship. They have to know you. And when they have thousands or millions of followers, it's not easy to get noticed. Adding them to your standard press release circulation is not enough.

IDENTIFY INFLUENCERS

Identify those influencers from whom you will benefit the most. As we have said, don't fixate on their number of followers. Look at the quality of the content they create (that's why people are following them) and how well it aligns with what you do. Going niche can often get better results than going big. These people are often called 'micro influencers' – but that refers to the size of their audience, not how much influence they have with that audience.

Find out what interests them; what excites them. Look carefully at where they engage the most with their audience: which topics work best for them.

Profile potential influencers. Look at all of their social media channels, collect contact and engagement information such as social media handles and e-mail addresses. Keep records of each contact. Your engagement should be meaningful and authentic – and you don't want to repeat yourself. This is not, repeat not, a means by which you send them continual advertisements.

You can use platforms such as Tapinfluence (tapinfluence.com) and Suzy (suzy.com) to help locate and engage with social influencers.

CONNECT

Take conversations to where influencers converse the most. They may well have multiple social media channels, but they are typically most *interactive* on one, or a few. That's where to reach them. As with any initial form of contact, those first steps aren't easy. It takes time – and they need to trust you. Share their content, adding comments when you do. Ask questions. Interact. This has to be natural; you're unlikely to succeed unless your interest and knowledge are genuine.

Don't suddenly interact, five times a day, on every social channel they use. It will look like an incursion.

Build relationships with the people your influencers engage with the most, following the same steps. Become part of the conversation group; part of the community.

When you are confident that you can ask them to review or promote something on your behalf, do so personally and out of the public forum – e-mail is usually best, and this may be the first time you reach them in this way.

Be clear about what you want – and be honest and upfront about it. You've chosen them because of the value they offer.

Feel free to compliment them, but don't be obsequious. Keep it real. Tell them why you'd like to work with them. Explain why your product or service will benefit them and their followers.

Be human. People like to hear about how a product or service came into being; what inspired it. Your company's founding may provide an interesting backdrop to your pitch. How customers use products and services, or struggle if they can't, can provide valuable insights.

It's especially productive if you are open to suggestions. They will know what works best with their audience; this may not be the way you'd originally envisaged things would work, but trust them. It's highly unlikely you'll get to 'own' whatever spot they create for you. If they're going to do a five-minute video on YouTube, be prepared for it not to be all about you. Influencers are not advertising channels.

Make sure you give them everything they need to work with you, including a campaign deadline, review products, background information, access to specialists, campaign hashtags and URLs.

DON'T DISAPPEAR

Don't turn them into a one-night stand. No one likes this. Be appreciative of their time. Let them know how the campaign is going and how they have helped. Thank them. They've done something significant for you. If you don't do this, you risk losing the influencer's sponsorship and friendship – and won't get a warm reception when you want their help again.

ONE-TO-ONE APPROACHES

Engagement works best when you connect with social influencers in a one-to-one way. Don't make them part of a campaign where you target others at the same time.

Remember: influencers are highly sought-after. Others will also be trying to court them. The more you treat influencers as individuals, as real people, the more successful you will be.

APPROACH OTHERS IN THE SAME WAY

Although we've focused on reaching social media influencers, you can reach many other influencers listed in the chapter *distribution channels* in the same way. It's time-intensive, so you'll pick and choose where this will be most effective.

> *Although an important part of publicity and marketing, influencer marketing isn't going to work by just adding influencers to your press release distribution list. You should connect with them directly, on a one-to-one basis.*

KNOW YOUR CONTACTS

Distributing press releases via mailing lists and newswires is essential,
but it's only part of the picture. Equally important is building media
relationships.

You will learn that:
- building media contacts is important for publicity success.
- using mailing lists and newswires doesn't obviate the need to create relationships.
- there are greater benefits to building relationships than just raising your chances of getting stories placed.
- media influence can come from less obvious places.

Mailing lists and newswires can quickly reach many people, but not everyone on a distribution list is equal.

Some people are more influential than others. Some will influence a particular community. Some may have a greater interest in your sector than others. Some may share your views. Some may be more open about placing your kind of news story. Everyone receiving your press releases is different in one way or another, yet companies very often send the same press release to their entire, unsegmented distribution list, regardless of the recipients' needs or interests. Press releases should be relevant and sometimes tailored.

HOW MANY RELATIONSHIPS?

Knowing everyone personally on a distribution list comprising hundreds or thousands of people isn't an option, and, when sending via a newswire service, it isn't even a possibility. But you don't have to know *everyone*, just a decent number of those with whom you can work a little more closely.

But with which people, from your vast distribution network, should you spark up a conversation?

Beware your ego taking you only to those who are 'most important', such as editors of large news outlets. Importance is relative and not necessarily a reflection of influence. Many influencers can easily have as much authority as a top journalist or editor. There's also the question of your effort; it can be far easier to engage with a specialist influencer than with the editor of a large outlet.

Research where you can gain most traction and have the biggest impact.

Since you may issue different kinds of press releases to different audiences, don't limit yourself to one type of contact. As an example, magazine-type websites may favour case studies over the product launches preferred by news outlets.

It's not all about what people can do for you or finding the ones with the most influence; it's also about finding those with whom you can most readily connect, who – for reasons of their own – are enthusiastic about working with you. Sponsorship can be a powerful thing.

As with life, it's impossible to force a media relationship into being. You get along with someone or you don't. In-between those two poles, you'll typically create relationships which are efficient and professional, and there's nothing wrong with that. It's not scientific; you can't always connect with those you desperately want to, while some relationships may spring almost out of nowhere and surprise you with their value.

Media and influencer relationships won't happen unless you make them happen, by sending an e-mail, connecting via social media or picking up the telephone. Have lunch, get to know them, get on first-name terms.

How many people you court is up to you. It's not as much a case of 'the more, the merrier' as it is about value. And, to be honest, just how many of these relationships can you manage? Perhaps one or two dozen truly close relationships, a far wider group more casually and with a middle ground of maybe a hundred or fewer? Invest your time where the reception is positive, and the results have the most potential.

FRIENDS WITH BENEFITS

The most obvious benefit of these relationships is increasing your odds of getting a story placed. For many, that's the only goal. True, press releases are more likely to get a positive response from an editor you know than from one you don't. But there can be greater benefits.

By building relationships, you can find out what's most relevant to your contacts: the kind of stories they like; the stories which deliver the best results for them. Feed that fire with exclusive stories too, or perhaps give them the jump on the rest of the media now and again. Find out how you can help *them*. These people *know what is newsworthy.* Outlets want content. But they want what *they* want, which is not always what *you* want to give them. Taking a steer from your connections will not only boost the chance of getting a story placed, but it will also *vastly* increase the likelihood of it being read and syndicated.

Having reliable contacts means it's easier to float the idea of potential stories. This can affirm a story's news value and, more importantly, it can shape how you write the story: editors, journalists, commentators and all manner of specialists will often readily advise you on what works best – if you have a relationship. Their feedback can sometimes be brutal, but it will always be honest. If your story isn't newsworthy, expect to be told so. If it's *nearly* news, they might say what's missing, or how you might approach it from a different angle. (And it's better to say to stakeholders, "I've checked with Emma and Simon and there's *no way* they'll run the story", than, "I'm *not sure* this will fly".)

Nurture and value your contacts, and you'll also have their mindshare when you're not selling a story: perhaps they'll ask you to comment on another story, or suggest a story for which they know there's a ready audience.

Finally, getting noticed by media outlets can increase chances of being noticed by others. You can move from nobody, to somebody, to mover-and-shaker with the help of just a few great contacts. The chances of enjoying the same success by just firing press releases out to an anonymous list are far, far lower.

> *For the serious publicist or marketer, media relationships aren't*
> *optional. They're an important means of making publicity work much*
> *harder.*

DISTRIBUTION SOFTWARE

*To be effective, press release distribution should be as
targeted and measured as any e-mail campaign.*

You will learn that using specialist distribution software enables you to:
- track and monitor each press release.
- build up a picture of which news stories are the most successful.
- reduce time spent administering mailing lists.

Most press releases are distributed via e-mail: for many companies, this means keeping a mailing list in a spreadsheet, and merging this data with an e-mail client.

A simple solution this may be, but it's not without considerable drawbacks.

For instance, it makes mailing list management cumbersome. For small distribution lists, a spreadsheet is feasible, but once you want to segment the list, or when the list grows, it becomes unworkable. Spreadsheets may have list-management features, but they're a poor tool for all but the simplest lists.

More significantly, spreadsheets only get part of the job done: storing contact details.

When you press send, the only statistical feedback you'll get comes from any e-mails which bounce back.

Without analytics – statistics on which people have read your story, forwarded it to others and so on – you have no intelligence with which to improve your publicity.

E-MAIL DISTRIBUTION SOFTWARE

It's time to enlist some e-mail distribution software.

This enables you to manage databases and send press releases from within the same application, which is usually Web-based, so there's nothing to install. You pay a fee, which may be monthly, or per mailing, or both.

The value gained from analytical data you'll get back more than makes up for the fees of such a service. Typically, you'll be able to see statistics on:
- how many people opened a press release.
- how many people forwarded a press release to another person.
- how many people clicked on links within a press release.
- in which countries your press releases are most read.
- any e-mail addresses which no longer work.

- who unsubscribes from your mailing list.
- how many e-mails didn't reach the recipient, because they bounced back as 'soft' or 'hard' bounces ('soft bounces' are when people have their out-of-office reply on or because their inbox is full; 'hard bounces' are when the e-mail address no longer exists, or the recipient is unknown).

Professional mailing services enable you to segment lists, so that you can choose which types of people receive specific press releases, while campaign analytics can tell you which types of press releases are most popular with which type of recipient.

Some distribution services also enable you to include a Google Analytics tracking code, or can fully integrate with Google Analytics, so that you can track results all the way from a click within a press release e-mail to a landing page on your website. That way you can more accurately, and easily, measure campaign results.

These services also help automate the management of your distribution databases. Unlike a spreadsheet, they allow people to unsubscribe without effort from you – so it's one less thing for you to manage. You can also embed a sign-up form on your website's press page, to enable people to sign up to your list (perhaps identifying themselves as a journalist, editor, commentator, etc when they do so).

It's important that distribution lists *are managed*. Using analytics data, you can proactively remove e-mail addresses which are dead (from which you get 'hard' bounce-backs).

Online services provide templates for e-mailing campaigns or enable you to upload your own. You'll want to use the simplest of these. Press releases don't need much in the way of design; they are not advertisements. It's best to include the press release text within the body of the e-mail, even if it's attached as a document, so the story can be read immediately.

Some e-mail distribution services may not allow you to send attachments. If this is the case, simply include a link within the e-mail, so that people can download any documents.

Some distribution services won't allow you to e-mail to generic e-mail addresses (such as info@, editor@ and enquiries@). This is a typically a good thing, as it's best to send press releases to exactly the right person – but it can be problematic if that's the outlet's preference. Choose a service which lets you do this.

There are lots of excellent distribution services online. Check out which has the features you want at a pricing level with which you're comfortable.

Start by looking at services such as:

- aweber.com
- constantcontact.com
- keap.com

- mailchimp.com
- myemma.com
- salesforce.com/products/marketing-cloud/email-marketing
- sendinblue.com

You can also get a similar (although sometimes more limited) service plug-ins to the e-mail client you already use. For example, Yesware (yesware.com) is a free plug-in for Gmail which provides statistics on when e-mails are opened, which links are clicked on, where the message is being viewed geographically, on which device the message is being read and so on. Typically, such plug-ins don't include any form of list management.

SOFTWARE BUILT FOR THE JOB

E-mail marketing tools provide a significant step up from using spreadsheets, but a better approach still is to use something built with press release distribution in mind.

Let's take a look at just one example of such a tool – Prezly (prezly.com). Prezly integrates e-mail distribution with customer-relationship management and online newsrooms. Prezly is used by companies such as Audi, Emirates Airline and IKEA.

Prezly provides an online newsroom to which you add news stories – including supporting media (such as images and videos) alongside SlideShare presentations and other resources, such as PDFs or trial versions of software.

Pages can be published or scheduled to go live on a specified date.

The visually customisable newsroom can be hosted by Prezly, using a personalised domain, or it can be integrated seamlessly into a company's own website.

The news story pages are designed for social media sharing to ensure that stories look their best on websites such as Facebook, LinkedIn and Twitter.

Newsrooms are optimised for mobile devices; Prezly says that around half of the first instances where people view a story is from a phone or tablet.

Once a story is in the newsroom, Prezly automatically creates an attractively formatted e-mail to distribute to the media and other contacts. The e-mail will include your text and any images (resized automatically from your high-resolution originals) plus links to any other resources, such as PDFs.

Prezly allows the e-mail to be personalised for specific audiences – and says that, based on its statistics, creating different pitches for different audiences (rather than sending the same thing to everyone) significantly improves engagement.

E-mails are sent to stored contacts. Contacts can be tagged in multiple ways (for example, 'press', 'journalists', 'bloggers', 'specialists' – you create your own tags and assign them as you wish).

Prezly doesn't provide a mailing list – when you begin using Prezly, you upload your current list. Prezly will look at your list and try to find your contacts online, linking to their social media accounts automatically.

After you send a campaign, Prezly provides tracking information such as e-mail opens, clicks, replies, unopened e-mails, undelivered e-mails and those contacts who unsubscribe. With this information, you can create follow-up campaigns (for example, to those who didn't open the e-mail) and continually improve what you do by learning which stories perform best.

Prezly's customer-relationship management system handles all contacts and interactions. If you've linked Prezly to your local mailbox or corporate e-mail system, you can see all conversations and marketing touchpoints (clicks, videos watched and so on) with each contact, even if those conversations are held by others in your team.

You can also add clippings to each contact – for example, if that contact is a journalist, you can clip the stories written by her or him to track coverage on a person-by-person basis.

A tool such as Prezly can help take publicity to the next level: you're not making do with something that works at a push, you're using something that's built for the job from the ground up.

Prezly isn't the only company to offer this kind of service and it's worth undertaking some online research to see what would work best for you.

Other publicity distribution tools include:

- cision.co.uk
- mynewsdesk.com
- pr.co
- presspage.com
- prowly.com

Publicity distribution products vary in functionality and are not necessarily directly comparable with Prezly; for example, they may focus more on social media analytics and less on detailed management of interaction with media contacts. You should review a range of tools and, if you decide these are for you, choose the one best suited to your contact database, campaign distribution and measurement needs.

BANISHING THE BLACK HOLE

Distribution is an essential part of the publicity process. How you distribute press releases will depend on many factors, but using a spreadsheet and e-mail client leaves you without vital analytics data. Unless you're using an e-mail distribution tool, you're throwing stories into a black hole. Who knows if they reached the other side?

For the publicity writer, banishing the black hole gives real purpose to the writing process. Analytics data enables you to learn what works, what doesn't, which markets and outlets prefer which kinds of stories – and much, much more. You can create campaigns, and write press releases, with far greater confidence of success.

The job isn't done when you've sent a press release. Analytics from each mailing can help you to refine your publicity, connect better with the media and other influencers – and continually improve your news stories, so that each release performs solidly.

MEASURING

MEASURING RESULTS

Measuring the effects of publicity has been notoriously difficult, with results ranging from imprecise to downright vague. But as publicity has evolved, so has the ability to measure it.

You will learn that:
- many traditional methods of measuring the impact of publicity have limited benefits, because they focus on the wrong things.
- the goal of linking publicity activities to financial outcomes is achievable.
- dedicated analytics systems can deliver a previously undreamt of ability to measure the effects of publicity.

Management thinker Peter Drucker said, "If you can't measure it, you can't improve it."

Advertising, marketing and publicity have long been notoriously difficult to measure. Before the Internet, most forms of measurement were really guesses dressed up as analytics. Good guesses perhaps, but guesses nonetheless.

The Internet changed much of this. The number of views of an advertisement; the number of clicks on it; the number of conversations or sales from it – it's been possible to calculate all of these, with precision, for quite some time.

We can't say the same for publicity, which has struggled to adopt measurement metrics as accurate as those used for other forms of marketing.

Part of this boils down to what you want to measure. Measuring the results of a mailing campaign can be clear-cut: the sale. Publicity is about far more than this. On the one hand, you might want to quantify concrete results – such as, "How many enquiries did this campaign generate?" On the other, you might want to understand something rather more abstract – such as, "Do our customers like us?"

For public relations, a measurement system evolved which was, at the time, probably the best possible: measuring 'the size' of what was published, which is often casually referred to as 'column inches' or, more correctly, Opportunity To See.

As a process of public relations measurement, it has an inherent flaw. It only measures the fact that something has been published. It doesn't measure *impact*. It measures *exposure*, from which you can only guess the *impact*.

Opportunity To See can also be considered as statistically anomalous: if a campaign gets a lot of traction, with extensive and repeat coverage, the numbers of 'Opportunities To See' can exceed the population available to see it. The number of Opportunities To See doesn't equal the number of those who have seen it.

Another traditionally popular means of publicity measurement is Advertising Value Equivalence, which measures the space gained by publicity coverage and compares it to the advertising cost of that space. If a press release spawned an article, then the Advertising Value Equivalence of the article would be the cost of an advertisement of the same size. Advertising Value Equivalence gained popularity because it compares what you could achieve with the same spend. But it brings value down to cost, whereas *value* is more about *impact*: the impact from an article can be potentially greater than that from an advertisement of the same size; for example, articles can often trigger more social shares and discussions.

Advertising Value Equivalence *can* look good, because when publicity works, the expenditure may be considerably lower than it would be for advertising – since, with advertising, you have to buy *every* space. Advertising's economies of scale are limited. With publicity, you create the source material once and oncosts are little – regardless of how much exposure it ultimately gets.

Since much more accurate systems of measurement were developed for other forms of marketing, publicity became somewhat marginalised – perhaps, to some degree, even mistrusted, especially as a driver of revenue. Many of us have been in conversations where 'generating exposure' was, in the absence of something more concrete, cited as a fallback justification for publicity.

Measurement of publicity still divides professional opinion, with some saying it is too complex to be accurately measured, while others say it can be measured with precision.

What shouldn't be in doubt is the need to set goals. Without goals, what is the point of your press release? We can debate endlessly what those goals should be, but if you're not aiming at some kind of target, what exactly *are* you doing? How can you know how well your press releases work if you don't measure *something*? What you measure, and how you do it, will depend on several factors: your budget, your available time, what's important to your stakeholders, what's relevant to the campaign, what's important to the business and its strategy, and so on.

Some forms of measurement can be easy to undertake while others can take a lot more work. Since this book's focus is on *writing press releases*, rather than publicity in its entirety, consider the following merely an introduction to each topic. We'd encourage you to explore these topics in greater depth.

WEBSITE TRAFFIC FROM MEDIA SOURCES

This is not difficult to measure, but it needs to be set up carefully, and be managed, so that hits from media sources are separated out from regular traffic.

Your website analytics software (for many, this will be Google Analytics) should be able to handle this, but you need to identify those media sources which are important to you. This isn't as simple as it sounds; initially, you might have a good idea of what *you think* these are, but, as your publicity grows, so does the need to expand your list of media sources. Otherwise, hits from media websites will be drowned out in the noise of 'normal traffic'. Remember, there is a wide range of potential outlets, so make sure that you go beyond mainstream media to include other influencers.

WEBSITE TRAFFIC FROM ALL CAMPAIGN RECIPIENTS

This is significantly easier to measure when you create a campaign URL or deploy a campaign-specific landing page. A campaign URL is easy to set up, even if you're driving people to a page which already exists, such as content.productions/know-how/publications – just add a unique query to the end of the URLs in your press release (for example, adding ?=c1 to the previous URL will give you the uniquely trackable URL: content.productions/publications?=c1). This will register as a distinct URL in your website analytics reports, separate from the 'normal' URL (without the query string), to which the campaign traffic goes. Your website won't flip out at the additional query string. It displays the page as it would normally, but your analytics software will help you to separate what came from your campaign and what didn't.

BACKLINKS TO YOUR WEBSITE

If you set up a landing page or campaign URL, you can use Google Search Console to check backlinks to those specific pages. There are also third-party tools which can help: search online for 'backlink tools'. These can tell you which websites link back to your campaign, allowing you to track the amplification of your press releases. Be aware that many of these tools are neither 100% accurate nor provide real-time results.

DOWNLOADS

These can be measured using your website analytics tools, just as you would measure page hits.

ENQUIRIES/SALES/SIGN-UPS

These can be measured on a campaign-by-campaign basis, using your website analytics tools.

SYNDICATION

You can measure this easily by setting up a Google Alert (google.co.uk/alerts) for the exact wording of your press release headline, contained within double quotes.

MEDIA OUTLET COVERAGE

In the past, this meant 'mainstream media' but now embraces other significant sources of online influence. Has the story been syndicated or republished? Has it led to new articles or interviews? This isn't as easy as tracking syndicated versions of the story, which will often be easily identifiable near-duplicates. When your story is covered in the media, it could be entirely new, written from scratch: inspired by your press release rather than being a duplicate of it. However, you can still set up Google Alerts for specific keyword combinations which are likely to be found in the resulting articles: perhaps a combination of a new product name, company name, spokesperson's name and so on. There are also online services which can do this for you, such as those provided by Kantar Media; these can provide cross-media monitoring which, in addition to news outlets, includes radio, television, printed and online publications. Other services include Brandwatch, Cision and CoverageBook.

SOCIAL SHARES

These can be measured using third-party tools. Search for 'measuring social shares'. These tools allow you to input the URL of a press release and then see how and where it was shared.

ACQUIRING PEOPLE INTO A CONTENT-MARKETING PROCESS

How you measure this depends on your strategy and content tools. For example, if you regularly post content on YouTube, then you might want to measure hits to your channel, or track the number of additional people who follow it. You may also cross-reference your website analytics for campaign periods to see if hits from a campaign lead to a rise in hits on other parts of your website. You might want to see how many people are encouraged to sign up for your newsletter, and so on.

MORE DETAILED ANALYTICS

Analytics software such as Google Analytics enables you to set up a 'multi-channel funnel' to see not just how many people downloaded an item, but how people reached that point. When someone visits your website and completes an important action – such as enquiring or buying – this is called a conversion. In analytics tools, conversions are typically credited to the visitor's last action. This could be searching for a page, clicking on a link to get to the page or clicking on an advertisement to reach the page. The problem with this is that users usually don't buy (or enquire) on the first visit to a website. More likely, it's after a few visits, perhaps after comparing your offering with those of competitors. Multi-channel funnels help you to understand the link between the first interaction, the last interaction and the final conversion. You can see how many days it took for customers to convert; which conversions take longer than others – for example, the difference between signing up for a newsletter and buying something – how many interactions were required for customers to convert and which conversion paths are most successful. Setting up a multi-channel funnel can be complex – but can provide rewarding, detailed information. If your organisation uses a customer-relationship management system, and this is integrated with your campaign analytics, then processes can be followed not only to the first sale *but beyond* – so you don't just measure cost of acquisition but also customers' lifetime value.

Many measurement tools are free and easy to use but, as they're not specifically built for the job in hand, they can be cumbersome to manage. When you need to measure several different things, juggling the variety of data presentation formats becomes a real chore, and worse if you need to compile these into a single report. This is fine for a small business or more casual publicist, but if you're active in publicity then you could easily spend more time measuring results than you do to generate them.

Many of these tools are more suited to measuring specific actions, perhaps conversions of some kind. While publicity can drive such actions, it can also achieve many things which other forms of marketing can't, and these need measuring too.

PUBLICITY MEASUREMENT TOOLS

You may want to measure something less immediately tangible: something that goes 'beyond the hit', such as customer perceptions, market awareness or share-of-voice. These valid publicity goals can be elusive to measure.

Just as website analytics have transformed our understanding of website visitor activity, so publicity analytics can transform understanding of publicity's value.

One such tool, Cision Media Monitoring, part of Cision's suite of services (cision.com), aggregates the online coverage generated by publicity campaigns, displaying the results in live, real-time, easy-to-understand dashboards.

It tracks mentions on millions of online sources – and customers can add their own target media outlets to Cision's lists. The focus for Cision Media Monitoring is not just the volume of coverage, but the quality of it. As an example, where Opportunity To See and Advertising Value Equivalence tell you where something has been published, Cision Media Monitoring also tells you the value of that publishing event: how many people read the article, how many shared it and whether their views were positive or negative (sometimes called 'sentiment analysis').

It can also measure your share-of-voice for a particular topic, service, product or industry: how much impact you're generating versus your competitors – or your performance can be benchmarked against your sector. It measures social amplification: those campaigns which generate the most buzz.

What about publicity outside the online arena? Cision Media Monitoring also handles broadcast channels, such as television and radio, print monitoring of national and local newspapers, social media monitoring and even tracks mentions of your brand across more than 20,000 news podcasts.

Cision Media Monitoring integrates with Google Analytics – so that, from one place, companies can immediately measure the traffic generated from a campaign. This can include common goals such as the number of page views, downloads, forms completed and even orders placed. But public relations isn't just about sales: it's called public relations for a reason. It's about building relationships. So yes, you can see a direct link between publicity and revenue generation, but you can also see your data in a far broader context, separating the impact of publicity from the general noise of both website traffic and online activity.

Each customer's Cision dashboard is custom-built, with widgets to measure what's important to that customer. Dashboards are interactive – and data can be easily drilled down into.

Cision's reports allow quick access to critical data – and not just in a format suitable for publicity professionals. Other stakeholders can drill down to the data that's important to them, without leaving a report.

A system such as Cision Media Monitoring allows you to more easily ascertain what works and what doesn't. Not just the kind of campaigns and content which create the most impact, but which media outlets work best for you. You can find out which of those websites covering your story attracted the most readers, where it was shared the most, generated the best positive influence, drove the most traffic back to your website, and even those websites which generated the most sales.

Cision Media Monitoring is not the only system of its kind. It would be impossible to profile them all equally or even compare their approaches (which can be radically different). We encourage you to undertake your own research and find the tools which best fit your needs and budget.

Public relations analytics tools include:

- brand24.com
- cision.com
- criticalmention.com
- hubspot.com
- meltwater.com
- onclusive.com
- trendkite.com

This isn't an exhaustive list nor a list of recommendations.

The Internet has driven lots of change in publicity, opening up opportunities beyond the large, mainstream media channels and enabling people to share/discuss content via social media. It has redefined 'influence', 'exposure' and 'impact'. Publicity analytics systems allow marketing professionals to quantify the impact of their publicity efforts properly, rather than just measure placement.

*There is always **some way** in which you can measure the effect of publicity, from the simple to the sophisticated. Quick and simple tools provide useful, if limited, data – while dedicated publicity-monitoring tools deliver an accurate, real-time picture of your online activity that can help you to build a powerful publicity strategy.*

VOICES THAT MATTER

EVERYTHING THAT COUNTS CAN BE COUNTED

Voices that matter: an interview with Erik Huddleston, president at Cision.

When William Bruce Cameron said, "Not everything that can be counted counts, and not everything that counts can be counted," he might well have been talking about publicity.

It's a problem that business leader after business leader has wrestled with. Publicity, perhaps more than any form of marketing, isn't always about the sale, so directly linking every penny of expenditure to a precise outcome can be challenging indeed.

This isn't a great way to run a business. Publicity, like other forms of marketing (and any business expenditure), should in some way justify itself.

The quantification of PR is the goal of Erik Huddleston, who is currently president at Cision, and was previously chief executive officer of TrendKite – which was acquired by Cision in 2019. Founded in 2012 by two former employees of Meltwater, TrendKite provided a sophisticated media-monitoring and intelligence platform specifically for marketing and publicity. TrendKite is now an integrated part of Cision, a platform which serves the full range of communicators' needs.

TrendKite's two founders, A.J. Bruno and Matt Allison, had seen technology within other forms of marketing flourishing, yet PR was stifled by a lack of innovation, something which threatened to make it irrelevant.

Huddleston, also from a background of marketing technology, joined TrendKite because he believed that the company could bring PR back into the sales and marketing fold – reversing the trend where, for many organisations, it has become what Huddleston calls a "disconnected island" – in contrast to other forms of marketing, which are tightly integrated with the business.

"We want to measure the return on investment – and impact – of PR as effectively as we do for other marketing disciplines," says Huddleston. "By measuring PR activities which, in the PESO model (where media is paid, earned, shared or owned), are 'earned', I believe that we can bring the PR leader back to the chief marketing officer's table – armed with meaningful metrics and an ability to demonstrate return on investment. We want PR – and other 'earned' activities – to be measured just as effectively as what is paid, shared or owned."

It's an ambitious goal, concedes Huddleston. "While organisations engaged in any meaningful PR activity typically measure *something*, perhaps placements and mentions, few PR professionals can look their boss – or client – in the eye and make a data-driven statement about the value that their PR delivers." He's confident that this will change. "The percentage of people measuring things in this way is low right now, but we're working to make it much higher."

This lack of measurement, entrenched in many organisations, has, says Huddleston, resulted in an erosion of confidence in PR. Yet it's a view he tempers with not just optimism, but certainty of change. "We should remember," says Huddleston, "that, historically, all marketing has been hard to measure. Years ago, John Wanamaker famously said, 'Half the money I spend on advertising is wasted; the trouble is I don't know which half.' This just isn't true any more. Every aspect of marketing has robust, proven measurement technology behind it – except PR. If confidence in PR has been eroded, it's because expectations for marketing measurement have changed – and PR hasn't kept pace. Since companies have rarely been able to directly attribute publicity activity to business outcomes, PR has become a silo, rather than being the key player it should be within the marketing mix."

A demonstration of Cision – seeing what's now possible in terms of PR measurement – can be a jaw-dropping moment, says Huddleston. "I love to demo Cision because of the reaction I see from PR professionals. Yes, they expect to see a media-monitoring platform, but immediately they understand that they are looking at something more. They see analytics that quantify impact, not a dry summary of press coverage. They see a framework that systematically links things which are meaningful to them – things which have been regarded perhaps as rather ethereal brand goals, such as reputation, mindshare and awareness – as well as more tightly defined outcomes such as traffic and sales. It's a picture of their world, their brand, their products, their competitors – not a complicated dashboard of Boolean queries. It instantly has real meaning. With a single click they can create a competitive mindshare analysis – something they used to have to really labour over."

Their enthusiasm at Cision demos shows that PR professionals – especially those who are focused on digital media – aren't resistant to measurement. They've just been waiting for something to properly measure the scope of their activities, rather than focus on the *ka-ching* of the cash register. "I think we underestimated how hungry people are for a better way of measuring things," says Huddleston. "We were initially surprised by the rapid adoption of new metrics – but it makes sense when you look at how much of what we do is aligned to the spirit of the Barcelona Principles. We measure what matters."

The Barcelona Principles are a set of voluntary guidelines established by the PR industry to measure the efficacy of PR campaigns. Agreed upon in 2010 at a summit convened by the International Association for Measurement and Evaluation of Communication (AMEC), the Barcelona Principles champion the end of Advertising Value Equivalence in favour of something more relevant – based on 'outcome', not 'output'. They also state that setting goals (and measuring results) is a fundamental part of any PR programme; that the effects on business results can (and should) be measured where possible, as should both quantity and quality – and social media. The Principles are perhaps the most significant step forward in PR thinking for decades, making publicity again relevant to today's more analytically savvy marketing teams.

Much of the business world is yet to catch up.

"Many businesses still measure the wrong things," says Huddleston, "primarily because the tools to measure the right things haven't existed. Those who have embraced digital marketing – or grown up with it – have to educate those who are old-school in their thinking. They need to demonstrate that it's now possible to measure things like sentiment, social amplification, customer acquisition through earned media, brand loyalty, share of voice over time, how PR is affecting attitudes and behaviours – and so on. These are still valid business objectives – but ones far more relevant in terms of the value PR delivers to a business."

Once organisations move to a better means of measurement, they can step up both the quality and quantity of their PR, believes Huddleston. "Proving the value of PR is a great way to improve a PR budget. It can shift the PR spend, too – for example, one of our clients found that a niche blogger drove significantly more traffic and sales than big, mainstream outlets. More accurate measurement like this enables organisations to find those influencers who can do far more for them. This increases both the quality and effectiveness of PR, leading to a virtuous circle of increased strategic relevance. Without real measurement, organisations tend to focus on outlets they've heard of rather than channels which genuinely drive results. They can end up applauding a press release pickup in a lightly trafficked corner of a big publication – which actually does little for them – and ignoring a mention on a niche site that a large audience has responded to. Data changes everything. PR has been a kind of 'dark matter' in the sales and marketing universe. Once its contribution is properly measured, PR's share-of-wallet naturally increases – shifting spend from less effective marketing channels."

Cision measures not only online PR, but also PR activity that takes place offline. "At one time, accurately measuring what happens online seemed relatively easy – but tracking offline activities was more complex; more elusive. Now we can do both with precision. We're measuring things which couldn't even be imagined just five years ago. Our ability to measure is always improving."

It's not just companies' publicity which improves with the use of tools such as Cision – Cision itself improves. "We are laser-focused on customer feedback," says Huddleston, "and we act on it. But, as with any emerging field, there are things our customers wouldn't know to ask for until they saw them. Marshall Field said, 'Give the lady what she wants,' but Henry Ford said, 'If I had asked customers what they wanted, they would have said faster horses.' So, we balance product development with what we're asked for and the innovation that only an experienced team can deliver."

Measurement shouldn't be seen as the end of the PR process or campaign, believes Huddleston, but rather the start of it. "You make PR more effective by thinking first in terms of what you want it to achieve. For example, which attitudes and behaviours are you trying to influence? Then not only measure this – but use it to create goals which define your campaign. If you aren't able to use a dedicated PR measurement tool, establish the best proxies you can to measure your progress against your objectives. There's always something you can measure, always. Most of all, learn from the data. Adapt. Be prepared to change your approach based on what the data tells you. Once you have effective measurement, you will have more effective PR. Right from the go, you can craft better press releases that you know, with confidence, will deliver better results – because you more fully understand the impact of what you write."

FEWER STORIES, BETTER TOLD

Voices that matter: an interview with Adam Parker,
non-executive chairman of RealWire and founder of Lissted.

As non-executive chairman of RealWire, Adam Parker knows better than most what can make a news story fly, or bomb.

Parker describes RealWire not as a newswire, but rather as a news distribution service. A key distinction, he says, is that, "RealWire doesn't accept just *any story*. If a story doesn't pass our editorial standards, we won't send it."

This approach is in contrast to most other newswires which, for a fee, will (within the bounds of their submissions policies) distribute pretty much anything. It's your business how good the stories are – or aren't.

RealWire doesn't simply 'use or refuse'. Where it spots opportunities to do so, it actively advises and helps customers to improve their press releases, based on hard-earned experience of what works and what doesn't.

"We always review – and question – everything that comes in," says Parker. "We want to know whether our clients are targeting the right people, whether the story contains any risks, whether the story is written in the best way – and so on. We want every story to do as well as it possibly can."

Proactive curation of press releases isn't the only thing to set RealWire apart. Parker believes that the company, founded in 2001, was one of the first news distribution services to focus on online media, rather than just on traditional printed publications – something now taken for granted but which, at the time, was groundbreaking.

In a world replete with free newswires, isn't it tempting to see a paid service, such as RealWire, as an unnecessary luxury? "If your story matters so much that you've taken time to write it," says Parker, "and you want people to know about it – why would you think it's best to send it out via free services rather than paid-for ones? Using free ones implies a lack of confidence in the story. In any event, when you factor in the time an organisation will have invested in creating it, professional distribution is generally a relatively small part of the overall cost."

Most free newswires grew more from their theoretical ability to deliver search optimisation benefits, by providing inbound links back to the owner's website. This practice of 'buying links' is something that Google now not only discourages but actively 'marks down'. Such benefits are therefore, at best, seriously limited, and not without risk.

Since free newswires still need revenue, customers often find that their press releases are surrounded by advertisements, sometimes – counter-productively – from competitors.

In any event, the reality is that free newswires seldom, if ever, provide a real route into mainstream media or to leading influencers.

For example, Google News only accepts input from a limited number of trusted sources, and the same is true of organisations such as the Press Association (which is a vital, direct channel to media professionals, especially in the UK). Real news outlets such as these can only be reliably reached by RealWire and services like it, an advantage that free newswires can't typically match.

Likewise, if you want to get a press release to Reuters, then the only dependable way to do so is via PR Newswire, Business Wire, GlobeNewswire or Marketwired; Reuters does not distribute journalists' e-mail addresses to the public.

"In the past, I'd suspect lots of stories sent to free newswires were really just 'search engine optimisation releases', bashed out to try to help with search engine rankings," confirms Parker. "In my opinion, I doubt that ever really worked, because free newswires are not typically of a good enough quality to be trusted by Google as a genuine news source – and their stories aren't usually newsworthy enough to be picked up by the media and real influencers."

Parker believes that the governing success factors for a press release are the quality of the story, the writing, the story's relevance to a specific audience, and the way in which it is distributed. "Stories fail because they aren't newsworthy, are written by someone relatively junior, are sent to a poorly updated database – or sent to absolutely everyone on a database, when they're only really suitable for a narrow audience. Too many companies see a press release as a quick win; something to get written, get finished and get out to as many people as possible. They should be thinking about the *best* ways in which the story can be written, the top people to reach with the story, whether the story has a geographic angle, if someone can be interviewed, if a video or infographic could support it – and so on. If it's a good story, its impact should be maximised rather than it just being batted out."

More than anything else, Parker believes that press releases fail when they're just not of value to others. "A story might be interesting to you and to the people in your business," says Parker, "but that doesn't necessarily mean it will be interesting to many other people. Using a newswire to reach more people will generally mean that more people will actually read it. However, it's still essential to put as much effort as possible into writing a great story – something that people would actually want to read. There's so much content out there, so much noise, you have to find a way to cut through it with something that people really want. To do that, it's vital to be absolutely clear on who you want to talk to and why. Then, to understand what they find interesting. Finally, to work out how to write your stories, your press releases, in a way which really resonates with them."

Part of the problem, believes Parker, is that few press releases are created with a specific outcome in mind. Without a defined outcome, you can't really measure results. Nor is it clear exactly what you would write or how you would write it. "If you define an objective," says Parker, "then you can actively write a story that is focused on meeting that objective. It then follows that you can properly determine who to reach – and the best ways of doing this. You can't meet an objective if you've not defined one."

In the ongoing debate about measuring today's publicity, particularly with ageing mechanisms such as AVE (Advertising Value Equivalence, which we cover in the chapter *measuring results*), Parker believes that there are still organisations who are behind the times. "AVE isn't useful," says Parker. "AVE hangs around because there are people who don't really know *what* to measure. It's essentially a vanity metric – OK, I could have achieved £100,000 of AVE but still not be able to demonstrate a meaningful outcome. AVE isn't an outcome measurement, it's a made-up value comparison. More enlightened organisations have dispensed with AVE and moved towards approaches which focus on evaluating the business outcomes their PR achieves. The recently launched Integrated Evaluation framework, from AMEC (International Association for the Measurement and Evaluation of Communication), is a good example."

Parker is also the founder of Lissted, a company which aims to provide a more meaningful measure of online influence. Lissted separates out those who simply appear to be influential (perhaps because they have lots of followers) and those who definitely are (possibly because they themselves are followed by, and interact with, *real* movers and shakers within a sector).

Despite the shift from print, radio and television to online media, the press release has stubbornly refused to die – even though many rally for it to do so. "I find it a little amusing when people talk about *the death of the press release*," says Parker. "The first time I heard this was in 2006, following a blog post by the journalist Tom Foremski – 'Die! Press Release! Die! Die! Die!' – and here we are years later and the press release still hasn't died. Cision's acquisition of PR Newswire for over $800 million is evidence of that. If you actually read Foremski's post though, you will find it was the style and format of press releases he wanted to kill. He wanted PR to provide more factual, spin-free releases and embrace the content and linking opportunities that the Internet provided. It's true that the traditional press release was written with *the press* in mind. But that was just the format of the media at the time – and the means to reach that media. We now perhaps tend to think of publicity as *influencer relations* – the art of talking to those people who have a disproportionate amount of influence within an audience – which, let's face it, still has a lot in common with reaching a journalist! There's no point in trying to reach *just anyone*, you need to reach people who are in some sense authoritative – perhaps in a certain market, or with a specific topic. Most influencers have influence in the real world – their online influence derives from that, even when they use social media to amplify it. We still use the term *press release*, which may well be dated or inaccurate, but the goal hasn't changed – nor has the means to reach that goal.

"With the rise of content marketing," says Parker, "marketers are creating content which they think will interest people. To get amplification, content marketers still need to reach influencers – and a press release remains an effective way to do it. OK, influencers are no longer *just the press*, so a press release should be more than it was – especially in terms of incorporating multimedia, for example. But the bottom line is that you need to connect with influencers and build relationships – just as you always have. There's also the same need to write a great story and create great content. The people you need to reach may have changed but the fundamental objectives haven't."

Indeed, Parker believes that too many people are focused on reaching the audience of yesterday, which is narrower than the real audience of today. "Marketing now talks about the PESO model," says Parker, "where media is paid, earned, shared or owned. Thinking just about mainstream media implies that your stories are only part of the 'earned' audience. This is self-limiting – whereas in actual fact, a news story is likely to be on your own website or blog, which is part of your 'owned' channel, it can be promoted through Twitter ads, LinkedIn sponsored posts or even be a component of an advertising campaign, making it part of the 'paid' channel – and a really interesting story will get picked up socially, so it's also 'shared'."

Parker believes that one way in which terminology such as 'press release' matters is because it reinforces the outmoded notion that there is a single audience for such content. "A RealWire press release goes to journalists – but, directly and indirectly, it can also reach lots and lots of other people through a multitude of other channels too," says Parker.

Interestingly, Parker believes that physics can teach marketers a thing or two about what matters in both publicity and content marketing. Physics tells us that matter can pass through four states – solid, liquid, gas and ionised (when it becomes plasma). Materials require different amounts of energy to reach each of these four states – it takes far more energy to boil most metals compared to water, for example. Parker contends that the same is true with news stories. "Sometimes a story is so compelling," says Parker, "it takes only a little energy, in the form of engagement, before it's reaching people who are many degrees removed from where it started. For other stories a great deal more energy is needed for word to spread, because the content just doesn't get people excited as easily. You see this with brands which are a little on the boring side; they often use celebrities to provide 'engagement energy' to their story, because even if people aren't that interested in the brand, they are interested in the celebrity."

But the real magic, says Parker, isn't just realising that some stories take more effort than others to fly (and, therefore, that a one-size-fits-all distribution method is fundamentally flawed). "The more interesting concept," says Parker, "is that very few stories actually reach their potential. Even a news story which has done really well and driven lots of engagement can almost always do better. Some people will invariably have missed it. In the physics analogy, if a story gets some interest and turns *liquid*, a lot of companies pat themselves on the back and consider the job well done. Yet few companies take such a story to the next level – gas – even though, at this point, it would probably take very little additional energy to do so. What generally happens is that the story sits there and dies – but with a bit more investment, perhaps putting some paid promotion behind it, the liquid story might turn into gas, or gas into plasma – and potentially influence considerably more relevant people. This is likely to take far less effort than creating an entirely new story."

Parker's central belief is that successful publicity is mostly about the quality of the story – and how effectively the story is promoted. "It's not about seeing how many press releases you can get out. Pumping out another story can just add to the noise," concludes Parker. "What we really need are fewer stories, better told – and to the right people."

CONNECTING CONTENT WITH CONTACTS

Voices that matter: an interview with Jesse Wynants, founder of Prezly.

It takes a brave person to bring something new to a long-established industry, but that's exactly what Jesse Wynants aimed for when he decided to build Prezly (prezly.com – reviewed in the chapter: *distribution software*).

Prezly was born of frustration. The digital lead working for Boondoggle, an advertising agency in Belgium, Wynants was involved in building digital tools, services and software for clients. One day, Wynants was given what seems a straightforward task: to write and distribute a press release. "The distribution was a very cumbersome process," says Wynants. "As with many companies, the contact list was kept in Excel. Distribution was through Outlook." Wynants could see immediately that there were far more efficient ways of doing the job. "I decided to develop something from scratch, as a personal hobby project. Once the development of Prezly took shape, I realised that if we built something better, we would have two clients immediately: my agency and that of my co-founder."

Prezly's initially small team decided that e-mail distribution alone wouldn't be enough to support the way publicity was evolving. "We realised that stories should live in an online newsroom. We saw the Web growing and growing. Social media was just around the block. We understood that if a news story is locked inside a Word document, a PDF or even in an e-mail, it isn't alive. It needs a URL."

Coming from a development background, Wynants feels that his team can approach PR distribution in a fresh way, unencumbered by legacy ideas or processes. "Our exposure to PR comes mainly through our clients," says Wynants. "In many ways that informs our product development, but it also helps us to ask some pretty challenging questions. We ask if sticking with the status quo is the best way forward? Whether features people think they want are actually useful? These questions come naturally to us because we're not traditionally schooled in PR. We didn't need to look to the past. We developed Prezly for a whole new world, one which, for example, includes social media. Reaching these new channels is just as important as hitting inboxes. We had to make sure Prezly works well with everything. New features – such as the ability to link online coverage to those media contacts which provide that coverage – are built and refined only through conversations with clients."

That new world is forever changing. Technological developments are fast. "I think we've seen things changing pretty rapidly," says Wynants. "Ten years ago, people didn't worry so much about where their PR content was stored and managed. Now, this is crucial. It has to be easy to distribute and share. Content now lives – distributed and interconnected – in an ecosystem called the Internet, where other elements such as your social media presence, engagement and personality are essential to success. That's a significant change.

"Another change is the type of people you need to reach with PR. If anything, that change is even more spectacular. A decade ago, or perhaps less, PR professionals had manageable lists of journalists – people they knew personally. It wasn't hard to reach someone and get a story covered. Now, this has exploded. Journalists are far from being the only influencers: there are social media influencers, sector or market influencers, employees, pressure groups, current customers and many others that you need to reach. Some are not professional writers – they may be blogging as a hobby, for example – but they have massive influence. PR distribution has become way bigger and far more complex. Excel just doesn't cut it any more. More than anything, you need to reach people you don't already know, you need to connect and build up relationships. It's hard to make sense of the data, the contacts, and to drill down quickly to reach a particular selection of people. But that's what needs to happen.

"I don't think enough companies are onboard with how PR is changing," says Wynants, "nor have they grasped all of the implications. For example, sending the same version of a story to a huge number of contacts may seem efficient, but it's actually ineffective. Instead of using one press release, it's better to write different versions of the same story, tailored to different audiences." This kind of personalisation, based on rapid segmentation of influencers, isn't possible when using a spreadsheet to manage contacts – but it's something that Prezly users can do easily. "The content and strategy remain the same," says Wynants, "but how you implement that strategy fundamentally changes. Customising press releases for different audiences makes it easier for you to stand out, and be relevant, in overloaded inboxes."

Prezly helps press releases to be striking in other ways, too. Having discarded the 'single sheet of A4/letter' approach, Prezly's online newsrooms and e-mails are attractively designed; it's not just optional for companies to use images and other media, it's expected. "This is something that is a no-brainer, but companies can initially find it difficult to implement. Data-driven businesses such as banks, for example, may tell us that 'we don't have any visuals'. We respond by saying, 'well, that's a great way to get started!' – any business can be illustrated visually, but everyone has to start somewhere. They can create infographics based on big data; they can retell their story in a more visual and entertaining way. Even if the visuals aren't perfect – say it's just a picture of the company's building – it's better than nothing. Press releases need visuals and other media, this is crucial. The creation of these assets needs to be a core part of how you generate press releases. Show people something that's relevant to the press release. Enrich stories with visuals."

When onboarding new clients, the Prezly team spends more time bringing them up to speed with 'new PR' than with using the software. "Our training is never much about the functionality of Prezly, which people take to very quickly," says Wynants, "it's always about best practice. For example, about how they should use visuals and the best way to create them. If they don't have visuals, then we introduce them to tools such as Canva (canva.com), which can be used to quickly create infographics without the need for a designer. It's always more of an inspirational session than it is about the tool; the tool is just the thing you happen to use. If you just use the tool, but carry on working as you used to, it might make you a little bit more efficient – but not more effective. We want to help make our clients successful."

Not that it's plain sailing when customers start to use Prezly. In fact, having real statistics about the effectiveness and reach of your press releases can be something of a wake-up call. "When clients send out their first release through Prezly," says Wynants, "they get a little bit of a cold shower. They perhaps believed that most of their e-mails reached a contact and were opened. Actually, they more likely find that their first press releases have a low open rate, and assume that something is wrong technically. We look at the analytics and see which e-mails bounced back, which couldn't be delivered and so on. We say: 'yes, it's a problem, but it's one that's been there for a long time – it's just that before, you didn't know it existed. Now that you do, you can fix it.'"

Being able to embark on a path of continual improvement is not only one of Prezly's strengths, it's also an intelligent way to approach publicity. "If your open rate isn't great, you can start working on it," says Wynants. "You can try different subject lines, sending at different times, using different introductions, more visuals, better personalisations and so on. Unfortunately, there isn't a silver bullet; it's hard work. Some things work and some don't; it's different for everyone. You build on what works and expand on it. People sometimes see trial and error as a negative approach, but we don't. We embrace it and encourage clients to do so as well. It takes time, but it works."

This process of building publicity that works is one with which most good PR professionals are familiar. Success is seldom instant. "The difference," says Wynants, "is that online tools provide evidence of what works and what doesn't, so you're not fumbling in the dark. You are responding to factual data. We encourage clients to try to A/B test subject lines – sending a press release with one subject line to half of the target audience and one with a different subject line to the other half. Depending on the type of influencer, writers might make subject lines a little bit more engaging – for example, including the recipient's name. Experiment with stuff; see what works. We also encourage people to go beyond e-mail and build audiences in other channels – to use LinkedIn, Twitter and so on – and not see e-mail as your only channel to reach all influencers."

Using social media to reach influencers isn't just a process of tweeting a press release and seeing what happens. It's identifying those who are interested and connecting them with the story – for example, tweeting directly to them. "It's important not to spam people," says Wynants. "If it's not relevant to a journalist, don't send it or tweet it. See where journalists are most active; follow them and connect with them there. See what journalists share. Build a relationship: in the end, there's nothing to replace the value of having a relationship with someone. When journalists know and trust you, they learn that you're not going to waste their time. Traditional PR people know how to do this; I'm not sure that the new generation of PR people have that talent. Software will never replace the core relationship – a system will never be able to deal with people in such a nuanced way, however far we go with artificial intelligence. That human touch is part of what makes professional PR. When you know editors, you find out what they are looking for. Asking questions helps you to tailor your pitch and give your story a better chance. When you know what influencers' agendas and challenges are, what they want for their media outlet, then you can tailor your stories for them. You can only do this if you know them."

The leaner, faster-moving industries often have an edge when it comes to PR. Less comfortable, they are adept at changing strategies quickly. "I think fast-moving businesses, especially ones that have been through some rough patches, seem to be much better at adopting a new approach to PR," says Wynants. "Like airlines – they've been under pressure so many times. They drive great conversations in social and publicity environments – and do fun stuff. When you come under pressure as an industry, then you do a lot of soul-searching. This pushes you to achieve better results."

As with any form of marketing, business leaders often want statistics. While Prezly delivers this for clients' campaigns, they don't set expectations for potential clients about standard performance levels. Rather, the Prezly team helps clients to improve their performance. "Our overall benchmarks are higher than e-mail marketing benchmarks. If you look at services like MailChimp, we're almost always higher. But even this isn't a fair comparison – our lists are smaller, they are better qualified, and our customers send a specific type of message to a specific type of recipient. Our mailers, by their nature, are more relevant to the reader."

Relevance and precision targeting is where Wynants sees the future of PR: publicists being able to reach the right people, without resorting to massive spray-and-pray mailings. "The future will be in having systems that make it easier to recommend the right people for a particular story," says Wynants. "This won't be about presenting them with lists of people they don't know, it will be about improving the performance of their contact lists, based on known previous behaviour. I'd also like to see technology work better with individuals, providing more guidance on why something is genuinely relevant to others. Putting 1:1 connections in place will be fascinating. Technology can do this by looking at what influencers write about, what they share. Having a system that can help you to learn more about someone in a small amount of time, based on information from multiple sources, would be very powerful. We firmly believe that the future is about the connection between content and contacts. We also want to make it easy to reach out through other channels such as WhatsApp and Snapchat and be less reliant on e-mail. For some contacts, it's better to engage with them on their terms. If they are active on Twitter, that's where we should reach them."

While Prezly sees social media and other communications channels growing, it doesn't envisage the death of e-mail. Indeed, the team finds that e-mail is the best route for clients to adopt its tools – and embrace the changing PR landscape. "We think e-mail will always exist," concludes Wynants. "We see our job as nudging people in the right direction, not forcing them to shift radically – so e-mail distribution remains important. We remain in step with established workflows because otherwise people wouldn't know how to start using us. But e-mail is just a first step to doing things better."

FACTS FIRST, OPINION OUT

Voices that matter: an interview with Martin Couzins,
experienced publicity professional, journalist and editor.

Martin Couzins has an uncommon and varied perspective on publicity. With a media career spanning more than twenty years, he has worked in many different roles. He worked for Reed Business Publishing as a journalist, subeditor, commissioning editor and editor. His credits include publications as diverse as *Doctor and Hospital Doctor* magazines, *Computer Weekly*, *Personnel Today*, *Xpert HR* and *Travel Weekly*. Couzins now runs his own company, Itsdevelopmental (itsdevelopmental.com), helping businesses with content and communications. He also manages his own learning and development website, LearnPatch (learnpatch.com).

"I currently run a website where I receive press releases," says Couzins. "I write them for others and I've been on the receiving end of countless press releases as a journalist and editor. I also help clients to write their own. In that sense, I have a holistic view of the press release."

Like any media professional, Couzins has long faced the daily challenge of an overflowing e-mail inbox. "Since my website is so specialist, I currently get perhaps five to ten press releases a day, but when I was managing magazines, I would have received far more – maybe between twenty and fifty."

Busy and pushed for time, editors review press releases quickly. Decisions are swift and unforgiving. "I look just at the subject of the news story before deciding whether to read further or to ignore it altogether," says Couzins. "I shouldn't have to open the e-mail to find out what the story is about. The only exception I might make is if the e-mail is from an organisation I think is interesting." E-mails may get little more than a cursory glance, but the editor's eye is an expert one. Good stories are few – and they stand out. "If the story's news value isn't immediately clear, it will be ignored."

Poor targeting is a problem. "I can't waste time on stuff that's not relevant to me," says Couzins. "Few PR people work out what I want and my audience wants – they just spam me with content that has nothing to do with my readership."

Introspective press releases also bite the dust quickly. "Many news stories are little more than vanity publishing," says Couzins. "Organisations write them for themselves and not for the audience; they're just not interesting to others. An editor thinks one thing: what do my readers want? It should be the same for the person writing the press release. A press release must be written for the reader.

"Many press releases are just opinion," continues Couzins. "We all like to think that our opinion counts, but it seldom carries that much weight. A political leader's viewpoint may well always be news. But for others, what does their opinion add? Who really needs to know it? What's going to change as a result of you voicing it?" Couzins believes that rather than turn to business leaders for comments, PR people should ask someone who counts, for example the specialists who work within the organisation. "Specialists know their stuff, they're the ones who get invited to speak at conferences. They filter information in their sector: they know what is going on. Often at the top of their game, writers should give a voice to them. But, because silos exist within most organisations, it can be hard to find these people. So PR writers go up the chain for the usual semi-fictional, glib management quote. That just doesn't work. Such quotations are usually a complete waste of time; perhaps someone saying that she or he is 'delighted to be launching this service', which has no impact or news value."

But the biggest issue is that many press releases are just not newsworthy. They simply don't warrant being published. "A lot of the time," says Couzins, "people don't think carefully about what constitutes news. So many press releases just aren't strong enough. An editor I once worked with was so right when he said 'well, whose news is it?' As a journalist you have to be careful – you can't assume that a story 'is news' based on your criteria, you have to put yourself in the mind of the audience. It has to be news to them."

For the few press releases that make it through, the quality of writing is something of a mixed bag. "Some are good and some less good. If I were to generalise, I would say that most are not very well written. They are often written in a pretty flat way, so lack punch. Writers tend to bury stories rather than highlight them. Their subject lines are awful most of the time, and tend to be written in all capitals to get shouty, which is just abhorrent to any professional writer. Some don't even use plain English: there can be so much jargon you can't understand what's being said."

Couzins feels that because publicists want everything to be positive, they pass over compelling news stories – stories that could give them substantial coverage. Of course, negative stories can be tricky to handle: they need to be well researched, avoid cynicism and (above all) remain objective. But they can create a lot of impact. "Organisations don't like to put a negative spin on things. Everything has to be positive – all of the time – and that's not right. For example, an organisation might do some research about the market or its customers which is quite damning, but then they put a positive spin on it. As an editor, you look at the story and say: actually the flip side of that is the real story; that's what would interest readers. So, while an organisation might write a press release which says that 20% of people think something is great, the real story is that 80% believe that it's terrible."

It's a common misconception, believes Couzins, that journalists sit waiting for press releases to come in; that press releases are their lifeblood. "Press releases sit alongside lots of other information that flows past me in the working day. They are a source of news, not the source of news. Journalists don't wait for the news. We follow people on social media, find stuff out through our connections and by monitoring topics." In this way, press releases compete not just with each other – they compete with many other news channels too. To succeed, they have to really stand out.

One way PR professionals can increase their chance of success is simple: contact journalists and editors and find out what they want. According to Couzins, this rarely happens. PR teams prefer to blast out press releases in large numbers, rather than concentrate effort where it can be most effective. "Only very occasionally will I be personally contacted. Many stories I cover come from strong relationships – and me talking directly to organisations. Where a relationship exists, the likelihood of a story getting published is much better. Yet it's very rare that I'm asked what I need and what my readers need. Frankly, that's amazing. I'd like an inbox full of people asking me what I want rather than one full of stuff I don't need. If people asked, their press release would be more relevant. It's a basic thing, but few do it."

When it comes to the format of the press release, and its role in a publicity or marketing campaign, Couzins feels that many organisations just aren't keeping up with changes in the media. "Companies haven't shifted fast enough," says Couzins. "Marketing departments sadly want to turn everything into a science. The science of content marketing is one of the latest. Funnily enough, that whole content-marketing trend is about companies wanting to write stories for their customers, not about their products – that's a shift away from product marketing. Well, guess who's been doing that just about forever? Journalists. That's what news stories are. Because marketing and publicity teams work mostly in silos, they aren't set up to spot a good story and exploit its potential with employees, stakeholders, customers and partners." So, at the same time that great stories slip – unnoticed – through their fingers, many organisations issue press releases that sit somewhere between opinion and fiction.

"Let's go back to basics. What is the point of a press release? A press release was originally designed to get your news into a publication. That was your route to market with your message. Now, an organisation has more control over that message and where that message goes. The press release has a fundamentally different role. The story is much more than a press release. The press release still has a job to do, but the story cuts across the whole digital footprint of the organisation. And its value is not just external. It's internal too.

"A press release is not what it was ten, twenty, or thirty years ago. It has the word 'press' in it, so people are fearful – because they don't know how the story will be used. There is a legacy view of what the press is, what the media is and how it works. That's a hangover from the days when there was no outlet other than the press. Now that companies own their media and have their own means of distribution, there is an opportunity to look at stories in an entirely different way. But the idea of what is useful to customers, what is engaging, what is factual, what is worth sharing – that's still at the heart of it. In that sense, the press release hasn't changed.

"People have to wake up to the fact that we live in a networked environment. Everything is leaky. PR used to be about controlling the story – you can't do that any more. Press releases were born out of packaging up a story to tell the world, through the media; now people share stuff about your company all of the time, whether you create it or not. You can either look at this and say, 'that's a bad thing', or you can say, 'what can we do with that?'"

The stories that get shared the most, according to Couzins, are what can perhaps be called traditionally good stories. "Research, facts and solid stories get shared the most. A lot of the time PR is just opinion, and that doesn't do so well. It's little different from fake news. Research performs better than product announcements, often, unless it's a massive game-changing launch. For a writer, it can be hard to get facts – perhaps for an event, how many people attended? How many exhibitors were there? Can we get quotes from people? These are the facts from the event; it's what makes solid news. Publicity shouldn't be fiction."

Whether news stories are fictional, weak, spin or too glossy is a moot point. In a time where fake news abounds and clickbait surrounds both news and advertising, trust is a pressing concern. "I think that we live in interesting times because of fake news. The Edelman Trust Barometer (edelman.com), which comes out every year, shows that organisations have a long way to go in terms of building trust with employees, communities and markets. One way to make that happen is through the type of content they put out. The accountability of news stories is becoming more important for an organisation. You don't want to be seen to be trotting out rubbish or voicing an opinion that doesn't count. It's not about volume. Sadly, this goes massively against the marketing need to regularly engage with the audience. So all kinds of stuff is pumped out all the time. Press releases can play a more prominent role in delivering the facts. Not the opinion. The facts. I'd love to see more of that from organisations. They can be the trusted source, instead of just spamming you with promotional stuff.

"One thing that journalism has taught me is that if you produce content that's fresh, timely and relevant, then people will read it. Nothing has changed with that. With all the rubbish on the Web, the stuff that gets reactions, whether it's hated, listened to, read or shared, is the real stuff. It rises to the top. I think that's what organisations need to focus on. Then add a social layer around your content and share stuff with your networks and influencers. Others then share it to a wider audience, saying this is useful, pushing it out further. Making this happen requires that PR people engage fully with stakeholders, coach them on what works, help them to understand how campaigns based on real news can get far more coverage than press releases which are just posturing or opinion. I think people are somewhat immature about understanding what this kind of conversation might be and how such campaigns could work for an organisation.

"It comes back to this: what genuinely useful information do you have that is worth sharing with your stakeholders, employees, influencers and with the media? That is the sort of questioning that needs to go first – rather than 'let's go and do a press release!'"

For Couzins, successful press releases are ones where the writer has gone back to the fundamentals. "What is the purpose of this? Is it news? Remember, what seems like news to you and what is news to your audience can be two different things. Who is your audience? Is it the media or is it your customers? Since it's called a press release you might assume it's for the media, but you're going to publish it everywhere – so it's for everyone. What are the facts? What is the new information? From these questions, you can establish what the story is. You can work out what the most useful, engaging information is. This matters before you write anything. The actual writing of the press release is far easier when you research a story well. When you don't have facts, you write like a fiction writer – because you're making it up. If you have data, you can write short, active sentences quickly. Finding real news stories is all in the research. Find the facts. Put them first."

CONCLUSION

IS IT NEWS?

Creativity is a habit, and the best creativity is the result of good work habits. –
Twyla Tharp

If there's one thing we'd really like you to take away from this book, it's the importance of the title.

We've said several times that the main failing of many press releases is that either the story isn't newsworthy, or the newsworthy elements of it aren't clear enough.

It's a question you should always ask yourself, a continual challenge for any and every press release you write: *is it news?*

As a writer, you'll labour to bring out the exciting elements of the story – but, at the end of the day, the story will sink or swim more because of its inherent newsworthiness than anything else.

Write everything as well as you can. When the story seems flat, drill down to what could make it newsworthy. Compelling stories aren't dull stories with spin, they are good stories well told.

Don't let anybody tell you that press releases don't work, when the opposite is true: today, more than ever before, press releases can work harder and reach further. They remain a great way to announce news; to tell your stories.

Hopefully this book will give your creativity a robust framework within which it's easier – and more effective – to work. It will help you work out what is and isn't news. It will help you work with others – getting them to understand what media outlets, influencers and the public really want. It will help you expand campaigns beyond the press release and make publicity more successful for you.

Above all else, we hope that this book will help you to excel.

There's a lot of noise out there. Don't add to it: rise above it.

Peter and Robert

RESOURCES

A collection of useful publicity templates.
These can also be downloaded from:
content.productions/publications/is-it-news/downloads

TEMPLATE: PRESS RELEASE

This template is a suggested press release template. Edit the template to suit your writing needs, and the requirements of your distribution. You may wish to add your company's logo.

Press release
For immediate release (or 'Embargoed until: date')
Insert location (usually: city, country)

[Headline]
Try to keep to a dozen words or fewer. Include just one key point: the single most important aspect of the announcement.

[Sub-headline (optional)]
Try to keep to a dozen words or fewer; avoid repetition from the headline. Note that not all outlets use a sub-headline so you can't depend on it being published. Provide an alternative angle for the single point expressed in the headline.

[Synopsis (or introduction)]
Try to keep to around 20–25 words or fewer. Avoid repetition from the headline. Try to include all of the key information of the announcement.

[Press release main body]
Try to keep to around 300–350 words or fewer. The whole press release, including headline, synopsis and body, should be around 300–400 words.

[Closing mark]
Signify the end of the press release content with *one* of these:
–30–
###
–Ends–

[Boilerplate]
About XYZ Company

Remove the word 'boilerplate' above, add in your company name. Describe the press release's owner in entirely factual terms. Keep to the most important facts and consider directing readers to a company page for additional information. Try to keep the boilerplate to 50–75 words at the most.

Remember to include the company's key contact information:
[Main telephone]
[Website]
[Generic e-mail]
[Twitter handle]
[LinkedIn URL]
[Facebook URL]

[Contact information]
For more information, please contact:

Include e-mail addresses, phone numbers and social media handles for key contacts. Use personal contact information, for example avoid company Twitter/LinkedIn handles. Outlets should be able to directly reach your contacts via these (remember, they are outside the body of the press release and therefore not intended for publication).

Do not provide too many contacts and ensure that those people listed are authorised and ready to talk to outlets. A good rule is to provide the details of those quoted within the press release, and the head of marketing/publicity.

If you have set up a campaign landing page for the press release, that should be cited *within* the body of the press release itself. If you have set up a media resources/landing page, that should be cited *outside* the body of the press release.

[Word count]
XXX words
The word count is the combined published amount of the press release: heading, sub-headline (where one is used), synopsis/introductory paragraph and press release body.

[Supporting media]
Remember to include supporting media for each press release. Thumbnails of images/videos provide a visual cue for outlets and can help prompt interest. Do not attach high-resolution versions.

E-MAIL TEMPLATE: REQUESTING MAILING LIST OPT-IN

This e-mail template is to be used when requesting people's permission to send your press releases to them.

E-mail subject:

News stories from [company name]

E-mail body:

Hi [recipient's forename]

I work for [company name] and am responsible for distributing our news. I took a look at your [publication or website] and think that our news may be of interest to you.

With your permission, I'd like to add you to our mailing list.

We send out around [insert round number] press releases each year – and you can opt out at any time, should you find that our news isn't relevant. However, I do feel that our news is of value to you, hence me writing personally.

If you'd like, I can send you our latest press release as an example – please just let me know.

I'm always here to chat at any time, either about our news or what's going on in the industry. Also, please feel free to connect with [company name] or me personally on social media.

Kind regards

[Your name]
[Phone number]
[Social media URLs]

E-MAIL TEMPLATE: SENDING AN UNSOLICITED PRESS RELEASE

This e-mail template is to be used when sending an unsolicited press release to someone – and asking them to opt-in to your mailing list.

E-mail subject:

News from [company name]

E-mail body:

Hi [recipient's forename]

I hope you don't mind me sending you our latest press release.
I work for [company name] and am responsible for distributing our news. I took a look at your [publication or website] and think that our news may be of interest to you.
If this is of interest, I'd like to add you to our mailing list.
(Although I've sent this news story, we won't send any more without your permission.)
We only send out around [number of stories] press releases each year and you can opt out at any time, should you find that our news isn't relevant.
I'm always here to chat at any time, either about our news or what's going on in the industry. Also, please feel free to connect with [company name] or me personally on social media.

Kind regards

[Your name]
[Phone number]
[Social media URLs]

E-MAIL TEMPLATE: OPT-OUT FOLLOW-UP

This e-mail template is to be used when following up an opt-out from your mailing list.

E-mail subject:

Your opt out from [company name]'s news list

E-mail body:

Hi [recipient's forename]

I noticed that you'd opted out of receiving our news stories.

I hope you don't mind me e-mailing you – I just wanted to say that I'm sorry you're leaving our list.

I'm assuming that our news stories aren't relevant to you, but if you have any other feedback, I'd welcome hearing it.

If we've been sending too many stories, you could also let us know and I can arrange to send you only the most important ones – otherwise we'll of course respect your request to opt out.

I'm always here to chat at any time, either about our news or what's going on in the industry. Also, please feel free to connect with [company name] or me personally on social media.

Kind regards

[Your name]
[Phone number]
[Social media URLs]

E-MAIL TEMPLATE: APPROVAL FOR PRESS RELEASE SIGN-OFF

This e-mail template is to be used to obtain people's approval for the press release. There are two versions: the first assumes that sign-off is given if the recipient doesn't respond; the second requires a response. Which you use depends on your organisation.

E-mail subject:

Final review of press release: [title]

E-mail body:

Hi [recipient's forename]

Please find attached the final draft of the press release: [press release heading] for your approval.

Could you please give this document one last read to ensure that you are happy with all of its content?

The press release is scheduled to be sent out on [date], so I need any comments on or before [date].

If I don't hear from you, I'll assume all is OK with it and proceed.

Kind regards

[Your name]
[Phone number]
[Social media URLs]

-or-

E-mail subject:

Final review of press release: [title]

E-mail body:

Hi [recipient's forename]

Please find attached the final draft of the press release: [press release heading] for your approval.

Could you please give this document one last read to ensure that you are happy with all of its content?

The press release is scheduled to be sent out on [date], so I need any comments on or before [date].

I can't proceed without your approval; if there's anything you'd like to chat about, please drop me a line or give me a call.

Kind regards

[Your name]
[Phone number]
[Social media URLs]

E-MAIL TEMPLATE: EXTERNAL APPROVAL FOR PRESS RELEASE SIGN-OFF

Getting approval from third parties for content within press releases can be problematic, as your publicity isn't likely to be their top priority. Follow up e-mails with calls, be positive and polite, but be clear about deadlines.

Only send the entire press release if it is appropriate to do so – in many circumstances third parties only need to approve their quote and the text which supports it. Unlike internal, implicit approvals (where you can provide a date by which any lack of response is taken as an approval), it's important to obtain explicit approvals for third-party contributions.

E-mail subject:

Final review of press release: [title]

E-mail body:

Hi [recipient's forename]

Please find attached the final draft of our press release: [press release heading] for your approval.

Could you please review this document to ensure that you are happy with it?

The press release is scheduled to be sent out on [date], so I really need any comments on or before [date].

I appreciate that this will take a few minutes of your time, and we're very grateful for your support and contribution.

I'll give you a call shortly to follow this up.

Kind regards

[Your name]
[Phone number]
[Social media URLs]

TEMPLATE:
CHECKLIST – TAKING THE BRIEF

*The more information you can get as part of the briefing, the better the
campaign will typically be – and the more likely stakeholders' expectations
will be aligned with yours.*

OVERALL
- What are the timescales for the press release? (Asking this first defines
  what is and isn't possible; if some activities are essential, for example a
  third-party endorsement, then timescales can be adjusted to suit.)
- Who is the main stakeholder?

PRESS RELEASE CONTENT
- What is the key point – the main message – of the press release?
- What are the supporting facts?
- Is there any research to support the release?
- Who from within the organisation would be the best spokesperson for the
  release?
- Who from outside the organisation could contribute to the release?
- Should the story be pitched in different ways to different outlets? What
  is the best angle for the media? What is the best angle for customers?
  What is the best angle for staff? Is there a different, more effective, angle
  for other audiences?

CONTEXT
- What are other companies/people doing that's similar to the press release's
  topic?
- Is there an upcoming event that would help with the timing of this press
  release?

OUTCOMES AND MEASUREMENT
- What is the desired outcome of the release?
- How will we measure the campaign/release?
- What can be done to boost response?
- Are the desired outcomes and measurement processes realistic
  and achievable?

SEARCH ENGINE OPTIMISATION

- What are the story's main potential keywords?
- How does this fit into the organisation's SEO strategy?

DISTRIBUTION

- How is this story best communicated on social media? How many updates, over what period?
- How can the story be broken down into smaller updates for social media?
- What would encourage others to share the story?
- What additional content would benefit the story (images/video/infographics etc)?
- Which distribution lists should the story go to?
- Are there any influencers who should have an early or exclusive view of the story?
- Which newswires should be used to distribute the story?

TEMPLATE: PREFLIGHT CHECKLIST

It's never too late. Use a preflight checklist based on this one to assess whether your story is good to go, or could be improved.

THE PITCH

- Has the right key point been identified and brought to the front and centre of the story?
- Are the supporting facts all in place? Are there too many?
- Will one release work for all audiences or would it be better to draft different versions?
- Does the press release have a clear call to action?
- Does the press release talk to the audience about their needs, goals and desires or does it glorify the organisation?
- Does the press release provide a resolution to a problem?
- Most of all: is this news? Is the story really newsworthy? Are the most newsworthy elements of the story clear enough? Is the impact of the story on others clearly explained?

CAMPAIGN COORDINATION

- Are all different versions of the story ready to go?
- Are all supporting elements in place and ready – such as a landing page and additional media?
- Are all social media updates – and their media – ready?
- Have you talked to other lines of business and marketing teams about their potential involvement and about other campaigns they are running, to identify any synergy or clashes?
- Are mailing lists clean and ready to be used?
- Are all contacts mentioned within the release available for interview by outlets?
- Do you have a plan to follow up the release with key influencers?

QUALITY

- Are all approvals in place?
- Does the written style and language comply with the organisation's content strategy?
- Has the story been proofread?
- Has the primary stakeholder signed off the story?

ENDNOTES

CITATIONS AND SOURCES

We've done our best within this book to provide citations for research and quotations. We've also tried to ensure that research is credible and relevant. However, the nature of the World Wide Web is that, by the time you read this book, some of the source material may have been changed, moved or removed.

ABOUT THE AUTHORS

Peter Labrow and Robert Clarke have worked together, in a variety of marketing roles, for around thirty years. They have devised and implemented marketing and publicity strategies which have helped organisations to become leaders in their markets. Together they founded an industry-specific newswire, Learning News, and they collaborate on many publicity projects.

PETER LABROW

Peter Labrow has over thirty years' experience in business-to-business marketing, content-creation and publicity. Peter's career includes managing creative teams within advertising agencies and working in marketing management roles up to director level within multinational companies. Over his career, Peter has written countless press releases and articles for magazines and news outlets. Today, Peter runs his own online content-creation business, Content Productions (content.productions). Peter has also authored a top-selling horror novel, *The Well*, which was voted 'Best Halloween Read' on Goodreads, just above *Dracula* – and therefore thinks his gravestone should read 'Trounced Bram Stoker in a fair fight'.

ROBERT CLARKE

Robert Clarke has marketed learning services over a thirty-year career; in 2001 he founded the learning-sector newswire, Learning News (learningnews.com). Robert has helped to build market-leading brands and start-up businesses – marketing IT training, performance support, project management, online learning and learning analytics. As part of running a newswire, Robert reviews a great amount of press releases and his experiences led him to co-write this book. Beyond the press release, Robert is a table tennis player and founded table tennis clubs in Warrington and in Stockport.

THANKS

PETER LABROW

I'm indebted to many people in my career; too many to list in full, but special mentions go to: my English teacher, Doreen Blake, who both pushed and praised me; Paul Webber, from whom I learned creativity at the (sometimes messy) sharp end; Colin Steed, then magazine editor, for giving me much latitude and many breaks – and Ken Hawes, a client who later hired me, before he became the best business partner anyone could wish for. Oh and Rob – I can't imagine not working with him.

ROBERT CLARKE

I'd like to recognise the influence on my career of four special people: David Tanham, my first boss, who was patient with me and helped me into the business world; Alan Thompson, from whom I learned a great deal about myself; Ali Parkinson, an inspirational coworker at three different employers over two decades; Peter, who has challenged and mentored me for over thirty years. That Peter has only managed to fire me once so far is testament to his patience.

FOR THOSE WHO HELPED WITH THIS BOOK

Special thanks to those who helped in various ways with the preparation of this book; we're especially indebted to Claire Andrews, Peter Clements, Gay Freeman, Joanne Nock, Lesley Jackson, Katie John and Lianne Mease. May your pens always have ink.

L - #0369 - 281120 - C0 - 229/152/13 - PB - DID2964875